Managing Collaboration in Public Administration

Managing Collaboration
in Public Administration
The Promise of Alliance among
Governance, Citizens, and Businesses

Eran Vigoda-Gadot

Westport, Connecticut
London

Library of Congress Cataloging-in-Publication Data

Vigoda-Gadot, Eran, 1966–
  Managing collaboration in public administration : the promise of alliance among governance,
  citizens, and businesses / Eran Vigoda-Gadot.
    p. cm.
  Includes bibliographical references and index.
  ISBN 1–56720–567–4 (alk. paper)
    1. Organizational change. 2. Public administration. 3. Public-private sector cooperation.
  I. Title.
  JF1525.O73V54 2003
  352.3′7—dc22   2003057989

British Library Cataloguing in Publication Data is available.

Library of Congress Catalog Card Number: 2003057989
ISBN: 1–56720–567–4

First published in 2003

Praeger Publishers, 88 Post Road West, Westport, CT 06881
An imprint of Greenwood Publishing Group, Inc.
www.praeger.com

Printed in the United States of America

The paper used in this book complies with the
Permanent Paper Standard issued by the National
Information Standards Organization (Z39.48–1984).

10 9 8 7 6 5 4 3 2 1

To Nimrod, a new light in our family

Contents

Preface

An old legend tells about three sons standing beside a bed on which their dying father is lying. Facing the critical condition of the family head, the sons are distraught and helpless, and concerned for the future. The father, troubled by the possibility of family separation after his impending demise, asks his sons to bring him a bundle of sticks. He calls the first son and motions him to break one stick. The son easily snaps the stick in two. The father beckons the second and third sons, asking them to do likewise, and they comply without undue effort. Thereupon the father gathers all the remaining sticks together in a bunch and asks his sons to try and break them like that. Naturally, this task is far more difficult and the sons can't accomplish it so easily. The father tells his sons: "When you are all alone, like the separated stick, anyone will easily overcome you. But when you stay together like these sticks, collaborating and covering for each other, then you will be able to do almost everything you wish and desire."

This is perhaps the essence of collaboration, which furnishes the ground for the writing of this book. I have stated elsewhere (Vigoda, 2002a) that during the last century modern societies accomplished remarkable achievements in various fields, many of them thanks to an advanced public sector. Yet at the dawn of the new millennium, new social problems await the consideration and attention of the state and its administrative system. To overcome these problems and create effective remedies for the new types of state ills, there is a need to increase cooperation and collaboration, and to share information and knowledge among all social parties—a need that acquired unexpected immediacy and support through the September 11 events in New York, Washington, D.C., and Pennsylvania. Collaboration among nations, organizations, and institutions has become vital and viable, and more people and leaders across the world treat it as the real challenge to free democracies in the coming generations.

Without doubt, we live in an era of great challenges for modern societies. The twenty-first century will necessitate enormous changes in our conventional perceptions of governmental activities and responsibilities. It will similarly require a reformation of the meaning of citizenship and a redefinition of the role of citizens, private sector firms, the third sector/voluntary organizations, the media, and academe. All these players, and others, will need to collaborate. Most important, they will need to collaborate with public administration as its impact grows, in order to provide the people with better services and high quality goods. They will have to collaborate because the economic, social, and human potential of "going together" is much more extensive and profitable than the option of "going alone."

This book attempts to develop a theory of the management of collaboration and to point out its usefulness for public administration systems and for other players in the national field. The two other main players identified and discussed throughout the book are private sector organizations and citizens as individuals or as collective forms of third sector bodies. The book argues that well-structured and comprehensive thinking on collaboration, combined with empirical evidence on its chances of enduring, is a powerful tool for policy makers and for public administrators and managers in developed democracies. The core assumption, as developed here, is that independent activity by public administration, governments, and other social players is no longer sufficient for our complex societies. Once adopted, the individual/independent strategy will fail to cohere with the growing changes and demands of modern life. The book accordingly attempts to conjoin the theory and practice of collaboration and to place them at the service of modern communities. To this end, we suggest a strategic managerial map for ascending to higher levels of collaboration and partnership, extending its impact on state leaders and decision makers, as well as improving its quality and effect in various social fields.

In sum, the book treats an inevitable process that most modern societies are going to experience, if they are not already doing so, in the coming years. The main goal of the book is to integrate theoretical, empirical, and practical data on the emerging field of collaboration management and to show their relevance for public administration. This knowledge may then be used in the service of decision makers, politicians, private entrepreneurs, citizens, and other members of modern society. We argue that collaboration is one of the most important processes in and around governments and public administration institutions. The aim of this book is to contribute to a better understanding of its essence and to a wiser implementation of its lessons in the years to come.

Acknowledgments

This book is a result of my interest in collaboration and partnership and in the challenges they present to modern nations. In recent years these topics have been the subject of much of my scholarly attention, research, and writing. I was especially impressed by intensifying calls for better understanding of the meaning of collaboration and its potential impact on our life on the national, local, and communal levels. Throughout the 1980s and 1990s, and on into the twenty-first century, the road toward collaboration and partnership in various state halls has intrigued academics, managers, public officials, and ordinary caring citizens. This interest was reflected in the large number of scientific publications and conferences on the topic. The media provided coverage and exposure for collaborative ventures and put collaboration on our public agenda. In fact, all who took part in this collaboration, in various states, cities, and communities, should be considered silent partners in the creation of this book. Among them are managers in the private and public sectors who were somehow involved in collaborative projects with other parties and, most important, those anonymous caring citizens who see collaboration strategies as an important tool to preserve lives and improve the quality of life in our communities.

Although it is impossible to mention everyone here, I feel that some people deserve my special gratitude. First, this book has benefited from the good advice and experience of many colleagues at the University of Haifa, and in many other schools and institutions in Israel and across the globe. I am also thankful for the comments and criticism of other members, reviewers, and professionals who offered ideas and information on the meaning of collaboration and the way of making it a strategic tool for public administration. All have done an outstanding professional job. They are Geert Boukaert, Tony Bovaird, Gerald E. Caiden, Aaron Cohen, Etai Gilboa, Robert T. Golembiewski, Arie Halachmi, Shai Litt, Bart Maddens, Kalu Kalu, Aaron

Kfir, Jack Rabin, Robert Schwartz, and Steven van de Walle. On the administrative side I express my appreciation for the proficient work done by the staff of Quorum Books of the Greenwood Publishing Group as well as for the support I received from the Research Authority of the University of Haifa. Special thanks go to Meira Yurkevich and Tali Shemesh-Birman. Obviously, the journey of writing this book could not have been completed without the help and support of these "partners," and I am grateful to all of them.

Finally, I hope that this book will contribute to the ongoing debate on the potential of collaboration for our nations and communities. Hence the book is dedicated to caring citizens wherever they are, and to professional managers in public and private organizations who are responsible for making the spirit of collaboration work in practice. It is also dedicated to my current and future students, who will have to deal, in class and in practice, with the public administration of tomorrow. Naturally, I bear full responsibility for the book's contents and orientations.

Introduction

THE NEED FOR COLLABORATION IN PUBLIC ADMINISTRATION

Public administration is entering an era of greater need for collaboration among various social players. However, quite ironically but unsurprisingly, it seems that once again we face future developments in our societies with no clear knowledge of what's ahead. In most of today's Western nations the free market doctrine is dominant in economic, social, and political affairs. Indeed, these nations have also woven an interesting and complex net of social constraints that are aimed at safeguarding human rights and providing minimum standards of living for their societies' less able citizens. Under the conventional title of "welfare states" or at least "caring states," the basic human needs of many are protected by central governments and by the law. Still, modern democracies of various types have adequately encouraged a tradition of competition, conflict, and contest over resources, and a high level of struggle over interests among all parties of the society. Based on the "Protestant Ethic" of Max Weber, competition has become a cornerstone in the ideology and philosophy of modern capitalist nations. The "competitive" jargon has been made commonplace by politicians, public sector officials, and businessmen alike. Consequently, this language has become the most common terminology to explain public policy and governmental decision-making. In a world where competition is the "name of the game," governments are expected to respond better to citizens' demands by choosing the best of many offers and by reducing costs and expenses to their minimum. Hence, in recent decades we have become familiar with the new tools of privatization, outsourcing, and contracting out, which represent a desire by policy makers to change old-style bureaucracies into more flexible, responsive, effective, and efficient bodies.

While the contribution of these methods, actions, and reactions is not disputed, criticism has arisen regarding the "next step" of bureaucracy development. Are we going on a one-way street toward greater fragmentation of our societies and communities, or is there an alternative to the rising level of competition? In many respects, competition is opposite to collaboration. In any situation where more than one person is involved, people may choose to compete or to collaborate in order to attain a goal or meet a need. It seems that today we know more and more about patterns and strategies of competition in public affairs, but we are still unclear about the potential power of collaboration in that regard. Collaboration has thus remained an underdeveloped area in managerial thinking, and the literature that has so far developed it is scarce. In a world of dominant capitalistic values competition takes the lead, and collaboration, at least in its public affairs aspect, is seen as less significant and more problematic.

Therefore a gap must be filled in managerial writing and in public administration thinking. What does collaboration in the public sector actually mean? What does it carry with it in terms of managerial concepts? Is it a rational and reasonable solution to various ills of our societies? If so, how can it be implemented wisely, and what strategy should be followed to achieve success in this process? Where should we start applying collaborative ventures, and who are the partners in this process? These questions are only a few of those with which I intend to deal in this book. Still, I must comment that the book will eventually raise many questions but provide a more limited number of answers.

ORGANIZATION OF THE BOOK

The book is arranged in six chapters. First I set the stage for the discussion by portraying the general evolutionary process through which public administration advanced as a science and as a profession in the last century. This chapter inclines to the assumption that, for several reasons, public administration of the "old type" worked independently and individually rather than in cooperation with other social players.

Chapter 2 sets out a politically focused analysis of collaboration and deals with the "spirit of collaboration." On the basis of earlier studies, I present and explain the meaning of accomplishing public managerial work "together" rather than "alone." This chapter also distinguishes close but different terminologies of mutual efforts, and it illumines the contribution of collaboration to our rapidly changing communities. It identifies the government and the public service as leaders and directors of such trends, and states the meaning of politics for the social action of collaboration. The chapter concludes with a strategic model of collaboration, with which the subsequent chapters deal more extensively. This chapter also elaborates on the responsibility of a key player, governance and public administration (G&PA), in the process of collaboration. I argue that both the centralized and the participatory strategies for collaboration rely heavily on state and administrative leaders, and that no successful collaboration can be achieved unless these parties are fully committed to their task.

Chapters 3 and 4 discuss two major types of collaboration processes in our societies: the public-private partnership and collaboration, and the public-nonprofit type of collaboration. An attempt is made to categorize different methods of collaboration, with their strengths and weaknesses, as well as each party's unique perceptions of public administration and management.

Chapter 5 makes a preliminary empirical effort to reach a better understanding of the meaning of collaboration and its existence in the public sector. This effort relies on an extensive survey of 244 senior Israeli managers who were asked to share knowledge of cases of collaboration in various fields, and their experiences with and attitudes toward such processes. The survey included public sector managers (PBS) and private sector managers (PRS). The results of this survey are diagnosed, interpreted, and contrasted with theory and strategic ideas presented in the earlier chapters. While it is clear that this survey is limited in its power and generalization potential, its foremost contribution lies in its behavioral, attitudinal, and empirical orientation, which reaches beyond mere theoretical development in the field.

The final chapter (chapter 6) attempts to assess the chances of better managing collaboration in public domains. It also summarizes my conclusion with the anticipation that future studies and research will narrow the gap between our need for a higher level of collaboration in public administration and our actual knowledge of the methods, tools, and rationality that may enhance it.

TARGET READERS

To advance a vision of collaboration in the public sector, this book needs to be targeted at the minds and hearts of various types of readers. I believe that the chief benefit of this book is for leaders of modern societies, be they politicians, public administrators, or CEOs of the business sector. These individuals, who constitute the elite of our nations, also carry the responsibility to advance collaboration and make it visible, effective, and useful for the citizens. However, there is no doubt that citizens themselves may also find the book enlightening and contributory to the formation of strong communities.

Moreover, like most authors of books of this kind, I anticipate that the first calls for change will be launched from academe and from the intellectual stratum of society. This book is thus aimed at scholars of business management, public administration, sociology, and political science. It is also intended for students, who will bear responsibility in the future for the development of our societies. An inclination toward higher and more sophisticated structures of collaboration among governments, citizens, and the public sector may prove to be the best safeguard against separation, alienation, and extremism of various groups. Accordingly, readers may come from various groups and sectors to fill the idea of collaboration with the vitality and optimism it needs in order to endure through the coming generations.

CHAPTER 1

*Public Administration: The State of the Art and the Call for Collaboration**

GOVERNMENTS, ADMINISTRATION, AND THE SEPTEMBER 11 EFFECT

The simultaneous terrorist attacks on New York, Pennsylvania, and Washington, D.C., on the morning of September 11, 2001, signaled the emergence of some striking changes in America and in the world. These events were in no way the reason for the writing of this book, which I had begun many weeks earlier, but their impact on my view on collaboration was remarkable. Perhaps one of the most interesting results of these terrorist actions was the sharp transition in U.S. public opinion on the role of government in day-to-day life, and on its size, responsibilities, and challenges. As this book will try to demonstrate, a significant aftershock of the September 11 events may turn out to be our view and perception of the need for collaboration in modern society.

High-level collaboration among many terrorist organizations and terrorist-supporting states like Afghanistan, Iraq, Iran, and Syria made the attack on the United States so effective and successful. It's my view that only a similar counterprocess of collaboration among democratic nations can resist these threatening forces and safeguard the free world. In this conflict, as in other socially oriented conflicts and dilemmas, it is public administration that has the primary role and responsibility to provide answers for the new needs. Today more than ever before, its purpose is to enhance collaboration among various social players and, as all agree, to protect democracy through this

*Some sections of this chapter are based on previous works by the author: *Public Administration: An Interdisciplinary Critical Analysis* (New York: Marcel Dekker, 2002); "From Responsiveness to Collaboration: Governance, Citizens, and the Next Generation of Public Administration," *Public Administration Review* (2002).

mutual effort. We have always expected national and federal institutions to do this, and for many reasons we expect them today to become even more energetic and involved in such trends and developments.

There are several reasons for our ongoing heavy reliance on the government and its executive branches. First, we simply have no other institution or body to turn to when our basic rights and needs are endangered. Second, in the last century governments and the public sector grew larger than at any time in the past, and they practically created citizens' high dependence on the services and goods they provided. Third, the public sector and its administrative heads proffer more services and goods than ever before, and they do so for larger populations with wide heterogeneity and expanding demands. In sum, we lean on governments and on public administration bodies because we believe that they hold the answers to our questions and the solutions for our needs. Put otherwise, citizens of modern states largely trust the systematic order and action of governments and their executive branches. If they can't do the right things for us, then who can?

RETHINKING PUBLIC ADMINISTRATION:
THE RISE OF AN INDEPENDENT, ECLECTIC DISCIPLINE

Our knowledge of public administration bodies increased remarkably during the last century. It grew, but it also changed over the years and in face of historical transitions. Today few will challenge the assertion that modern public administration is entitled to its independent position among other disciplines of the social sciences. However, this justified independent position does not contradict the fact that the field is also far more eclectic than might be thought.

The science of public administration was born toward the end of the nineteenth century, when the business of the state started to attract social-academic attention. The revolution that turned public administration into an independent science and profession is traditionally related to the influential work and vision of Woodrow Wilson (1887) and Frank J. Goodnow (1900). These scholars were among the first who advocated the autonomy of the field as a unique area of science that drew substance from several sources. In the first years, law, political theory of the state, and several "hard sciences" such as engineering and industrial relations were the most fundamental and influential mother disciplines. Over time, these fields strongly influenced the formation and transition of public administration, but the extent and direction of the influence were not linear or consistent. In recent decades, however, public administration has benefited greatly from the knowledge and methods of other sister disciplines. The call for an independent science of public administration was balanced with other needs to share knowledge and explanatory models in order to put together a "greater theory" of the social sciences. It became clear that despite the unassailable independence of public administration as a science and as a profession, further progress was not possible unless more collaboration was gained among all those who study, teach, direct, and run the public sector in its multiple facets.

INTERDISCIPLINARY SCIENCES AND THE VISION OF COLLABORATION

To understand better the meaning and potential of collaborative work in and around the public sector, one may benefit from an interdisciplinary approach to the field. Such a view identifies the possible sources of knowledge that surround the discipline. Otherwise stated, learning about the uniqueness of public administration and the potential of its collaboration with other parties necessitates a firm identification and typology of those disciplines that may serve as possible contributors to the field. As proposed by Goodwin (1998), there is a rapidly growing need for reorientation of research to reevaluate the old distinctions among markets, state, and civil society. This trend may recognize the importance of new dependencies and relationships, and involve new understandings about the structures as well as the fissures.

Going back to the late nineteenth century, one is not surprised to find that the judiciary system and the law actively shaped the essence and boundaries of public administration as an awaking scholarly field. Kettl and Milward (1996:7) argued that traditional public administration, as advocated by the progenitors of the discipline, consisted in the power of law. Representatives of the people make the law and delegate responsibility to professional bureaucrats to execute it properly. Highly qualified bureaucrats, supported by the best tools and resources, are then expected to discharge the law to the highest professional standards, which in turn produces good and accountable managerial results that best serve the people. According to Rosenbloom (1998), the legal approach views public administration "as applying and enforcing the law in concrete circumstances," and is "infused with legal and adjudicatory concerns" (p. 33). This approach derives from three major inter-related sources: (1) administrative law, which is the body of law and regulations that control generic administrative processes; (2) the judicialization of public administration, which is the tendency for administrative processes to resemble courtroom procedures; and (3) constitutional law, which redefines a variety of citizens' rights and liberties. Several legal definitions argue that public administration is law in action and mainly a regulative system, which is "government telling citizens and businesses what they may and may not do" (Shafritz and Russell, 1997:14). Thus, the law furnishes the grounds for the operation of the public service, and it is a potential first partner in the creation of a useful collaborative process.

However, through the years it has become obvious that law in itself does not maintain satisfactory conditions for quality public sector performances to emerge. Constitutional systems furnish platforms for healthy performance of public administration, but do not account for its effectiveness or efficiency. Good laws are necessary but not sufficient conditions for creating a well-performing public service. The road was then open to other disciplinary influences to sound their voices and make their contribution to the emergence of greater collaboration with public administration.

One such important contribution came from the classic "hard sciences" of engineering and industrial relations. In its very early stages public administration was heavily influenced by dramatic social forces and long-range developments in the Western world. The ongoing industrial and technological revolution in the early 1900s, which was accompanied by political reforms, greater democratization, and more concern for the people's welfare, needed highly qualified navigators. These were engineers, industrial entrepreneurs, and technical professionals who guided both markets and governments along the elusive ways to economic and social prosperity. Various fields of engineering, the subsequently arising area of industrial studies, and other linked disciplines such as statistical methods became popular and crucial for the development of management science in general, and were also gradually found useful for public arenas. The link between general management and public administration had its roots in the understanding of complex organizations and bureaucracies, which have many shared features. Hence, the push toward incremental integration of knowledge was led by these hard sciences. Collaboration of knowledge, ideas, and methods appeared more robust, and convinced many that answers to social problems may be awaiting in other arenas.

With time, dramatic changes occurred in the nature, orientation, and application of general organizational theory to public administration of modern societies. A major transition resulted from the exploration by the Hawthorn studies in the 1920s and 1930s, conducted by a well-known industrial psychologist from the University of Chicago, Alton Mayo. A behavioral apparatus was used to drive a second revolution, beyond the revolution that originally produced the theory, which swept the young science into its first stages of maturity. Still, in those days of revolution in progress, many barriers were raised against another step toward social science integration and collaboration in knowledge. This became the activity mainly of those parties who advocated the independent development of public administration and were concerned by too great an orientation toward behavioral sciences. The cognitive approach drew much of the fire, being criticized by those who argued that individuals' attitudes, perceptions, and beliefs were unreliable sources of knowledge. Instead, many suggested the pure behavioral method, where only actual behaviors counted and were considered for a better understanding of social activities and policy affairs.

Nonetheless, trends and developments in the public sector today cannot be fully grasped without adequate attention to attitudinal, perceptual, and behavioral issues, as well as social and cultural ones, which represent an essential part of this book. These aspects conjoin with questions of policy-making, policy learning, and policy evaluation, as well as with managerial, economic, and organizational contents, better to illuminate public systems. The human and social side of public organizations became central and critical for all seekers of greater knowledge and comprehension of the state's operation. During the 1960s and through the next decades, collaboration in social sciences was practically created. Moreover, individuals and groups were set at the heart of the discussion on organizational development and managerial methods. The human side of organizations was made an organic part of the art of administration. Still today, it is an indispensable facet of the craft of bureaucracy. All who are interested in the healthy future and sound progress of public organizations and services, both as a science and as a profession, have to incorporate humanistic views into their basic managerial ideology. Hence, another important step toward greater collaboration of knowledge was taken.

However, major transitions still lay ahead. International conflicts during the 1930s and the 1940s forced immense changes in national ideology and democratic perspectives in many Western societies. Consequently, public administration and public policy had to be transformed as well. During the Second World War theoretical ideas were massively supported by advanced technology and higher standards of industrialization. These were pioneered by professional managers and accompanied by new managerial theories. Ironically, the two world wars served as facilitators of managerial change as well as accelerators and agents of future developments and reforms in the public sector. The political leaders and social movements of the victorious democracies were convinced that the time had come for extensive reforms in the management of Western states. The assumed correlation of social and economic conditions with political stability and order propelled some of the more massive economic programs in which the state took an active part. The rehabilitation of war-ravaged Europe involved governmental efforts and international aid, most of it from the United States. In many respects, this was a time when productive collaboration took place to remedy some of the damage of the global conflicts. Wounded Europe devoted major attention to the creation of better services for the people, long-range planning, and high-performance public institutions capable of delivering quality public goods to growing numbers of citizens. Building better societies was the goal. A larger and more productive public sector was the tool.

In many respects the utopian vision of a better society generated by the postwar politicians and administrators in the 1940s and 1950s crumbled during the 1960s and 1970s. A large number of governments in the Western world could not deliver to the people many of the social promises they had made. The challenge of creating a new society, free of crime and poverty, highly educated and morally superior, healthier and safer than ever before,

remained an unreachable goal. So during the 1970s and 1980s, citizens' trust
and confidence in governments, and in the public administration as a professional agent of governments, suffered a significant decline. The public no
longer believed that governments and public services could bring relief to
those who needed help, and that no public planning was good enough to
compete with natural social and market forces. The promise of modern administration, running an effective public policy, seemed like a broken dream.
Political changes took place in most Western states, largely stemming from
deep frustration among the public and disapproval of government policies.
By the end of the twentieth century, the crises in public organizations and
mistrust of administrators were viewed as both a policy and a managerial
failure (Rainey, 1990). In addition, this practical uncertainty and disappointment with governments and their public administration authorities naturally
diffused into the scientific community. Theoretical ideas for policy reforms
in various social fields, which once seemed a key for curing malaise in democracies, proved unsuccessful. Within the last decade the search for new
ideas and solutions for such problems has reached its peak; premises originally rooted in business management have been increasingly adapted and
applied to the public sector. Among these ventures are reengineering bureaucracies (Hammer and Champy, 1994), applying benchmarking strategy
to public services (Camp, 1998), reinventing government (Osborne and
Gaebler, 1992), and the influential movement of New Public Management
(NPM) (Lynn, 1998; Stewart and Ranson, 1994). These receive growing
attention, accompanied by large measures of skepticism and criticism.

In light of the above, the scientific background of public administration
in the late 1990s and early 2000s is still not stable and has not overcome its
childhood ailments. On the contrary, identity conflicts have only intensified
with the years. Waldo's (1968) diagnosis in the late 1960s of public administration as a science in formation, struggling with a pernicious identity crisis,
has not changed much. The evolution of alternative subdisciplines inside and
around the field (e.g., policy studies, public personnel management, information management, etc.) carried both promise and risk for public
administration's position and role as a central field of social study. As noted
by Peters (1996a, 1996b), modern public administration greatly reflects lack
of self-confidence both as a science and as a profession. This lack is expressed
in many ways, the most significant being incapacity to guide governments
through a safe circuit of public policy change.

Much of the accumulated wisdom in the science of public administration
has been obtained through social experiments, the commission of policy
errors, and sometimes even learning from them about better ways to serve
the people. But mistakes cost money, much money, money that is paid by
the citizen-taxpayers. Like good customers at a neighborhood supermarket,
citizens should, and have, become aware of the services they deserve, of the
high prices they are asked to pay, and of governmental actions that should

be taken to produce useful changes. Demands for better operation are generally aimed at governments, but they should be, and are, also targeted at science and at academe. Science has the potential for exploring new knowledge, generating better explanations for relevant administrative problems, applying sophisticated and useful professional methods, and, most important, directing all available resources to produce successful and practical recommendations for professionals. Its prime goal is to design a comprehensive theoretical view of public systems that is clear, highly efficient, effective, thrifty, and socially oriented at the same time. This cannot be achieved without extensive understanding of the diversity, complexity, and interdisciplinary character of the science of public administration. But, most important, these targets are unlikely to be accomplished without collaboration among various social parties simply because the tasks facing modern societies are too great and demanding for one sector, as powerful and dominant as it may be, to manage. Thus, it may be argued that modern public administration is really seeking to do more for citizens and to provide them with better services and goods. This necessitates higher levels of cooperation and collaboration among public agencies, but also, and more importantly, among other social players such as the private sector and the third sector. Unfortunately, these processes are still not widespread enough in most of the Western world.

THEORETICAL FRAGILITY AND CITIZENS' MISTRUST IN GOVERNANCE: MAJOR CALLS FOR COLLABORATION

The eclectic nature of public administration as a science, its marked theoretical fragility and instability, together with persistent citizens' mistrust of governmental services and institutions, may be described as major calls for change in the public service. Such calls seek a different spirit among various social players. This spirit calls for better management of public assets, values, and needs, and for advancing the collective idea of going "together" rather than going "alone." In fact, this is what I define as "the spirit of collaboration." As will be explained later, this idea in no way contradicts liberal values or the free market principle of self-derived activity or individual entrepreneurship. It is merely a necessary extension of its boundaries to our modern times and complex environment.

The fragile status of the theory of public administration may serve as one point of departure for our discussion, which is broader and multiperceptional. Here, my core argument is that one can find many ways to depict the administrative system, its functionality, and its relationship with other social players, such as the (organized or nonorganized) public or the private sector. But the identity crisis of public administration and its ability to join forces with others cannot be solved until many approaches are combined and coalesce to explain the very basic constructs that modern societies encounter at the start of the new century. A major assumption of this book is that only mutual efforts and quality combination of critical knowledge from a variety of social disciplines and methods can yield a real opportunity for overcoming public administration's postchildhood problems. Such a crisis of identity, which has existed for more than a century now, carries risks, but also promises, that must be properly isolated, assessed, analyzed, and only then fulfilled. The translation of science into operative acts by government must rely on such wisdom, which can be accumulated from various social branches. Hence, the contemporary fragile theoretical status of public administration may eventually result in higher interdisciplinary collaboration, which can lead to a more extensive reform in practical collaboration. The contribution of this book is thus its effort to bring these views together and to analyze their managerial and social impact, as well as to engender and facilitate collaborative trends in and around the halls of government and public administration.

The desired comprehensive understanding of public administration, as portrayed earlier, should rely on the accumulated wisdom and knowledge of its sister disciplines (and not necessarily the conventional mother disciplines) in the social sciences. Unfortunately, most writing on public systems to date has adopted a unidimensional viewpoint. Public administration was frequently understood through the eyes of policy analysts or political scientists. Alternatively, it was considered a specific field of management science or a domain of organizational studies. While the roots of the administrative process are definitely, and with much justification, identified with political science, policy studies, and managerial constructs of public institutions, it would be most imprecise to point solely to these arenas in portraying the boundaries and nature of public administration. An integrative approach has much merit and potential in this case, and it must be well developed to conform to the complex reality of serving the public.

Administrative science is a discipline in transition that seeks to integrate various scholarly fields for the purpose of better collaboration of knowledge. It involves politics, but not only politics. It deals with policy, but reaches much farther and deeper than policy questions. It incorporates sociological and cultural aspects that change rapidly in a mass communicative global world, but it goes beyond these issues. It deals with people as workers, citizens, clients, and consumers, as leaders and managers, as well as with a variety of other human constructs that merge into a unique branch of knowledge. A multidisciplinary approach is evidently required to explain better what every scholar already knows from his or her personal perspective: that the truth about public administration has many faces, and no monopoly exists any longer over the discipline's status and orientations. Moreover, the multidisciplinary approach, as widely developed in my recent book (Vigoda, 2002a), is an essential theoretical grounding for the idea of practical and successful management of collaboration. As noted above, I identify three main disciplines that serve today as core sources of knowledge in the study of public administration. These are political science and policy analysis, sociology and cultural studies, and organization management and the business sciences, which also comprise organizational behavior and human resources as subdivisions. As will be explained below, these disciplines represent multiple sources of knowledge applicable to the general idea of collaboration by various partners. Similarly, they serve as core elements in our revised thinking of collaboration as a powerful tool for modern governments and public administration.

Politics, Policy, and Collaboration in Public Administration

The political approach to public administration was depicted by Rosenbloom (1998) as stressing the values of representativeness, political responsiveness, and accountability to the citizenry through elected officials. These values are considered necessary requirements of democracy, and they must be incorporated into all aspects of government and administration. Wallace (1978) argued that ultimately public administration is a problem in political theory. It deals with the responsiveness of administrative agencies and bureaucracies to the elected officials, and through them to the citizens. Shafritz and Russell (1997) provide several politics-oriented definitions of public administration: it is what government does (or does not do), it is a phase in the policy-making cycle, it is a prime tool for implementing the public interest, and it does collectively what cannot be done so well individually (pp. 6–13). Hence it is impossible to conduct a politics-free discussion of public administration.

The political system in modern democracies, here defined as "governments and public administration," obviously works for the public, but at the same time it also needs to work with the public by reason of securing democratic values. Similarly, governments and public administration in modern societies work under the free market doctrine. These actions are reflected by extensive action for the private sector that safeguards the idea of free economic choice. Yet to do so, governments and public administration also need to work continuously with the private sector. This mutual effort better defines boundaries for the economic system, and thus advances collective social interests.

Politics is clearly the heart of public administration processes; hence, it is also expected to play a critical role in collaboration management. Politics focuses on citizens as members of groups or on highly institutionalized organizations that sound the public's voice before political officials and civil servants. The politics approach to public administration involves strategies of negotiating and maneuvering among political parties, public opinion, and bureaucracies. In many respects this dynamic is fundamental for the emergence of healthy collaboration at all levels. It involves an incremental change in society, which relies on open debate, a legitimate power struggle that frequently leads to compromises, the distribution and redistribution of national resources and budgets, and a heavy body of legislation and law to regulate these processes.

Still, perhaps the most obvious linkage between politics and public administration stems from policy-making and policy implementation processes. It is naive to distinguish political systems from professional administration systems in regard to public policy. Politicians and administrators need to collaborate as much as other social players need to collaborate with governments and public administration in order to reach their ambitious goals. As Rosenbloom (1998:13) suggested, "Public administrators' involvement in the public policy cycle makes politics far more salient in the public sector than in private enterprise. Public administrators are perforce required to build and maintain political support for the policies and programs they implement. They must try to convince members of the legislature, chief executives, political appointees, interest groups, private individuals, and the public at large that their activities and policies are desirable and responsive." In many ways, these activities are built upon the covert assumption that collaboration is needed among various players in the political as well as the social system in order to move bureaucracies forward. These assumptions are also the essence of collaboration and the road to success in public policy-making.

The theoretical contribution of political science to the study of public administration is therefore multifaceted. It invokes better understanding of the power relations and influence dynamics that take place within and among bureaucracies (Pfeffer, 1992), and determines their operative function as well as outcomes. Here, party politics acknowledges that the investigation of pressure and interest groups, and the better understanding of conflict relationships among various players of the state, are used to build models of decision-making and policy determination that are rational and realistic. In addition, political psychology is implemented more thoroughly to explore personality traits of political leaders as well as of public servants. For the same reasons, budgetary studies and policy analysis methods are an integral facet of the political approach, which assumes limited rationality as well as high constraints of time and resources on the administrative process.

From a somewhat different perspective, Ellwood (1996:51) argued that political science has simultaneously everything and little to offer public management scholars, hence also public administration scholars. Everything, because both fields deal with political behavior, processes, and institutions. Little, because political science deals only with the constraints forced on the administrative process, with no practical contribution to the managerial improvement of public systems. Ellwood further agrees that both fields rely on other academic disciplines, employing techniques of anthropology, economics, game theory, historiography, psychology, and social psychology, as well as sociology. In line with this it would be only natural to conclude that the relationship between political science and public administration is described as an on-again, off-again romance. Kettl (1993:409) suggested that "the importance of administration lay at the very core of the creation of the American Political Science Association . . . when five of the first eleven presidents of the association came from public administration" and played a major role in framing the discipline. As Ellwood puts it, with the years, public administration became public but also administration. It shifted its focus to a more practical and client-service orientation, which necessarily incorporated knowledge from other social disciplines, such as personnel management, organizational behavior, accounting, and budgeting.

The methodological contribution of a political approach to public administration studies is also meaningful. Here a macro analysis is necessary if one seeks an understanding of the operation of large bureaucracies and their coexistence with political players. A political approach delivers these goods by means of comparative studies, policy evaluation methods, rational choice models, and simulations, as well as content analysis techniques and other tools useful for observation of the political sphere. Put another way, a vast process of knowledge accumulation was needed to move the discipline forward. In many respects this is actually another form of collaboration, where one field of knowledge contributes directly or indirectly to the development of another. While this is not a deliberate progression, hardly anyone disputes its positive impact on social structures.

The political and policy view of collaboration will thus put at the center of our discussion all those who are part of political processes. According to this perspective, no collaboration can endure if it is not controlled and monitored systematically and significantly by the state and by its administrative branches. The politics-policy view will also expect that politicians and bureaucrats will have a key role in launching collaboration and making it work. To attain collaboration, a strategic policy decision is needed that signals to all other social players that this is a desirable road for the state. Similarly, it means that politicians will be willing to share power with others to reach the collective targets. This is exactly why many actually doubt the potential of a politics-policy approach to collaboration. Assuming that politicians will not readily share power with others, unless they are forced to do so or are guaranteed that their interests will not be harmed, the politics-policy-driven initiative for collaboration is unrealistic.

The Social and Cultural View of Collaboration in Public Administration

The second approach that is highly relevant to the understanding of public administration bodies and the collaborative processes within them rests on a sociological apparatus. It has a very close relationship with the political approach, so it is sometimes defined as a sociopolitical view of public systems or as a study of political culture (Shafritz and Russell, 1997:76). Yet its core prospects are beyond the political context. The voice of society has a special role in the study of public administration arenas, not only for democratic and political reasons but also because of its fundamental impact on informal constructs of reality such as tradition, social norms and values, ethics, lifestyle, and other human interactions. As will be explained later, the social and cultural view of collaboration in public administration relies on the function of several players. Among these are citizens as individuals, organized and unorganized groups of citizens, the third sector, and other nongovernmental parties such as the media and academe.

The theoretical contribution of a sociological and cultural approach to public administration consists of several elements. An essential distinction must be drawn between inside and outside cultural environments. An outside cultural sphere incorporates informal activities and behaviors of small groups as well as of larger social units that interact with the administrative system. Included in this category are customers' groups, private organizations, nonprofit volunteering organizations, and citizens at large. Considerable attention has been paid to communities and to the idea of communitarianism (Etzioni, 1994, 1995), as well as to the emergence of the third sector, as rapidly changing conventional structures and beliefs in modern societies. An inside cultural environment is related to internal organizational dynamics and to the behaviors of people as work groups. Thus, it is sometimes termed organizational culture or organizational climate (Schein, 1985). Like the outside organizational environment, it has some observable constructs, but it mostly expresses many covert phases. In many ways, culture is to the organization what personality is to the individual—a hidden, yet unifying theme that provides meaning, direction, and mobilization (Kilmann et al., 1985). It includes basic assumptions as to what is right and what is wrong for a certain organizational community, norms and beliefs of employees, unseen social rules and accepted codes of behavior, as well as tradition, language, dress, and ceremonies with common meaning to all organizational members. All these distinguish "us" from "them," promote group cohesiveness, and improve common interests.

Several sociological sources can be effective in analyzing public administration dynamics. The first is group theory, which is closely related to the study of leaders and leadership. The second is ethnic studies, which concentrate on minorities and race questions such as equity, fair distribution of public goods, and integration in productive public activity. The third is communication and the technological information revolution, which have had a radical effect on society, public policy, and public administration units and structure. Information networks and communication have become immanent features of the cultural investigation of bureaucracies. For many years a plausible approach in management science and in the study of public administration called for the formulation of a universal theory in the field, one that is culture-free and applicable across all nations. With the passage of time and with giant technological developments, this perception became ever more anachronistic.

Today, the goal of a universal administrative paradigm is hardly achievable. An alternative viewpoint is more balanced and contingent. It argues that basic similarities do exist among public organizations in various cultures, but at the same time intraorganizational and extraorganizational cultures fulfill a major mediating role. Culture in its broad context constantly affects the operation of bureaucracies as well as political systems that interact with them. Examples like Theory Z of W. G. Ouchi (1981) and lessons from more recent Chinese and east European experiences stimulated the scientific community and initiated culture-oriented ventures in general management inquiry (Hofstede, 1980, 1991). They especially promoted the investigation of work values and culture-oriented management in private as well as in public arenas. Many scholars became convinced of the necessity of incorporating social and cultural variables as core elements in the administrative analysis of public arenas. A sociological and cultural approach to public administration also made an important methodological contribution. It initiated culture-focused surveys of individuals and groups who work in the public sector or of citizens who receive services and goods. Culture-focused observations and analyses possess the merit of being sensitive to people's (as citizens or employees) norms, values, traditions, and dispositions, and sometimes they overlap other politics- and policy-oriented studies so as better to explore dynamics in public organizations.

However, in contradiction to the politics-policy view, the social and cultural approach to collaboration concentrates on social players who, strictly speaking, are not politically oriented. According to this perspective, successful collaboration can make progress by the involvement and participation of citizens as individuals, citizens in organized or unorganized groups, and the contribution of the third sector. This is basically a grassroots/bottom-up approach to collaboration, which is far different from the bureaucracy-rooted/top-down model for collaboration best depicted by the politics-policy approach. It relies on personal engagement of people who care, and on their genuine contribution to the community. These individuals and groups have already given power to the political system and to policy makers, but have come to a point where they feel that the political system is unable or unwilling to go the extra mile for them. In other words, the sociocultural view of collaboration concerns a change that is fostered by the power of individuals and collective groups. Citizens are expected to play the most significant role in any collaborative process—its launching, development, and evaluation. They will thus need practically to reclaim power from politicians to make the collaborative ventures work. For this purpose they must rely heavily on the collective public voice as reflected by the media. However, even then the power of governments and public administration, and its impact on a state's collaborative culture, is much stronger because citizens are naturally less organized than bureaucracies, and therefore less powerful. In addition, most citizens of modern democracies are usually passive and apathetic (Almond and Verba, 1963; Verba et al., 1995), and thus have less influence on the emergence and development of collaborative ventures. Hence, the socio-cultural approach to collaboration as reflected in bottom-up dynamics is problematic. It makes an important contribution to the process of collaboration, but it is definitely not the only possible or effective model that can bring governments, public administration, and other social players together in a mutual effort for modern societies.

Organizational and Managerial Views of Collaboration in Public Administration

In recent years organizational and managerial theory has become relocated in the study of public organizations. The New Public Management philosophy has emphasized the need to better manage the public sector in order to cure some of its pandemic illnesses. Following this, I argue that organizational and managerial theory deserves much more attention in the study of the idea of collaboration in public administration.

A managerial definition of public administration proclaims that it is the executive function in government or a management specialty applied in public systems (Shafritz and Russell, 1997:19–23). Although public sector management is distinct from private sector management, in many ways the two systems share a surprisingly broad area of similarities (Rainey, 1990). For many years differences stemmed from the nature of services each sector provided, from diverse structures and functions, but mainly from discrepancies in the environment. However, when the environment started to change rapidly, organizations had to change as well. Modern societies have become more complex, flexible, and dynamic. Cultural, industrial, technological, economic, and political environments of organizations have undergone speedy transformations that are still in progress. On the one hand, public and private organizations have to adjust to and comply with similar changes in the environment to safeguard their interests and existence. But on the other hand, the starting point of public organizations is far inferior and urgently calls for rethinking and reinventing (Osborne and Gaebler, 1992).

Conventional wisdom accepted a classic assumption regarding the relatively stable and invulnerable structure of public organizations. Drawing on the Weberian approach, hardly anyone disputed the need for large bureaucracies in modern democracies. Moreover, the advantages and disadvantages of large bureaucracies were well known among academics and practitioners. A weighty bureaucracy was considered an axiom of public administration. Only with the emergence of new management trends in old bureaucracy were these basic assumptions questioned. For example, Kettl and Milward (1996) stated that management in the public sector matters. It matters because citizens' demands increase and because the standards of performance expected from governments are higher than ever before. Performance is related in the minds of people and in scientific studies with quality of management, quality of managers, and the administrative process between them. Accordingly, it has much to do with the human aspects of administration. Perhaps this perception has led to some recent developments in public administration, making it client-oriented and more businesslike. Scholars frequently define these shifts as the principal change in public administration and its transition into a revised field of study named public management.

In all, modern public administration decidedly benefits from the inputs of managerial and organizational theory. It gains additional profit from traditional political and policy analysis prospects, as well as from a wider society- and culture-oriented theory. Modern societies question current obligations of public personnel to citizens, and urge them to put the people first by treating them as customers or clients. Yet these tendencies draw fire from those who argue that a client orientation of the public sector breeds citizenry passivism and a lack of individual responsibility for the state and its agencies. It is further assumed that today these obligations and commitments are not clearly decoded and manifested or satisfactorily implied. Much more can be done to improve responsiveness to citizens' needs and demands, without the active role of citizens in the administrative process being abandoned.

Moreover, the application of multidisciplinary approaches (political, social, and managerial) to public service is essential before further advances can be made. It is argued that some tenets of administrative culture and democratic values need to be explored, in order to propose higher levels of social theory synthesis and integration. These may also be the milestones on the way to better linkage, partnership, cooperation, and collaboration among state leaders, public officers, and citizens in modern societies. Here lies the main challenge of public administration in the coming years: the invention of a new, vitalized administrative generation tightly bound up with modern participatory democracy and willing to join forces with other social players for the increase of common social goods.

Figure 1.1 demonstrates a triangle of disciplines that construct the very basic essence of collaboration in public administration. According to this figure, to acquire collaboration in public administration, an interdisciplinary platform should be developed, based on shared knowledge and experiences. The most influential fields of knowledge that are relevant are political science and policy studies, social and cultural understanding, and managerial and organizational wisdom. An effective philosophy of collaboration thus relies on three core constructs: (1) the creation and integration of common political views and shared policy targets; (2) the development and formulation of common social norms, views, and cohesive cultural outlook; and (3) the encouragement of common managerial strategies and organizational views.

Figure 1.1
Collaboration by Disciplinary Origins: A Basic Structure

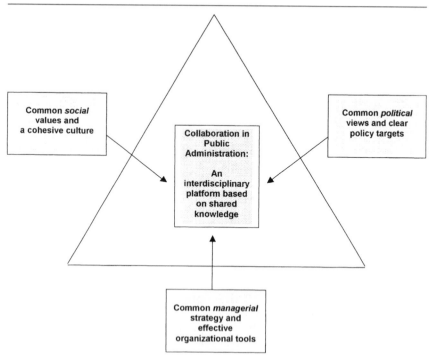

COLLABORATION BY DISCIPLINES:
SEVERAL THEORETICAL PERSPECTIVES

Our knowledge of collaboration may also benefit from a comparison with other close or similar concepts that are frequently used by scholars from the three disciplines. Figure 1.2 presents a typology of criteria, by disciplinary origin and theoretical perspective, that contribute to our understanding of the meaning of collaboration. Beyond the disciplines and perspectives explained in the previous sections, I have used two additional criteria: (1) structure and (2) interaction. Structure refers to the arrangement and formation of power relations; interaction refers to the types of contacts, interfaces, and relations among units. Let us examine the meaning of these criteria by each of the disciplinary origins and theoretical perspectives. Together they are expected to shed light on the meaning of collaboration under the political, managerial, and social apparatuses.

First, a conceptual and practical conflict exists between public administration in its classic bureaucratic framework and the nature of democracy in which it should operate. Some will say that this is an inevitable conflict

Figure 1.2
An Analysis of the Meaning of Collaboration by Three Disciplinary Perspectives

Discipline and Perspective / Criterion	Politics and policy: State level analysis	Organization and Management: Managerial level analysis			Social and Cultural: Community level analysis
		Organization focused	Labor focused	Business focused	
1. Structure	Bureaucracy	Centralization	Cohesion of work	Private money and ownership	Social power and stratification
2. Interaction	Democracy	Decentralization and participation in decision making	Division of work	Public money and ownership	Pluralism and communitarianism
3. Collaboration	Cooperation	Coordination	Integration	Partnership	Association

between administration and politics in free societies. Others will note that bureaucracy does not necessarily contradict the democratic ethos. On the contrary, it guards democracy and makes it work. Unless a strong bureaucracy is present, democracy may lose its essence and be perceived as a weak and ineffective governance mechanism. When collaboration is brought into the discussion, things become even more vague. Democracy proudly encourages freedom of choice, which can be used by social players in many ways, only some of which are collaborative. Yet to guard against centrifugal forces, social players need also to enhance cooperation to gain the best political outcomes. While I will further discuss the meaning of cooperation in the later chapters, it is essential to mention at this point that cooperation reflects a mutual effort on the assumption that there are close or similar political interests which can be gained through collective action.

The sociocultural view is set out on the extreme right of figure 1.2. It illuminates how the bureaucratic-democratic conflict is implemented in the social arena. Hence, social power and stratification are confronted with the ideas of pluralism and communitarianism. Modern societies generally seek more pluralism and heterogeneous inputs by citizens and various ethnic groups. Social leaders also mention individuals' involvement, voluntarism, and social responsibility as momentous for the healthy development of communities. However, modern societies simultaneously need to operate against conservative structures of stratification and rigid social clusters. Frequently, the power of economic, cultural, and political elites delays pluralistic processes and preserves old structures of governance and mobilization. The term *association* thus reflects a need for compromises among various social players and the search for mutual interests that can work in behalf of citizens and communities.

Finally, when we take an organization-management perspective, we enter a more complex arena. The conflict between democracy and bureaucracy is close in type and in nature to the conflict between social power or stratification, on the one hand, and to pluralism or communitarianism, on the other. The striving for (political) cooperation and (social) association is close to several other terms coming from the organization-management agenda, such as (organizational) coordination, (work) integration, and (business) partnership. Decentralization in bureaucracies ultimately means conveying power to other stakeholders and limiting the power of public agencies. Organizational management theory usually denotes such processes as participation in decision-making or, better, empowerment (Sanderson, 1999). In fact, this is one critical obstacle to more collaboration in government. As bureaucratic theory suggests, governors and public administrators do not graciously yield power and authority to others. Moreover, organizations confront various centrifugal forces: (a) centralization versus decentralization, (b) cohesion of work versus division of work, and

(c) private money and ownership versus public money and ownership. As will be elaborated later, these elements, which appear so contradictory, can be brought together by means of (a) coordination, (b) integration, and (c) partnership. Together with the political idea of cooperation and the social idea of association, they may build an inclusive vision of collaboration in public administration.

SOCIAL PLAYERS IN COLLABORATIVE DYNAMICS

According to the three disciplinary views presented above, it is now possible to identify and define some of the key stakeholders who take part in any collaborative process, be it on the local-community, state, or national level. The roles, functions, responsibilities, and perceptions of these players will be discussed in detail in the following chapters, but a brief overview of these players may prove useful for the reader.

Government and Public Administration

The terms "government" and "public administration" (G&PA) refer to all agencies that are fully or partly governmental or government-owned. This includes all government ministries, government authorities, public companies that are government-owned, and other institutions where the government holds a major share in budget or in management. "Governments and public administration" also includes local authorities and agencies that work under the supervision and control of these bodies. In addition, the term covers boards and structures of national projects that were created ad hoc for a local-level or state-level task (e.g., transportation, energy, infrastructures). Governments and public administration represent all individuals who work for these bodies and are paid by them directly.

Businesses and the Private Sector

The next category of social players who will enjoy special attention in our discussion is the powerful business/private sector. This is perhaps the largest and most influential sector in every open democracy and free market society. It accounts for most of the economic activity on the national level and provides a field test and laboratory arena for many organizational and managerial experiments later applied in other organizations and in the public sector. Included in this sector are all firms, companies, and businesses that are privately owned, privately sponsored, or privately managed. They all seem to transact with other bodies on a business-based rationality that is profit-oriented. Furthermore, the sector includes organizational bodies, but in fact it refers to individuals who work primarily in such bodies. This sector, like the public one, is also highly structured and formal, but it is much less centralized and thus free for entrepreneurial inputs that are innovative.

Citizens, Communities, and the "Third Sector"

Citizens and the third sector represent a third player of high importance for our discussion. In many respects this group is more complex than the group of governments and public administration due to its lack of formal structure and its mass orientation. In fact, and as will be elaborated in chapter 4, we should distinguish three sections or subgroups that deserve attention here: (1) citizens as individuals; (2) citizens in small and unorganized groups; and (3) citizens who are part of larger groups or communities that are usually also more formal and long-lasting, and may be defined as third sector bodies. The third sector has some characteristics of an organized-structured body and is exceptional, but the other two subgroups represent sporadic action by individuals or small, informal groups of individuals that are more difficult to study and examine.

While most if not all of the figures included in the governments and public administration section can be also defined as "citizens," here we focus also, but not exclusively, on those who are not formally included in government bodies and public administration organizations. Citizens of the state may be defined in many ways, yet the simple way is to define this group as "the people." Such a broad definition includes all those who are legally members of a nation, a state, or a city/town/village. For reasons of scientific clarity and simplicity, we are not able to include in this group all those who may be part of the "community" or are not formal or legal residents or citizens. However, informally these "illegal" members of the community are definitely part of the voice of the collective citizenry. Their opinions, attitudes, and behaviors should be taken into account together with those of the legal citizens, especially in societies where their relative number in the population is significant. Similarly, formal and informal citizens may choose to create a short-term or a long-term structure of groups and action forces. As will be elaborated in chapter 4, the theoretical distinction of various types of citizens' groups is meaningful for our knowledge on collaboration. It is noteworthy, however, that the most developed organizational construct of citizenry action is represented by the nonprofit sector, which is better defined as the "third sector" to distinguish it from the other two sectors, the profit/private-business one and the public one. Furthermore, one may also observe that most individuals who are included in this category are simultaneously part of the governments and public administration category and the business and private sector category.

AN ELEMENTARY INTERDISCIPLINARY MODEL FOR THE MANAGEMENT OF COLLABORATION IN PUBLIC ADMINISTRATION

Without doubt, various core disciplines have served public administration and contributed greatly to its modern formation and development. Nonetheless, a collaborative scientific effort that is well structured and supported theoretically and practically may become even more influential in the years to come. The idea of better managing scientific collaboration may advance what various social scientists study and understand independently, and combine these mutual sources in the service of modern society through better achievements and higher performance of public sector agencies.

In my view, the most prominent players who operate in the service of modern society are (1) governments and public administration, (2) citizens and the third sector, and (3) the private and business sector. It is therefore argued that each disciplinary approach highlights the role of a different player in the collaborative effort.

Figure 1.3 presents this idea graphically. According to this scheme, there are three types of analysis that enhance our knowledge of the idea of collaboration: (1) political-national level analysis, (2) community level analysis, and (3) managerial level analysis. These types are driven by three disciplinary origins and the same three categories of social players.

Political-National Level Analysis of Collaboration

The state-level analysis of collaboration will lean on government and public administration branches as the prime initiators and leaders of collaborative ventures. The focus here is on what the state wants to do, can do, and does do in practice to advance the idea of partnership and collaboration among various players. Naturally, each of these questions deserves separate consideration. Bringing state leaders and senior public officials to the conclusion that collaboration is needed is a first stage. It should be followed by the recognition that these institutions have the power to change. Finally, it is in the hands of officials of all levels, mainly in the halls of public administration, to allocate resources and make them available for the process. According to this analysis, governments and their executive branches coordinate the actions of other social players, such as citizens and the third sector (line A), as well as businesses and the private sector (line B).

Communal Level Analysis of Collaboration

The community level collaboration incorporates a less organized structure of activity that is built upon loose contacts among most of the players.

Figure 1.3
An Interdisciplinary Spectrum of Collaboration Perspectives

Social player Disciplinary origin	Governments and Public Administration (G&PA)	Citizens and the Third Sector	Businesses and the Private Sector
1. Politics and Policy	*Political-National level* *analysis of* *collaboration*	*A* *B*	
2. Social and Cultural	*C*	*Communal level* *analysis of* *collaboration*	*D*
3. Organizational and Managerial	*F*	*E*	*Managerial level* *analysis of* *collaboration*

Conservative ⟶ Modern

An evolutionary continuum of collaboration

While contacts between individual citizens may be close, unless they assume a formal structure of voluntary and nonprofit organization, they remain informal and should be considered ad hoc, voluntary activities. The community level analysis of collaboration needs to classify the various patterns of citizenry involvement. Such activities can take place on the federal or national level, on the local level (i.e., neighborhoods and cities), or at the workplace. As will be explained later, all these activities may be considered "good citizenship behaviors" that flourish only in a collaborative and supportive social environment. Public administration is in contact with citizens as individuals as well as with groups of citizens, and its primary goal is to elevate these relations to the stage of organized collaboration where the main benefit goes to the people as clients. Nonetheless, the community level analysis of collaboration implies that governments and public administration (line D) and business and the private sector (line C) support and reinforce grassroots activities that are initiated and monitored by citizens as individuals or groups.

Managerial Level Analysis of Collaboration

The managerial level of analysis makes use of current organizational theory and business experience to discuss issues of conflict management, allocating business potential for growth and innovation, and wisely handling human resources in both the private and the public sectors. While the private sector serves as a benchmark for public organizations, there are still mutual benefits for both parties. The idea of public-private partnership (PPP) imparts practical meaning to the symbolic slogans of collaboration. These models of alliance, which will be presented in chapter 4, allow transfer of resources from one sector to the other and improve both parties' flexibility and responsiveness to customers and citizens. However, the philosophy of PPPs is mostly economic in nature. An alternative pattern of collaboration has emerged in the last few years with the creation of Businesses for the Community (BFC) projects. This alternative is a more authentic one that best correlates with the social movement of communitarianism and voluntarism. As will be explained later, it is based on a spontaneous orientation of good citizenship that partly derives from economic considerations—but is mostly community-rooted. Obviously, according to the organizational and managerial level of analysis, businesses and the private sector are the central engines for collaboration, supported by citizens and the third sector (line E) and by governments and public administration (line F).

An Evolutionary Continuum of Collaboration

A better understanding of the differences among the three types of analysis can be gained when an evolutionary perspective is included. As will also be argued in subsequent chapters, the state level analysis is the more conservative-classic approach to collaboration, followed by the community level analysis, which is closely identified with the idea of communitarianism (Etzioni, 1994, 1995). The managerial level of analysis is the most recent, modern, and complex one. This last view is also the focus of this book. In the following chapters I will try to explain why the managerial perspective is the most promising of all the approaches, and how its advantages can be applied in service of the public.

COLLABORATION, BUREAUCRACY, AND THE OLD TYPE OF PUBLIC ADMINISTRATION

For many years conservative public administration and the conservative perception of the role of bureaucracy were noncollaborative by nature. As suggested in figure 1.2, the politics-policy approach allocates responsibility for providing public services to governments and to public administration. It relies heavily on the authoritative power of bureaucracy and on its patronage position toward other social players. Hence, the state level analysis is elementary for the study of collaboration in public administration. No such process is possible unless governments and public administration are ready to initiate it, to invest effort and resources to advance it, and psychologically to recognize the enormous advantages that such a reform carries. The political support is no less important. While administrative officers are more likely to become engaged in such a mind change, the political realm is less likely to identify its advantages.

What are the foundations of this approach? The old type of public administration is identified with the very basic nature of classic bureaucracy, with roots dating back thousands of years. The Bible mentions a variety of hierarchical and managerial structures that served as prototypes for governance of growing populations. Ancient methods of public labor distribution were expanded by the Greeks and the Romans to control vast conquered lands and many peoples. The Persian and Ottoman empires in the Middle East, like imperial China in the Far East, paved the way for public administration in the modern age, in which European Christians, and later Christians of the New World, were in the ascendant. All these, as well as other cultures, used a remarkably similar set of concepts, ideas, and methods for governing and administering public goods, resources, and interests. They all employed professionals and experts from a variety of social fields. They all used authority and power as the cheapest control system for individuals, governmental institutions, and processes. All of them faced administrative problems close in type and in nature to problems of our own times: how to achieve better efficiency, effectiveness, and economy in government; how to satisfy the needs of the people; and how to sustain stable political hegemony despite the divergent demands and needs of sectoral groups.

Not surprisingly, all the above cultures and nations also used similar managerial tools and methods aimed at solving problems of this kind. They all applied, fairly effectively, division of labor, professionalism, centralization and decentralization mechanisms, accumulation of knowledge, coordination of jobs, complex staffing processes, long-range planning, controlling for performance, and so on. Intuitively, one feels that nothing has really changed in the managerial and administrative processes of public organizations for centuries, possibly millennia. But this feeling is of course exaggerated. Some major changes have taken place in recent centuries to create a totally different environment and new rules, to which rulers and citizens must adhere and by which they must adjust their operation. In fact, a new kind of governing game has taken shape, in which public administration plays a central role.

Despite basic similarities, public administration of our times is an organism entirely different from public services in the past. It is larger than ever before, and it is still expanding. It is more complex than in the past, and it is becoming increasingly so by the day. It has many more responsibilities to citizens, and it still has to cope with increasing demands of the people. It is acquiring more eligibilities, but more than ever before it must restrain its operation and adhere to standards of equity, justice, social fairness, and especially accountability. Moreover, modern public administration is considered a social science, a classification that carries high esteem but also firm obligations and rigid constraints. For many individuals who decide to become public servants, it is a profession and occupation to which they dedicate their lives and careers. But most important, public administration is one of the highly powerful institutions in modern democracies. It wields considerable strength and influence in policy framing, policy-making, and policy implementation. Hence it is subject to growing pressures of political players, social actors, and managerial professionals.

INTEGRATING COLLABORATION WITH THE NEW PUBLIC MANAGEMENT PARADIGM

To understand better the (dis)integration of the idea of collaboration in the new public management (NPM) paradigm, one should first define the boundaries and meaning of NPM. Since the early 1980s, much work has been conducted in public administration theory and practice that claims to go beyond the conservative approach in the field. This "liberalization" of public administration is recognized today as the "new public management" trend. The self-identity problem of public administration was greatly aggravated by the launching of the idea of NPM. As noted by Kettl and Milward (1996:vii), "Public management is neither traditional public administration nor policy analysis since it borrows heavily from a variety of disciplines and methodological approaches." Mainly drawing on the experience of the business/industrial/private sector, scholars have suggested taking a more demanding attitude to the dynamics, activity, and productivity of public organizations. However, "Competing academic disciplines dueled to establish bridgeheads or, worse, virtually ignored each other as they developed parallel tracks on related problems" (p. 5). Consequently, a cross-fertilization, which could have accelerated learning and improved performance of public systems, was delayed.

What are the roots of NPM, and in what way is it actually a new arena in the study of the public sector? Several theoretical foundations, as well as practical factors, can answer these questions. The first, and probably the deepest, source of NPM emerges from the distinction between two proximate terms or fields of research: administration and management. As noted earlier, since the late 1880s the monopoly on the term "administration" has been held by political scientists. Scholars like Goodnow and Wilson were those who perceived public administration as a separate and unique discipline that should consist of independent theory, practical skills, and methods. However, the term "management" referred to a more general arena, used by all social scientists but mainly by those who practice and advance theory in organizational psychology and business studies. Consequently, conservative administration science tends to analyze the operation of large bureaucratic systems as well as other governmental processes aimed at policy implementation. Management, on the other hand, refers to the general practice of empowering people and groups in various social environments and in handling multiple organizational resources to maximize efficiency and effectiveness in the process of producing goods or services.

A consensus exists today that NPM has become extremely popular in the theory and practice of public arenas. But can we define it as a long-range revolution in public administration theory? No comprehensive answer exists to this question. Some will say that NPM has only revived an old spirit of managerialism and applied it in the public sector. Others will argue that this in itself has been a momentous contribution to public administration as a discipline in decline. Relying on an extensive survey of public management research in America, Garson, and Overman (1983:275) argued that this increasing popularity was due to the more virile connotation of the term "management" than of "administration." Over the years, a growing number of political scientists have perceived public administration as an old and declining discipline. It was unable to provide the public with adequate practical answers to its demands and, moreover, it left the theoreticians with a vast number of social dilemmas waiting for exploration. Interesting evidence of this process could be found in many schools of public administration that during the 1980s and 1990s decided to become schools of public management. In the search for alternative ideas, management theory was proposed as the source for a new and refreshing perspective. It was suggested that public management rather than public administration could contribute to a new understanding of how to run the government more efficiently and thereby to surmount some of its ailments.

In an attempt to understand and advocate this inclination more fully, Perry and Kraemer (1983) proposed that a greater impact of new ideas and methods from the field of public management on the administrative science was essential and natural. It reflected a special focus of modern public administration that was not to be ignored. Rainey (1990:157) claimed that this process was a result of the growing unpopularity of government during the 1960s and 1970s. Ott et al. (1991:1) stated that public management was a major segment of the broader field of public administration because it focused on the profession and on the public manager as a practitioner of that profession. Furthermore, it emphasized well-accepted managerial tools, techniques, knowledge, and skills that could be used to turn ideas and policy into a (successful) program of action.

Since the 1980s many definitions have been suggested for NPM. However, nothing seems wrong with the relatively old perception of Garson and Overman (1983:278), who defined it as "an interdisciplinary study of the genertic aspects of administration . . . a blend of the planning, organizing, and controlling functions of management with the management of human, financial, physical, information and political resources." As further discussed by other scholars (e.g., Lynn, 1996:38–39), six differences exist between public administration and public management that make the former a new field of study and practice. These are (1) the inclusion of general management functions such as planning, organizing, control, and evaluation in lieu of discussion of social values and conflicts of bureaucracy and democracy; (2) an instrumental orientation favoring criteria of economy and efficiency in lieu of equity, responsiveness, or political salience; (3) a pragmatic focus on midlevel managers in lieu of the perspective of political or policy elites; (4) a tendency to consider management as generic, or at least to minimize the differences between public and private sectors in lieu of accentuating them; (5) a singular focus on the organization, with external relations treated in the same rational manner as internal operations, in lieu of a focus on laws, institutions, and political bureaucratic processes; (6) a strong philosophical link with the scientific management tradition in lieu of close ties to political science or sociology.

While the emergence of NPM is frequently related to the increasing impact of positivist behavioral science on the study of politics and government (e.g., Lynn, 1996:5–6), the practical aspect of this process should also be considered. Practical public managers (Golembiewski, 1995), as well as political scientists, will refer to the difficulties in policy-making and policy implementation that confronted many Western societies in Europe, America, and elsewhere during the 1970s. These practical difficulties are viewed today as an important trigger for the evolution of NPM. Reviewing two recent books on NPM (Aucoin, 1995; Boston et al., 1996), Khademian (1998:269) argues that American and British advocates of the field find common ground in explaining why such reforms are necessary. The problem of an inflexible bureaucracy that often could not respond efficiently and promptly to the public needs conflicted with basic democratic principles and values in these countries. Peter Aucoin elegantly summarizes a "trinity" of broadly based challenges with which Western democracies have struggled, and will probably continue to struggle in the future, partly through management reform. These are (1) growing demands for restraint in public sector spending; (2) increasing cynicism regarding government bureaucracies' responsiveness to citizen concerns and political authority, and dissatisfaction with program effectiveness; and (3) an international, market-driven economy that does not defer to domestic policy efforts. It seems that these challenges have led governments in America, Britain, New Zealand, Canada, and elsewhere in the West to the recognition that sound reforms and changes in the public service should be made.

Scholars agree today that at least some of the accumulated wisdom of the private sector in these countries is transferable to the public sector (Pollitt, 1988; P. Smith, 1993). In an attempt to liberate the public sector from its old conservative image and tedious practice, NPM was advanced as a relevant and promising alternative. NPM literature has tried to recognize and define new criteria that may help in determining the extent to which public agencies succeed in meeting the growing needs of the public. NPM has continuously advocated the implementation of specific performance indicators used in private organizations to create a performance-based culture and matching compensatory strategies in these systems. It has recommended that these indicators be applied in the public sector (e.g., P. Smith, 1993; Carter, 1989) because they can function as milestones on the way to better efficiency and effectiveness of public agencies.

Moreover, citizens' awareness of the performance of public services was suggested as a core element of NPM because it can increase the political pressure exerted on elected and appointed public servants, thereby enhancing both managerial and allocative efficiency in the public sector. Scholars who advocate NPM liken this process of public accountability to stakeholders/citizens to the role adopted by financial reporting in the private/corporate sector (P. Smith, 1993). As in the private sector, increasing exterior-related outcomes can have a profound impact on internal control mechanisms, as managers and public servants become more sensitive to their duties and more highly committed to serving their public customers.

Following these, Lynn (1998:231) suggested that the NPM of the late 1990s had three constructive legacies for the field of public administration and for democratic theory and practice. These were (1) a stronger emphasis on performance-motivated administration and inclusion in the administrative canon of performance-oriented institutional arrangements, structural forms, and managerial doctrines fitted to a particular context—in other words, advances in the state of the public management art; (2) an international dialogue on and a stronger comparative dimension to the study of state design and administrative reform; and (3) the integrated use of economic, sociological, social-psychological, and other advanced conceptual models and heuristics in the study of public institutions and management, with the potential to strengthen the field's scholarship and the possibilities for theory-grounded practice. While the first two "legacies" are widely discussed in contemporary literature, the third is greatly understudied and needs further theoretical development, empirically guided research, and practical implementation. Its importance lies in pointing to the potential advantage of mutual effort for the purpose of creating modern societies that work better, serve better, and fulfill the expectations of citizens better.

Finally, Kettl and Milward (1996) argue that one of NPM's most significant contributions to public administration as a discipline in transition is the focus on the performance of governmental organizations. According to their analysis, this scientific orientation needs to draw on "a wide variety of academic disciplines for the full and richly textured picture required to improve the way government works. Only through interdisciplinary cross-fertilization will the picture be rich enough to capture the enormous variety and complexity of true public management (and administration) puzzles" (p. 6). I further suggest that the interdisciplinary effort needs to be effectively integrated with a well-grounded managerial plan of collaboration. Such a managerial strategy for collaboration among various social players will be of merit not only for the public sector but also for the private and third sectors.

THE MIND CHANGE OF NEW PUBLIC MANAGEMENT: RESPONSIVENESS TO CITIZENS AS CLIENTS

One important theme highlighted by the NPM approach has been the responsiveness of governments and public administration to citizens as clients. A previous work by Vigoda (2000b) identified two approaches to understanding public administration's responsiveness. These approaches can be defined as controversial but also as complementary. They provide distinct views of responsiveness, but in addition each approach contains checks and balances missing from the other. According to one approach, responsiveness is at best a necessary evil that appears to compromise professional effectiveness, and at worst an indication of political expediency if not outright corruption (Rourke, 1992). According to this line of research, responsiveness contradicts the value of professionalism in governments and public administration because it forces public servants to satisfy citizens even when such actions run counter to the public interest. In the name of democracy, professionals are almost obliged to satisfy a vague public will. Short-term considerations and popular decisions are put forward while long-term issues receive little and unsatisfactory attention. In addition there is a risk that powerful influences of some may ring out loudly, and wrongly pretend to represent the opinions of many. Such influences can result in an anti-democratic decision-making pattern and may not represent the true voice of the majority. The other approach to responsiveness suggests that democracy requires administrators who are responsive to the popular will, at least through legislatures and politicians, if not directly to the people (Stivers, 1994; Stewart and Ranson, 1994). This approach is more alert to the need to encourage a flexible, sensitive, and dynamic public sector. In fact, it argues that only by creating a market-derived environment can governments and public administration adopt some necessary reforms that will improve their performance, effectiveness, and efficiency.

While responsiveness is occasionally considered a problematic concept in public administration literature, it is undoubtedly critical for politicians, bureaucrats, and citizens alike. A responsive politician or bureaucrat must be reactive, sympathetic, sensitive, and capable of feeling the public's needs and opinions. Since the needs and demands of a heterogeneous society are dynamic, it is vital to develop systematic approaches to understanding that society. Undoubtedly, this is one of the most important conditions for securing a fair social contract between citizens and governmental officials. Hence, scholars and practitioners suggest the elaboration of performance indicators based on public opinion. The opinions of service receivers must be seriously considered good indicators of public policy outcomes (Palfrey et al., 1992; Winkler, 1987; National Consumer Council, 1986; DHSS, 1979). This information can help one to (1) understand and establish public needs; (2) develop, communicate, and distribute public services; and (3) assess the degree of satisfaction with services (Palfrey et al., 1992:128). Consequently, the NPM approach advocated the idea of treating citizens as clients, customers, and main beneficiaries of the operation of the public sector that is today more oriented to assessing its performance (Thomas and Palfrey, 1996). In essence, the motivation to meet the demands raised by citizens is equivalent to satisfying the needs of a regular customer in a regular neighborhood supermarket. According to this view, responsiveness in the public arena closely complies with business-oriented statements such as, "The customer is always right," and, "Never argue with the client's needs" that every salesperson memorizes from his/her first day at work.

But what does responsiveness actually mean? How can we best define and operationalize it for dependable social research? In essence, responsiveness generally denotes the speed and accuracy with which a service provider responds to a request for action or for information. According to this definition, speed can refer to the waiting time between a citizen's request for action and the reply of the public agency or the public servant. Accuracy means the extent to which the provider's response meets the needs or wishes of the service user. Yet while speed is a relatively simple factor to measure, accuracy is more complicated. Beyond the recent trend of analyzing public arenas in terms appropriate for the marketplace, public service accuracy must take into consideration social welfare, equity, equal opportunities, and fair distribution of "public goods" to all citizens (Vigoda, 2000b). These values are in addition to the efficiency, effectiveness, and service that characterize market-driven processes (Rhodes, 1987; Palfrey et al., 1992). To test the accuracy of government and public administration endeavors, several methods may be applied:

1. Examining citizens' attitudes and feelings when consuming public services; this can be achieved by means of satisfaction measures indicating the outcomes of

certain activities and the acceptance of public administration actions as fruitful, beneficial, equally shared among a vast population, effective, fast, and responding well to public needs.

2. Examining the attitudes and perceptions of others who take part in the process of planning, producing, delivering, and evaluating public outcomes. These "others" include external private and nonprofit firms, suppliers, manufacturers, constructors, etc.

3. Comparing objective public outcomes with absolute criteria for speed, quality, and accuracy. The absolute criteria need to be determined in advance within a strategic process of setting performance indicators (Pollitt, 1988). Such a comparison is even more effective when conducted over time, populations, cultures, geographical areas, etc.

4. Comparing the distribution of services and goods with moral and ethical criteria as set forth by academics and professionals.

Subject to several restrictions and balances, responsiveness has a potentially positive effect on social welfare, and it improves the process of modernization in the public sector. Recent managerial positions such as the NPM approach also suggest that, as in the private sector, increasing external-related outcomes (i.e., responsiveness of governments and public administration to citizens' demands) will have a profound impact on internal control mechanisms (P. Smith, 1993). It implies that managers and public servants become more sensitive to their duties and highly committed to serving the people.

To increase responsiveness in public administration organizations, it is essential to constantly evaluate the perceptions of citizen-clients toward various service providers (Vigoda, 2000b). However, responsiveness cannot be maintained unless these perceptions accord well with the expectations and perceptions of public administrators in all levels. The idea of having a certain level of fit between what clients expect and what public officials are ready, willing, or able to deliver is crucial. Vroom (1964) emphasized the meaning and importance of expectations inside the workplace. He argued that meeting employees' and managers' expectations is essential for obtaining proper individual outcomes and general organizational performance. In many ways, the theory of expectations may be transferable to the complex relationships between service providers and citizens as consumers. Supporters of the cognitive discipline (e.g., Lewin, 1936) have long argued that perceptions of reality, and not reality itself, determine people's behavior and attitudes toward other individuals and toward the environment. Following this, the citizens' view of the public service depends on their interpretation of reality and not on public administration actions per se. Likewise, responsiveness is far from being measured in absolute figures. Put another way, the "sense of responsiveness" counts differently in various administrative cultures, and consequently should be treated as a relative rather than an absolute measure. Furthermore, as with responsiveness, relative measures may also be applicable to other important properties of public administration activity, such as responsibility, accountability, fairness, and equity. For example, waiting five minutes on the phone for the response of a public servant may seem reasonable to a British citizen. However, it may be perceived as less reasonable by an American citizen, and may appear totally unreasonable to an Israeli citizen.

In line with this, a comparative-relative approach based on cross-cultural understanding needs to be considered if one seeks a reliable evaluation of modern public administration. As will be explained below, a preliminary platform for such a specific initiative exists, and is being examined in the Israeli sphere. Moreover, beyond its interesting comparative merit, this approach of continuous responsiveness evaluation has meaning for the advancement of collaborative ventures among public administrators, policy makers, business firms, and citizens as individuals, groups, or active members in third sector organizations. In other words, responsiveness may be seen as an additional step toward higher levels of collaboration in public administration. The wider context and importance of such collaboration is discussed in the next section.

COLLABORATION: ONE STEP BEYOND RESPONSIVENESS

Mounting interest in the idea of NPM has put serious pressure on state bureaucracies to become more responsive to citizens as clients. In many respects NPM has become the "religion" and responsiveness is the "law." However, recently bureaucracies have also been urged/forced to progress beyond responsiveness and extend collaboration with other social players, such as private businesses and third sector organizations as well as citizens. Without doubt, these are important advances in contemporary public administration, which finds itself struggling in an ultradynamic marketplace. Some may even define the shift toward collaboration as an additional "law" in the "religion" of NPM. Like any other call for reform, it was built upon a necessary change in the minds and hearts of the players involved. In order to bring collaboration into the central halls of public administration, many old perceptions and attitudes need to be revised and reframed.

Despite its envisaged advantages, the idea of collaboration attracts heavy fire from those who believe that it is merely a utopian idea with minimal impact on the administrative process. At most, opponents suggest that collaboration is a welcome change in theory-building and in practical culture reconstruction, but they add that modern societies still confront a growth in passivism in citizens, who tend to favor the easy chair of the customer over the sweat and turmoil of participatory involvement. Thus, the critics conclude, collaboration remains a utopian idea with only minimal impact on the nature of modern administration and on its activities.

A swelling current in contemporary public administration seeks to revitalize collaboration between citizens and administrative authorities through various strategies. In fact, such trends are not so new. The need to foster certain levels of cooperation among political governmental institutions, professional agencies of public administration, and citizens as individuals or groups has been mentioned before, and was advanced in several ways. Among these philosophies and strategies one should mainly consider the following:

1. Greater cooperation with the third sector (A. A. Thompson et al., 2000; Gidron et al., 1992; Grubbs, 2000).
2. Greater collaboration with the private sector and initiation of plans aimed at supporting communities through various services in the fields of internal security, transport, and education (Glaister, 1999; Collin, 1998; Schneider, 1999).
3. Encouragement of state and local municipality initiatives that foster values of democratic education, participation, and involvement among citizens (e.g., the local Democratic Club established in Culver City, California: www.culvercityonline.com, accessed 6/25/01). This pattern also coheres with the idea of a communitarian spirit that transfers some (but not all) responsibility for civic development from the central government to local authorities in states and cities, as well as directly to individual citizens (Etzioni, 1994, 1995).
4. Innovation by original citizenry involvement through nonprofit civic organizations that help to establish a culture of participation and practice of voice (see the examples of "citizens' conventions" in Denmark and Israel: www.zippori.org.il/English/index.html, accessed 6/25/01).

Still, advocates of the NPM approach continue to claim that the main instrument to restore ill-functioning governments and public administration systems is better responsiveness to citizens as clients or customers. According to this line, which is rooted in political economy rationality and social choice theory (Kettl and Milward, 1996; Hughes, 1994), only better compliance with people's wishes can steady the wobbly interface between citizens and rulers in contemporary democracies. But is a market-driven responsiveness really the best answer for crises in governance, or is it only an oversimplification of wider problems in modern society?

RESPONSIVENESS AND COLLABORATION: A QUEST FOR HATS AND LADIES

What are the advantages of citizens' being treated as clients/customers over the perception of them, and others, as equal partners in the process of governance? A metaphor of ladies and hats may prove useful here to examine two competing options: (1) there are two substantially separated faces of government and public administration (two ladies), one that adopts the idea of responsiveness and one that favors collaboration; (2) the discipline of governance and public administration is more coherent (only one lady) than we might think, and at most it changes colors over time (two hats).

Above I portrayed two themes in current public administration research as separate and dissimilar perspectives. I argued that responsiveness is of the essence in NPM, and I further suggested that NPM seems detached from the idea of collaboration. Therefore, it may be suggested that there are two different types of public administration; like two ladies, one is attired by the supporters of responsiveness, the other by supporters of collaboration. These two ladies differ substantially because, as explained earlier, they advocate independent views of the roles of governments, public administration, and citizens in the process of running states and societies. Yet we may in fact be suggesting only one lady with two hats. One hat, an older-style classic, is more oriented to bureaucratic tyranny and concentration of power in public agencies. It reflects a situation where public administration is the right hand of politicians, and thus must preserve power through maximum centralization and control over decisions as well as resources. This hat/attitude implies minimal care for either responsiveness or collaboration because both mean depriving governments and public administration of their power. The other hat, however, is newer, and more receptive to and more appreciative of de-concentrated managerial ideas, such as better responsiveness and improved collaboration with citizens, which effect a wider process of modernization. This hat signals a continuous change in public administration systems and, maturing with time, it implies more participation of the people in the administrative process. The lady of public administration wearing the newer hat is less concerned about bureaucracy losing power and control; instead, she favors sharing responsibilities and dialogue with citizens, which may lead to cooperation and partnership on a higher level.

In addition, the "two ladies" version is a more classic approach to the understanding of responsiveness and collaboration in public arenas, so it has received wide scholarly attention over the years. As noted earlier, one group of studies has concentrated on the first "lady" of public administration, the idea of responsiveness (e.g., Stivers, 1994; Rourke, 1992), while the other group has focused on the other lady, who represents the idea of collaboration and partnership (e.g., John et al., 1994; A. A. Thompson et al., 2000; Nalbandian, 1999). In fact, hardly any attempt has been made to try to integrate these views or to suggest that they may be better seen as stemming from one another. The "two hats for one lady" image inclines to this integration, but it is less frequently developed and needs more extensive explanation and elaboration. According to this image, responsiveness and collaboration are inherently related. They designate different points on a continuum of a citizens–government/administration interaction that are constantly shifted and reframed with time and social events. Thus, a framework of interaction with citizens is better presented here by one evolutionary continuum (one lady) of public administration. Along this continuum, responsiveness and collaboration are only different "hats" on one line of symmetry.

THE ESSENCE OF COLLABORATION: NOT NEW, NOT SIMPLE, NOT IMPOSSIBLE

Recent criticism of the responsiveness-oriented thinking of NPM as described here and elsewhere has called for a theoretical and practical shift toward increased collaboration in and around public administration (Vigoda, 2002b). According to this criticism, NPM breeds passivism among citizens as clients by overstating the idea of responsiveness. Putting the citizen-client in the center sends a hidden social message to the people, saying, "Make your wish . . . it is our goal to serve you"; yet it adds, "But please don't bother us . . . leave the professional work to us." In other words, NPM and the ethos of responsiveness put citizens as clients at the center by asking them for their needs and demands. But similarly they ask citizens to keep their distance from the administrative work and the decision-making centers. The hidden message is thus, "Bureaucracy needs to work for you, so keep away." In so doing, modern public administration wins the battle of responsiveness but doesn't even try to fight the battle for collaboration with the people.

Consequently, I find it essential to induce an intensive turn toward collaboration in the public sector. In many respects such a progress carries all the typical symptoms of an additional administrative reform, one that is directed at the minds and the hearts of policy makers, policy implementers, and other social players, such as private entrepreneurs, third sector organizations, and citizens in general. Doing (good) administrative work for the public also means doing it with the public, as well as with all those who are concerned with the formation of modern/prosperous societies. Hence, despite some serious obstacles and difficulties, the idea of a "collaborative public administration" may be defined as a reform in progress. It is a reform that has the potential of revising our old, conventional view toward government by making government and public administration more willing to share ideas, knowledge, and power with others.

While theory is equivocal when dealing with various recommended models of reform in public administration, there are still two major types of such reforms: (1) bureaucracy-driven models and (2) grassroots-driven models. Both of these models suggest an infusion of change in the public sector, and each does it using a different starting point. Bureaucracy-driven models view governments and public administration as those who are responsible for the initiation of change and for making it work properly. The grassroots-driven models, on the other hand, put more demands on the people with an expectation that they, instead of governments and public administration, will make the first move toward reform. These models demonstrate how various reforms became successful when starting from urging needs of individuals or groups, or from the spontaneous collective support of an original street-level leader. Naturally, there is no ideal model integrating both of these approaches in policy planning cycles. However, there may be an ideal-type model for a collaborative reform. In the following chapters I will try to better explain the meaning of these theoretical models and to elaborate on their contribution to the creation of a "spirit of collaboration" in and around public administration. My core argument is thus that an ideal managerial type for collaboration should, and can, be portrayed.

CHAPTER 2

The Spirit of Collaboration and the Role of Governments: A Politics-Focused Analysis*

THE MEANING OF COLLABORATION UNDER MODERN GOVERNANCE: THEORETICAL OVERVIEW

A politics-focused analysis of collaboration emphasizes the role of governments and executive branches of the state, generally referred to as public administration bodies. In our rapidly developing world, the face of governments, public administration, and communities across the globe is changing. The term "governance," once meaning the power of rulers and state leadership, is slowly but surely coming to signify higher levels of collaboration with other partners in markets and in civic society.

For example, recent conceptualizations of governance suggest a new interdependence of governmental agencies, nongovernmental organizations, and semigovernmental institutions, elsewhere defined as quasi-nongovernmental or QUANGOS (e.g., Rhodes, 1996, 1997; Stoker, 1997). This process reflects what Cloke and his colleagues (2000) define as "a new collectivity of action and a move from assumption about primacy of the state as the site of political activity" (p. 112) or, alternatively, a "blurring of boundaries" (Stoker, 1996) distinctly demarcating private sector, public sector, and third sector activities (Cloke et al., 2000). Under the condition of greater power separation, higher levels of competitiveness, and stronger demands for quality services by citizens, a wider range of actors and organizations is required and is self-motivated to contribute resources, skills, knowledge, and experience to the process of policy-making.

*Some sections in this chapter are based on E. Vigoda and E. Gilboa, "The Quest for Collaboration: Towards a Comprehensive Strategy for Public Administration," in E. Vigoda, ed., *Public Administration: An Interdisciplinary Critical Analysis* (New York: Marcel Dekker, 2002).

Still, a more elementary need at this point is to clarify the essence of collaboration for our reinvented governance. Here, some major critiques on the vision of collaboration see it as an unrealistic pattern for our democratic states and for our liberal culture. So are we presenting a utopian approach, unlikely to function in a competitive environment and a free market society? Perhaps collaboration should remain as a merely theoretical prototype for the ideal society we all seek, but can never attain. I considered these questions time and again prior to the decision to write this book. And I must admit that I have no definitive answers. A "spirit of collaboration" in public administration may indeed survive as an unreachable goal, at least in the short or midterm. Still, the decision to write this book was taken on account of many national and international experiments in collaboration that have evinced a certain measure of success.

Theoretically, collaboration draws substance from various disciplines and fields of knowledge, even more than those mentioned in respect of the eclectic nature of public administration. Actually, it would be unreliable and incomplete to treat collaboration solely from an economic, political, sociological, or even psychological point of view. Rational choice theory, the conflict resolution approach, communitarianism, or real-politics analysis provide additional theoretical tools that should be wielded in a useful manner if one seeks a higher level understanding of the collaborative process as well as its chances to endure.

A CONCEPTUAL BOUNDARY BETWEEN PARTNERSHIP AND COLLABORATION

The literature is preoccupied with close but different terminologies for mutual effort by social players. In this sense, collaboration is only one concept that needs to be assessed in relation to others such as partnership, cooperation, integration, and joint ventures.

In the next section I try to elaborate on the meaning of a strategic collaboration process as stemming from the latest theoretical thinking and practical experiences. I undertake a theory-guided analysis of ever-increasing and challenging collaboration ventures, and provide a general map of effective collaboration processes as demonstrated in the field of local government. My expectation is that this doubly anchored synthesis, both practical and theoretical, will be of value for the disciplines of governance studies and participatory democracy, and particularly will reframe innovative thinking in contemporary public administration.

COLLABORATION AND HUMAN NATURE: RATIONAL CHOICE THINKING AND THE WIN-WIN ALTERNATIVE

Rational choice theory suggests that humans are motivated by self-interests. On the grounds of utilitarian philosophy and game-theory arguments

(Boschken, 1998; O'Toole, 1995), it has been posited that individuals, as well as groups and institutions, mostly operate according to desired goals and objectives. These may be formal or informal, but they always aim at maximizing personal benefits and minimizing costs (Ostrom, 1986). On the assumption that social players constantly seek more revenues, and at the same time attempt to reduce expenses and negative retaliations, collaboration between state agencies and other social players basically contradicts human nature. This contradiction evolves with the rapid increase of public interests, divided ambitions, and the potential of conflict among all players.

Opposed to this rationality, healthy and prosperous civic societies in practice seek higher levels of cooperation among their members to increase general "public goods" and to improve the welfare and well-being of large communities. Thus, collaboration is frequently referred to as another mechanism for conflict management. For example, Fredericksen (1996) elaborated on the usefulness, but also the fragmentary nature, of analyzing conflict management methods in public domains as a continuum running from competitive to cooperative techniques. While the former represent a win-lose game, the latter are better described as win-win alternatives. Between the two extremes several other alternatives exist, such as litigation, arbitration, mediation, facilitated problem-solving, and collaboration.

Analyzing the nature of partnership, Cigler (1999) suggests a slightly different continuum of networking, cooperation, coordination, and collaboration. According to this definition, collaboration has six main characteristics: (1) being a strategy rather than a limited tactic, (2) involving strong ties among participants, (3) involving groups from different sectors (public, private, third sectors), (4) involving a group of members who are committed to a long-run activity, (5) having a formal pattern of running the process and a clear method of documentation, and (6) inclining to transparency and encouraging involvement and contribution of other citizens and public groups.

In light of the above, I suggest that cooperation usually denotes a limited, low-level, and mainly tactical assembly of forces to achieve a defined goal, while collaboration reflects a wider and more extensive stage of cooperation with strategic, far-reaching, and integrative significance. As suggested by Cigler (1999), "Collaborative actions involve strong linkages among stable membership in specific and often complex purposes, and usually are long term" (p. 86). Beyond cooperation of organizational units, firms, or other interest groups in society, collaboration represents a longer-range ideology that, to be successful, must gain the support of senior decision makers, leading public officials, and experienced managers in governmental agencies. According to the social ecology theory and the strategic management approach, organizations (and other parties in public alliances) benefit from collaboration by reducing uncertainty in their environment (Berman, 1996).

Moreover, evidence does exist today that such collaboration is possible and effective, and thus may be described as a win-win alternative for all partners involved (Fredericksen, 1996; Fisher and Ury, 1983). In fact, the plausible contradiction between utilitarian human nature and the desirable altruistic nature of civic societies is not necessarily contradictory. For the emergence of reliable and honest collaboration, mutual self-derived interests and shared goals must be allocated to all parties. These goals and interests are primarily egocentric and self-directed, but when they cohere with supplementary or similar aspirations of others, they acquire meaningful collective power. Indeed, many issues are still unlikely to become win-win situations in public policy or public administration ventures (e.g., budgetary conflicts, staffing and promotion of public personnel, competitive business ventures).

Nevertheless, the space for effective collaboration is wide enough to include many public initiatives that frequently and mistakenly seem to be win-lose games. The principle of rational choice is well learned by all players. According to this rationality, the greater this collaboration, the bigger and better the benefit to each participant and to the entire community. Furthermore, when public agencies and bureaucracies are involved, their stability, sustainability, effectiveness, and general success are better served. Consequently, healthy collaboration in public domains counts on rational choice, on social/economic exchange theory (Blau, 1964), and on the collective vision of communal solidarism. Therefore, true collaboration exists only in liberal environments and prosperous societies, those abundant in mutual understanding and acceptance of others' needs and aspirations, but that also highlight the idea of free markets and free exchange mechanisms among people. Wherever such acceptance and approval are sparse, there is a greater likelihood of diversification, intolerance, conflict, and self-derived activity rather than social-oriented concern or public solidarity.

Accordingly, pessimists will note that collaboration runs counter to human nature. They will turn to basic assumptions of self-derived activity, utilitarian rationality, and egocentric logic to support this claim. By this rule, the effect of collaboration on public administration and on citizens in general is marginal. Collaboration is of no use in a free market society, where individual interests collide and most of them do not conform to the collective public interest. However, the more optimistic will argue that collaboration among various players in public domains is possible, even if not easily accomplished. According to Gardner (1991) and Berman (1996), broad-based strategies work because people do not resist their own ideas and because they find support, reinforcement, and identity from like-minded people.

Collaboration thereby breeds commitment of participants and yields improved policy advocacy, grantsmanship, increased coordination of resources and know-how, and effective countermeasures against opponents (Coleman, 1989; Roberts and Bradley, 1991; Berman, 1996). For the attainment of collaboration, and for the certainty of its positive long-term impact, serious difficulties need to be overcome. Among these, crossing mind bridges is perhaps the most challenging. A psychological willingness to cooperate and become honest partners in the collaborative process can be secured by convincing the involved parties that it is in their best interest to join forces. The cognitive barrier is thus crucial, and proves even more complicated in the public arena due to the large number of players and the diversity of issues and interests involved, as well as the long-range and extensive impact of the issues on citizens, organizations, markets, and societies.

COLLABORATION AND THE POWER OF BUREAUCRACY

At first glance, collaboration and cooperation between governments, public administration, and citizens seem to contradict the essence of bureaucracy. The ideal type of bureaucracy, as set out by Max Weber, has clearly defined organizational characteristics that have remained relevant down the years. Public organizations have undergone many changes in the last century. But they are still based on the Weberian legacy of clear hierarchical order, concentration of power among senior officials, formal structures with strict rules and regulations, limited channels of communication, confined openness to innovation and change, and noncompliance with the option of being replaceable. These ideas seem to be substantially different from the nature of collaboration, which means negotiation, participation, cooperation, free and unlimited flow of information, innovation, agreements based on compromises and mutual understanding, and a more equal distribution and redistribution of power and resources. According to this utopian analysis, collaboration is an indispensable part of democracy. It means partnership where authorities and state administrators accept the role of leaders who need to run citizens' lives better, not because they are more powerful or superior but because this is a mission to which they are obligated. They must see themselves as committed to citizens who have agreed to be led or "governed" on condition that their lives continuously improve.

In support of the above recognition, D. Thompson (1983) stated that "democracy does not suffer bureaucracy gladly. Many of the values we associate with democracy—equality, participation, and individuality—stand sharply opposed to hierarchy, specialization, and impersonality we ascribe to modern bureaucracy" (p. 235). Bureaucracies, like other organizations, constitute a worksite that is anything but democratic. According to Golembiewski and Vigoda (2000), bureaucracies embody a firm hierarchy of roles and duties, a vertical flow of orders and reports, accountability to highly ranked officers, fear of sanctions and restrictions, and sometimes even lack of sufficient accountability dynamics. All these signal that the "natural state" in public administration is authoritarian.

Hence, it seems odd to ask for genuine collaboration between those in power and those who delegated power. In many respects, growing involvement by interest groups, political parties, courts, and other democratic institutions may only vex politicians in office and state administrators. Too broad an involvement, in the eyes of elected politicians and appointed public officers, may be perceived as interfering with their administrative work. The freedom of public voice is thus limited and obscured by the need of administrators and politicians to govern. The public consequently lacks sufficient freedom of voice and influence. While mechanisms of direct democracy are designed to show such impediments the door, modern representative democracy lets them back in through the window. Representative democracy frequently diminishes the motives for partnership with governance. Constitutions, legislatures, federal and local structures, and electoral institutions are in slow but significant decline in many Western societies. They suffer from increasing alienation, distrust, and cynicism among citizens; they encourage passivism and raise barriers before original individual involvement in state affairs (Eisinger, 2000; Berman, 1997).

But what is the meaning of a "wise collaborative process"? Are there any rules and guidelines that distinguish right from wrong actions in turning a collaborative initiative into an effective process? Theory in this field is quite vague, or at least equivocal. On the one hand, studies focus on the importance of collaboration as another tool in conflict resolution management and on its contribution to the management of public organizations (e.g., Weber and Khademian, 1997; Bardach, 1999; Cigler, 1999; Fredericksen, 1996). On the other hand, this literature is frequently supported by case studies that contribute to our experience and understanding of actual collaborative ventures (e.g., Toregas, 2000; Snavely and Desai, 2000) but that fail to paint the entire picture or move toward reliable generalization.

As far as I could find, no satisfactory attention has been paid so far to the configuration of a strategic process for collaboration in the public sector. Some effort has been dedicated to developing integrative collaboration methods in urban planning or local housing programs (e.g., Nicol, 1998; Kermit, 1994; Cole and Goodchild, 1993), but these attempts have been limited in scope. An inclusive strategic approach should establish a common denominator of various collaboration ventures to promote a more comprehensive theory. Accordingly, the following sections will attempt to fill the gap in this field, and present a general map for strategic collaboration in public administration agencies.

A STRATEGIC MODEL OF COLLABORATION

Despite the growing number of collaborative ventures in government and the knowledge that has subsequently accumulated, only slight regard has been given so far to the need to develop a comprehensive strategy for collaboration in and around public administration. As suggested by Cigler (1999), collaborative actions frequently emerge from disastrous events that trigger fiscal stress or perceived stress. In light of this inconsistent/ad hoc approach to collaboration, it is easier to understand why the literature lacks a more strategic orientation to the field. The potential advantages of collaboration as a strategic apparatus for public agencies are many. It can contribute to the mutual power of public programs, increase commitment of players to a specific idea or initiative, stimulate productivity and performance of people and institutions, enhance the image and legitimacy of players in the eyes of citizens, augment trust in government, and secure democratic values (Nye et al., 1997).

In fact, we have presented our view of the need to foster a strategic approach toward collaboration (Vigoda and Gilboa, 2002). We claimed that like any other administrative or managerial strategy, our suggestion rests on several assumptions. The first is that public administration, its agencies, and its personnel should seek higher levels of collaboration with other social players wherever possible and wherever the public interest may benefit. Another assumption, as will be explained below, is that the local government arena is a good habitat for such experiences, at least in their first steps. However, beyond the first two assumptions, which are normative, the third is much more realistic. It argues that rationalism, as rooted in human nature, permits collaboration only in a limited, albeit increasing, number of public ventures, and that collaboration is best described as a complex process with both advantages and drawbacks.

There are also several preconditions for a strategic approach to collaboration. Generally I adopt Cigler's (1999) suggestion of nine such preconditions: (1) a disastrous event, (2) fiscal stress or perceived stress, (3) a political constituency for cooperation, (4) supportive capacity building, (5) early and continued support by elected local officials, (6) visible advantages of cooperation for participating government, (7) existence of a policy entrepreneur, (8) early focus on visible effective strategies, and (9) emphasis on collaborative skill building. These conditions set the stage for a collaborative venture and make it a relevant mechanism to deal with a public issue.

A better understanding of the collaborative process is based on systematic analysis platforms. One such platform is presented in figure 2.1. Here a general map of collaboration between public administration and others on the national, communal-local, or organizational levels is suggested. This map is based on five main stages and check-points of the process: (1) deciding on a fitting issue for collaboration, (2) characterizing the issue by "what and where" inquiries, (3) finding out who is involved, (4) finding out how to implement, (5) launching implementation, and (6) evaluating the process. These stages will be broadly developed below.

Note also that collaboration can be analyzed from various perspectives. I will try to illuminate how collaboration with public administration is

Figure 2.1
Strategic Map of an Effective Collaboration Process

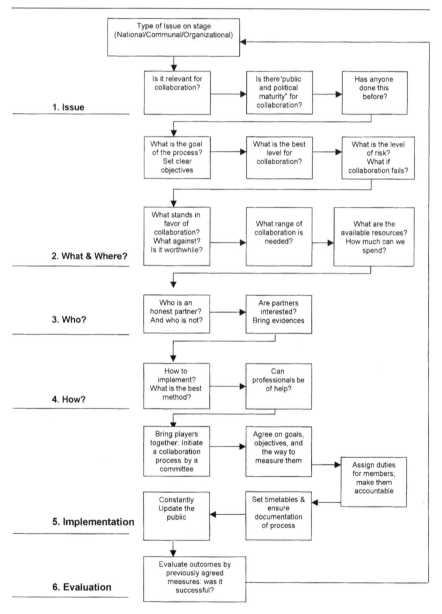

implemented on various social levels, but I have decided to focus on the local government level. Beyond the global, regional, national, and even the organizational level, a local governance view is the most applicable and realistic for practical and theoretical reasons. To date, most collaborative projects reported in the scientific literature have been conducted in this environment, so our present knowledge relies heavily on such experiences. Moreover, as suggested by Sobel (1993) and Etzioni (1994, 1995), the local/communal level is ideal for increasing citizenry involvement in government. It has the potential of bringing together individuals, groups of citizens, private and third sector organizations, and public agencies, and helping them cooperate in a microcosm. The outcomes of collaborative programs in local government are manifested directly to the people. The results are more clearly observed by public stakeholders, who also develop a sense of attachment, concern, and criticism toward these programs. In the longer run these endeavors may evince relevance and compatibility in national or federal domains.

Issues for Collaboration

A good collaboration process starts with an appropriate and worthy issue. From a professional angle the most complex and critical task in a collaboration venture is to classify which public issue really deserves collaboration and which does not. Collaboration can prove successful under two main conditions: (1) when an issue merits investment of effort and making alliances work, and (2) when there is good reason to believe (but not yet confirm) that the power and influence of those who join an alliance are significantly greater than the power and influence of their opponents. This said, I certainly do not assume collaboration to work under sterile conditions. A collaborative process can work even if there are opponents, but only when their power and influence remain markedly low. Moreover, collaboration will not reach fulfillment when another, cheaper, and more elegant solution presents itself that involves a minimum of players. In other words, when another good and economical solution for a social problem is available, collaboration is not needed.

Another criterion is legitimization. A desirable issue for collaboration is one that wins wide-ranging approval among citizens, in addition to support expressed by other public stakeholders. In representative democracies, public opinions very frequently diverge from the opinions of electorates or public personnel. Issues that receive much attention from the public but do not seek public legitimization in response are less likely to be suitable for collaboration. Thus, prior to any decision taken regarding issues for collaboration, a thorough examination of alternatives and stakeholders' interests is recommended. Moreover, as can be seen in figure 2.1, these initiatives must rely on adequate public and political maturity. This is expressed as (1) cultural acceptance of collaboration as an effective mechanism to deal with public concerns, (2) trust in the "goodwill" and sincerity of potential participants, and (3) willingness to take an active or at least a passive part in this process.

Huxham (1993a, 1993b, 1994) addressed the issue of collaborative capability and maturity and its effect on the effectiveness of collaborative ventures. The notion of collaborative capability arose from work with an enterprise development agency concerned to develop strategic relationships with its local authorities. It may be thought of as the capacity and readiness of an organization to collaborate. Some of the dimensions of collaborative capability are the following:

a. Degree of organizational autonomy
b. Degree of individual autonomy
c. Cohesiveness of organizational structure
d. Development of strategic processes
e. Degree of elaboration of their own strategy statement
f. Degree to which collaboration is an issue
g. Level of adult behavior
h. Degree to which the organization has a trusting attitude.

Huxham's argument is not that a greater level of each of these factors in the organizations involved necessarily leads to more successful practice, but that consideration of them may indicate whether, at this time, the organizations are capable of working together on a specific project.

Collaborative capability focuses attention on the individual organizations involved in the collaboration. Associated with this is the notion that the intraorganizational concerns of each participating organization will have an effect on the effectiveness of the collaboration. These factors are therefore of importance to those considering, or involved in, collaborative activity. They may affect the choice of partners or the way in which partners are interacted with.

The dimensions of collaborative capability may also be thought of as indicators of the maturity of each individual organization. By contrast, collaborative maturity—a concept which has emerged from work with a community sector collaborative group—is concerned with the maturity of the collaboration itself. Collaborative maturity does not necessarily reflect the amount of time that a certain collaboration process has been in existence; a collaboration can remain collaboratively immature forever if the members of the participating organizations who are supposed to drive the collaboration fail to learn how to work together effectively.

Therefore, collaborative immaturity may develop from a number of causes; inexperience and poor leadership are two of the most obvious. Collaboratively immature groups are unlikely to have the collective sophistication to understand, and hence to address, process issues concerned with the way in which they work together. They are thus in a vicious circle: because they are unable to address their ways of working together, they are unable to test and experience alternative processes and thereby acquire a greater degree of sophistication.

Finally, issues for collaboration may be raised by different players in the social system, be it public or political institutions, other nonprofit or third sector organizations or groups, private or business firms, or ordinary citizens as interest groups or as individuals. However, as the literature review shows, most current initiatives of collaboration are initiated in local government, by the authorities, and by their public administration cadre (e.g., Cigler, 1999; Berman, 1996; Boschken, 1998).

Analyzing the Problem: What Is Involved and Where Should One Begin?

A comprehensive analysis of the issues set forth involves several questions: What is the goal of the process? What is the best level for practice? What is the level of risk (what happens if the entire process fails to achieve its goals)? What range of collaboration is needed? What are the available resources for collaboration? What are the available financial resources for collaboration?

First, goals and objectives must be clearly defined. Collaborative ventures that are too vague may miss their target. Such goals and objectives need to be measurable; otherwise it will be impossible to evaluate results effectively when the process approaches final stages. As will be explained later, the goals, the objectives, and the way to measure them must be agreed by all partners involved.

When an issue is defined as "potential for collaboration," the next task is to find what is the best level for such a process. As mentioned earlier, in recent years more responsibilities and decision-making power have devolved to local municipalities and to communal public sector agencies, with central government playing mainly a supervisory, coordinating role. Thus, much of our knowledge on collaboration with public administration is driven by local government experiences. Environmental issues, cultural ventures, welfare responsibilities, education, transportation, planning and development, and sometimes even health care services are provided by or with the assistance of local governments and their administrative cadre. In Britain, for example, such trends were associated with the renewal of local democracy and more direct forms of participation (Sanderson, 1999).

However, even issues that deserve collaboration should not necessarily be treated at the local government level. For example, when powerful interests of other players that reach beyond the local government arena are involved, a different level of collaboration may be preferable. In addition, when an issue captures a higher level of public attention, or when it is subject to wide public criticism (e.g., at the national or federal level, through the media, by state comptrollers, or in the courts), limited collaboration in the local government arena will probably be useless or at least ineffective. In this case, the national level may prove more realistic, although it carries some serious considerations resulting from lack of knowledge and experience in this arena and from the restrictions of representative democracy. On the other end of the continuum lies a minimal level of collaboration as implemented inside organizations or among a few agencies. This is more of a partnership model, to which the literature, as well as this book, refers separately.

Local governance will then be ideal for collaboration on communal topics such as urban planning, rural development, limited ecological problems (e.g., water use and purification, waste treatment), welfare initiatives, education projects and initiatives, or transportation plans that concern residents of a defined area. The local government level is frequently inappropriate for collaboration where wider projects with greater impact beyond the local geographical area are concerned. In such ventures the decision-making power of local authorities is low or nonexistent. Still, theory and experience frequently suggest that smaller-scale initiatives at the local government level have the advantage of becoming indicators or facilitators of wider initiatives in national or federal circles (John et al., 1994).

Like any other strategic decision in public domains, collaboration involves a certain level of risk for potential parties. The most visible source of risk is the need to share information among players. As suggested by Weber and Khademian (1997), "Sharing information creates opportunities for participants to discover more numerous and innovative solutions . . . that otherwise would be beyond their reach. But when that information is revealed, participants become vulnerable in a number of ways" (p. 397). Commitment to the process may decline, participants may withdraw, information may be used to advance self-interests at the expense of the interests of others, and defectors may use information they gathered during the process to advance contradictory initiatives. Moreover, a collaborative process gathers more information from various participants and thus extends the realm of possible policy outcomes. This may finally produce an agreement that is less predictable and harder to accept by partners. However, beyond the risk of shared information, poor management or unprofessional handling of a collaborative process may produce meager results. Failure to meet the desired goals can discourage future collaborative attempts, increase antagonism among parties, reduce willingness for future cooperation, and, most important, portray an image of public leadership unable or unqualified to direct such projects. These outcomes may inflict long-range harm on citizens' trust in government and raise the levels of pessimism and delegitimization of democratic institutions in general.

Other "what and where" questions concern the required range of collaboration and the available resources that permit its implementation. The range of collaboration is usually linked to the number of participants; this issue is elaborated more in the following section. However, prior to any decisions on partners, the leading group and initiators of the process (usually elected officials and public administration servants) need to decide on relevant circles of potential contributors. These circles may be geography-anchored, profession-anchored, or task-anchored. For example, collaboration in local governance may be conducted in neighborhoods, in larger local areas, or throughout the entire local municipality district. Collaboration may also be assigned by professional groups interested in the process, such as teachers', parents', and children's councils for education initiatives (Fredericksen, 1996). It may involve traders' associations, customer groups, and business experts for commercial ventures. A decision on the range of collaboration is meaningful because it determines the level of required resources and helps in focusing on relevant social groups that may have an effective say. It is useless to enlarge a collaborative process to involve disinterested, irrelevant, or hostile partners, just as it is problematic to overlimit circles and exclude participants who may raise productive ideas, share experience and information, or introduce challenging viewpoints that enrich the process.

While the financial issue may seem merely technical, it is of great importance and needs to be clarified at a very early stage to ensure that efforts are not wasted and resources are available (Harrison et al., 1995). As with other organizational and public ventures, expenses for a collaborative process are not marginal. Prompt financing is required for all stages from initiation to completion, including public relations, information gathering, and organizational expenses, as well as for the evaluation, method, and lesson-learning mechanism. The directors of the process are responsible for furnishing answers to these questions prior to implementation. Assuming that public administration takes the lead in initiating collaborative processes, it has the duty to allocate resources for, but not necessarily to finance, the process. In most cases the financing body will be a business concern interested in making the process work or a joint effort by several bodies capable of and interested in moving a certain venture forward. Public money will be involved only in projects that disengage private firms. For example, collaboration between the public sector and third sector/voluntary bodies necessitates spending more public money to launch and sustain the collaborative process because the third sector lacks its own resources. In addition, public money will be used in cases where public administration and individual citizens are the only partners involved.

Analyzing the Players: Who Is Involved?

Honest partners in collaboration projects are those who favor and are interested in a long-range activity that promotes their interests together with the interests of others. These players must also show a high level of commitment, trust, and belief in the general goals set by directors of the process.

Not infrequently, players contribute to the redefinition of goals and targets, again on condition that changes are accepted by all parties.

First, partners need to have an interest in the goals and objectives of the process. They are expected to grasp correctly the mutual benefit of self-interests and social interests. Second, potential players must be singled out and assigned to the collaboration process on the basis of their interests or according to their representation of different public sectors. An effective process engages a limited number of significant players concerned to make collaboration work. Players may often hold conflicting interests, yet at the same time they should believe that the social interest can coexist side by side with their personal interests. Moreover, only as long as the benefit is perceived by each player as greater with than without collaboration is the collaboration process worthwhile and possible. Thus, it is necessary to identify players well and to define their actual interests properly. Also, actual interests should be distinguished from overt-formal interests, and reflect the net benefit to the players in personal or in organizational terms.

Relevant players must likewise exhibit commitment to the collaboration process and a strong belief in its usefulness. This is not an easy requirement, especially when the general culture in local government is authoritarian and individuals are unfamiliar with the advantages of the collaboration process. To increase players' commitment, it is recommended that seminars conducted by professionals be held, that successful examples of collaboration processes used in other places be presented, and that a greater sense of openness and transparency be fostered by local agencies of public administration. The term "honest partner" denotes a party that has self-interests but is willing to share whatever is needed on the way to successful collaboration. A typology of players may run from individual citizens through smaller (formal or informal) citizens' interest and ad hoc groups (e.g., neighborhood committees, parents' and students' councils) and professional councils, to organizations of the private and third sectors (Vigoda and Golembiewski, 2001). A central player in all collaboration ventures is public administration, which bears responsibility for coordinating players and directing them toward the appointed goals.

Moving Toward Implementation: How Is This Activated?

Successful implementation of a collaboration process relies on good programs and appropriate methods. A literature review reveals a wide range of alternatives, each differently formulated in accordance with the players' desired goals and objectives. However, similarities exist among these methods that permit a higher level of generalization. For example, Nicol (1998) suggests a version of liaison groups. These are forums of public officers and representatives of business firms that discuss a variety of issues concerning urban planning programs. They allow a clear presentation of policy issues and exchange of useful information in an amenable atmosphere that is problem-solving-oriented rather than conflict-focused. Mandell (1999) notes a different structure, termed *network structures*; these involve private, public, and third sector organizations as well as individual citizens in discussions on topics that are relevant to community welfare. However, network structures cannot operate by traditional managerial methods, but must rely on conflict management methods, empowerment, and trust-building among parties (Sanderson, 1999). The network structure method can thus take the form of a limited task force, a coalition activity, or a coordination group; all these forms rely upon mutual commitment of the parties to each other and to their common goal. Vigoda and Golembiewski (2001) review other platforms of collaboration with citizens, and elaborate on the idea of citizenry conferences as applied in several countries, such as Denmark and Israel. Citizens' conferences and citizens' committees deal with actual public interests and try to influence decisions on issues that are not fully addressed by governments but that the government is willing to promote. Here, too, governments and public administration are encouraged to maintain their advisory position, providing the citizens with sufficient conditions and experience to elaborate on their spontaneous ideas and sound counsel.

The move to implementation of a collaboration process also calls for the potential contribution of professionals. Experts in process management, project control and assessment, public financing, taxation law and policy, engineering and architecture, marketing and market research, statistical analysis and surveys, communication media, and arbitration and law are not always available inside the local authority or even in central government bodies. Therefore they need to come from the free market or from external institutions that possess specific knowledge. Over the years evidence has accumulated that professionals' support, as provided by individuals, private consulting firms, or academic institutions, is beneficial for collaborative negotiations and community training interventions (Fredericksen, 1996). The contribution of the professional is threefold. First, it has the important role of developing skills such as cooperation and collaboration talents (Palvolgyi and Herbai, 1997; Bianchi, 1997). Since many of the collaborative ventures initiated in public administration have no specific background to rely on, participants must be trained prior to launching the program. As theory of conflict resolution shows, lack of such training may cause damage or even the collapse of the entire process due to ineffective group dynamics or hazardous conflicts among participants. Professionals thus take the responsibility of leading the process on its methodological side and assisting the leading administrative cadre in running the program more effectively and smoothly.

Second, professionals provide frontline information and initiate ideas and knowledge that enrich the collaboration process. They can furnish examples of close or similar ventures tested elsewhere, and learn their lessons. Last, professionals serve as a reliable and mostly disinterested party, to whom other participants can turn in times of crisis or when the potential for conflict looms larger. Professionals in conflict resolution and in the field of collaboration enjoy the general image of objective players. They are concerned for the success of collaboration as a democratic process that stands for itself. They usually take no side in debates because they are not experts on education, housing, environmental affairs, or other specific fields. Their contribution consists of escorting others through the difficulties of compromising and working out a plan that best responds to the needs of everyone, particularly of the public.

Collaboration in Practice: Implementing a Program

In general, approaches to collaboration are inherently biased by having the implementation stage placed at the heart of the entire process. While it is indeed a core stage, it would be quite misleading to concentrate on implementation alone unless it is well rooted in the planning and predevelopmental stages. The implementation process deals with several targets: bringing players together under any method chosen; rethinking and redefining goals, and determining performance indicators for the entire process; assigning duties to members with timetables set for various tasks; keeping documentation to create accountability; and ensuring that the public knows, and is continuously updated by all possible means.

The first step of this stage may be defined as the initiation of action. A committee of players' representatives is convened and chaired by a leading public administrator who has been assigned to and trained for the duty. Decisions of the committee need to be taken democratically but with strong emphasis on a consensus; otherwise collaboration is meaningless. This process is time-consuming, and thus can use professional ad hoc advice from time to time. Second, participants rethink and redefine goals to make them measurable by various means. An extensive literature on performance indicators provides the logic and tools for the creation of measurable goals (e.g., Pollitt, 1988). Unless PIs are strictly agreed to by all members, there will be no effective way to evaluate the process in its final phases. Only when the entire implementation stage is clear to all participants is it possible to assign duties to members, to set timetables, and to approve reliable documentation to make accountability possible. An effective and honest collaboration process applies transparency and open gates to the public. When the work of a committee is accomplished, but the public is unaware of the process, a central effect of public encouragement is missed. A strategic process of collaboration differs substantially from limited partnership or short-range alliances by referring to enduring ventures that inspire other initiatives in the future. Therefore, it is important to explore the benefits as well as the difficulties of the process, and to create a culture of a learning environment.

Evaluation: Was It Successful?

The evaluation process is required mainly for future learning and lessons of similar or identical projects. As with many other organizational ventures and policy programs, evaluation represents a feedback mechanism that provides for improvement and advancement. Adjustments in a collaboration project are an indispensable part of the entire strategy. They need to be made because reality transforms the conditions under which the collaborative process operates. In fact, a rigid strategy is no strategy. Unless a collaboration strategy is sufficiently flexible to cohere with transforming reality, its contribution is in doubt.

An extensive arsenal of evaluation methods and techniques can be found in various disciplines. For example, organizational development and organizational behavior tools may assess the inner dynamics and attitudes of parties directly involved, while policy programs analysis and public opinion methods may be applied to evaluate more general outcomes. It is important, however, to create a knowledge bank for relevant collaboration experiences. Prior to launching new collaboration ventures, it is recommended that lessons be learned from past experience and that the necessary amendments be made according to specific requirements, as determined by the project leaders and other parties. Here, too, professionals and academics can be of help. Many existing collaborative projects use such knowledge at the evaluation stage, as well as at other stages, to monitor and revitalize the process.

Evaluation primarily has the instrumental role of controlling results. However, it has another significant aspect: assessing the symbolic-cultural impacts and change for affected organizations, for organization members, or for the citizens they serve (Grubbs, 2000). While the literature usually assesses an evaluation process in terms of "getting the job done," it is crucial that more attention be given the cultural and symbolic waves initiated by a collaboration process. Beyond making a project more effective and responsive to citizens' needs and demands, one should keep in mind that collaboration breeds citizenship involvement and changes people's mind-sets regarding their part in building flourishing communities. A successful collaboration process may persuade pessimistic citizens that public administration can operate better, replace its old orthodox image with a modern responsive one, and draw up new frontiers for effectively managed democracies. The symbolic impacts of collaboration programs and their evaluation are perhaps the objectively hardest to pinpoint on a strategic map. They are the most challenging ones due to their wide-ranging influence and long-term sustainability for generations to come.

IN SEARCH OF THE "SPIRIT OF COLLABORATION"

Recent works on collaboration have encouraged public administration agencies and leaders to adopt new models of alliances among diverse groups and individuals in society. Similarly, collaboration has become a necessity in local governance owing to its growing responsibilities and the continuous devolution of central governance, which transfers more tasks to local authorities. A process of reinvention in local government has thus been inspired by the increasing need to enhance collaboration. Alliances have become strategies for institutions of governance to do more with less, to create leadership systems based on steering rather than rowing, and to treat citizens as customers (Grubbs, 2000) or even partners equal to state and local authorities (Vigoda, 2002b). It has been pointed out that the future of modern public administration depends heavily on joint forces and improved patterns of collaboration among various social players. Citizens' needs and demands, increasing complexity of public programs, and magnification of various social problems serve as main accelerators that bring citizens, public and private sector bodies, and third sector/nonprofit organizations together. This process reflects both self-derived interests and a collective viewpoint of win-win alternatives.

For this purpose, a strategic agenda of collaboration needs to be rebuilt. Its power may draw substance from theory-anchored models and from practical and empirical experience as presented here. A core assumption of the strategic approach is that public administration can no longer settle for a limited level of cooperation between sporadic players, and thus tends to collaboration. Public agencies, both governmental-political and organizational-administrative, will need to adopt a culture of mutual effort and to put more energy into joint ventures that are inclusive and long-term. The strategic platform presented above may contribute to the development of such interdisciplinary orientation and increase the impact of public-private-nonprofit alliances, both instrumentally and symbolically (Grubbs, 2000).

A theoretical gap exists today in the administrative and political science literature, which frequently classifies collaboration as another technique of conflict management, conflict resolution, or rational choice mechanism (Fredericksen, 1996). By contrast, I attempt to treat collaboration as a separate phenomenon, one that deserves its own theoretical attention that is different from other writings on straightforward conflict management theory. I will argue that the option of collaboration is becoming highly relevant for public administration and that it proves useful in a growing number of social issues. The strategic view may serve as a useful managerial tool for the encouragement of collaboration but, more important, it may stimulate a fresh spirit of collaboration, wider and more influential than ever before. Collaboration thus needs a spirit. While many other managerial and administrative actions may well function by a set of formal procedures and bureaucratic orders, it is unlikely that collaboration will work equally well unless it is enriched and vitalized by a unique "spirit." Yet while we all seem to understand that such a spirit is necessary, it is essential to better explain its meaning and contribution.

In this book I would like to enrich the discussion on the current state of new managerialism in public administration and to criticize it for obscuring the significance of citizen action and participation through overstressing the (important) idea of responsiveness. In light of this criticism I propose an alternative to the "responsive" public administration and challenge it with the idea of a "collaborative" administration. I argue that inducing a spirit of collaboration in and around the public sector is essential and possible. It relies heavily on interdisciplinary managerial experiences and on cooperation with the business and the third sectors, as well as on the participation and involvement of individual citizens. I will further argue that the collaborative model, whether it is bureaucracy-driven, citizen-driven, or private sector–driven, is realistic and beneficial even if it cannot be fully applied. To prove successful, however, it must rely on intensive participation and involvement by various social players and on their collaboration with governments and public administration.

THE RESPONSIBILITY OF GOVERNMENTS AND PUBLIC ADMINISTRATION

The present starting point of citizen-government/administration relationships as well as business-government/administration relationships is not very encouraging. King et al. (1998) argued that "although many public administrators view close relationships with citizens as both necessary and desirable most of them do not actively seek public involvement. If they do seek it, they do not use public input in making administrative decisions . . . [and] believe that greater citizen participation increases inefficiency, delays, and red tape." Following this Peters (1999) elaborated on the common belief that today public institutions are structured to prevent effective participation. Given this, the implications for collaboration need no further interpretation. They only emphasize the change and challenge facing modern bureaucracies.

In light of this, the prime responsibility of governments and public administration is to define strategic goals that can enhance partnership with and empowerment of citizens. This partnership must conjoin with resources available in the private and third sectors, which for diverse reasons become more willing to engage in actions for the community and for the public. To respond to the demands for effective participation by the public, these institutions may engage in future structural and cultural changes and extensively use the tool of "empowerment" by which collaboration develops. Empowerment may encourage authentic voluntary behavior by citizens that is not manipulated by the state. Governments can only stimulate environmental conditions that are necessary to generate spontaneous behavior by citizens as individuals and groups, or as part of organized institutions. Programs of involvement and collaboration need to be governed by citizens and administered by practitioners who understand them. However, public service practitioners will fulfill their duties by becoming citizens' honest advisers and helpers rather than controllers of public organizations (Box, 1998, 1999; Rimmerman, 1997). As suggested in previous studies, several programs and techniques can be applied to achieve these goals.

First, volunteer programs in the fields of health, welfare services, education, and security need to receive national and federal support (Brudney, 1990). Adequate training programs for volunteers, as well as for volunteer leadership and management, need to be developed and implemented by professionals. Second, educational efforts that emphasize the importance of individual-level and organized entrepreneurism may start in the very first years of school and create awareness in the very young of the high values of citizenship involvement. Without such an extensive educational effort, long-term initiatives will remain limited and incomplete. Governments will also be responsible for coordination of cooperation among voluntary groups and institutions. This coordination may increase the efficiency of volunteer groups and third sector organizations to get more value for effort. However, the role of governments and public administration must remain consultative. Using their delegated authority, governments can establish public volunteers' committees to coordinate the voluntary activity at the local and national levels. Governments and public administration will maintain their advisory position, providing the citizens with sufficient conditions and experience to work out their spontaneous ideas.

Public administration may also become more active and entrepreneurial in the initiation of the partnership between public servants and citizens. In some countries (e.g., Britain, Germany, Australia) public servants, in contrast to governments and elected politicians, usually enjoy a less political image in the eyes of citizens, so they may gain more public trust and participation than politicians. In other countries, such as the United States, public trust can be gained differently, perhaps through higher transparency of governments and public administration, more involvement of the media, and communal administrative ventures that bring citizens closer to the daily administrative process. The focus of new public management in collaborative spheres will benefit from adjusting more vigorously to include transformation of "goodwill" into "effective operations." Public administration, through its professional cadre, can lead the operative involvement of citizens by improving the partnership between governments and citizens. Investment in spontaneous behavior of the people is low-cost and economical compared with other reform efforts, and thus must be encouraged (Brudney and Duncombe, 1992). Another responsibility of public administration is evaluation. All programs of citizens' involvement will benefit from continuous evaluation by unbiased professionals. These can be found in academe or in the private sector.

LOCAL GOVERNANCE AT THE FRONT

The New Right ideologies of the 1980s, both in Europe and in America, promised a rolling back of government, and thus contributed to the move toward a more businesslike public sector. However, some scholars suggest that instead of a real decrease in governments' involvement in social affairs, a shift was made in the form of governments characterized by the rise of QUANGOS and the (re)creation of the third sector (Cloke et al., 2000). Moreover, much of this activity was directed at the local governance level and at communities that were asked/urged to provide answers for citizens where the central government was unable or unwilling to deliver services and other public goods. Thus new actors and agencies from the private and voluntary sectors became part of local governance policy-making and policy implementation, which resulted in higher motivation for cross-sectoral collaboration.

Similarly, the work of public managers in local governance became highly demanding. Given their central position in the municipality and community, they play a crucial part in creating the right balance and climate for effective partnership and collaboration. Today's organizational environment is constantly changing, and the local government arena is also in transition. Local governments in America, Europe, and elsewhere have undergone significant changes in recent years. These changes were largely caused by the dynamic nature of modern business environments. This is evidenced in a rise in citizens' demands for better services and goods; an increase in decentralization processes within bureaucracies; among the latter, the introduction of advanced technologies into the private and public sectors; and diverse economic conditions such as globalization and open markets policy that leave their imprint on today's managers. These managers need to enhance skills of corporate work and collaboration with as many relevant individuals and organizations as possible. Thus the managerial skill of collaboration becomes an essential tool for today's local government administrators. Here the ethos of collaboration may provide the answer to the growing demands created by a turbulent environment.

Therefore, in recent years collaboration has been successfully utilized in many fields associated with local governance activities. Studies found that wider involvement of public agencies, private organizations, and third sector bodies in community-based strategies was positively associated with the use, effectiveness, and targeting of various social programs, such as care for the homeless (Berman, 1996), pollution control, ecology, and environmental protection ventures (Weber and Khademian, 1997), and with the general responsiveness of local governments to citizens' needs (Crook, 1996).

These studies and others suggest that many local authorities in America, Europe, and other Western states have adopted new concepts and strategies of power-sharing, community-based policy-making, and participatory management processes in community affairs aimed at extending decision-making circles in the local arena (Berman, 1996; Bryson and Crosby, 1992; Wheeland, 1993; Ostrom, 1993). What is the reason for such trends? Advocates of collaboration argue that the complexity of many contemporary social problems requires increased cooperation among social players. These include public and private organizations (Berman, 1996), public agencies, nonprofit organizations of the third sector, nongovernmental organizations (NGOs) and QUANGOs (Grubbs, 2000; Arsenault, 1998; Bardach, 1999; Sarason and Lorentz, 1998; Gidron et al., 1992), as well as citizens as individuals or as informal smaller groups (Vigoda and Golembiewski, 2001). By this approach, cooperation becomes a necessity even if it basically contradicts many of our fundamentally skeptical assumptions of human nature. In fact, individuals, organizations, and bureaucracies remain highly self-focused and self-centered, but to secure their needs and interests, they are obliged to collaborate. To keep abreast of modernity and secure legitimization in the eyes of their customers/citizens, they need to join forces. No public bureaucracy or public agency today is powerful enough to foster its strategies and policies independently. It frequently lacks sufficient knowledge, experience, motivation, technology, legitimization, or other resources that foster the successful initiation and implementation of serious cutting-edge public programs.

CHAPTER 3

Public-Private Partnership and Collaboration: A Business-Focused Analysis

THE COLLABORATIVE PRIVATE SECTOR

For many years, the private and the public sectors of democratic societies were managed almost independently. In the United States a leading doctrine was maximum separation of state/public affairs from business/individual entrepreneurship to allow the latter complete freedom of choice in a liberal environment. In European countries, where the idea of a welfare state was more prevalent, the private sector was also treated as desirable and vital. However, politicians armed the state with regulatory power that many times prevented a private sector monopoly. Social leaders searched for better ways to eliminate the private sector's predatory orientation and to create effective checks and balances that safeguard individuals' welfare, rights, and interests. Other democratic states shared these views, and in fact encouraged a clear border and distinction between what should be considered "public domains" and a "private sphere." Hence, the possibility that public sector bodies should look for better ways to collaborate with the private sector was at times contradictory to the philosophy of free markets and greater competition.

During the late 1980s the idea of new public management emerged, based on the assumption that competition was beneficial for citizens as clients. According to this view, state bureaucracies should seek higher levels of competition to satisfy the needs of citizens as clients or customers. These institutions should operate where the private sector was unable or unwilling to be involved. Yet the option of collaboration, which for many years was perceived as unrealistic and theoretical, became more relevant. It grew rapidly, and proved useful in many countries and fields where separation of work between public and private agencies emerged as insufficient, ineffective, or unsatisfactory. With the passage of time two main platforms of collaboration were created and developed. The first was public-private partnership, which is rooted in the economic view of collaboration. The second may be titled Businesses for the Community initiatives, relying on a social and communal approach where private firms voluntarily become involved in citizenry actions and innovations.

PUBLIC-PRIVATE PARTNERSHIP

Public-private partnership (PPP) may be defined as an arrangement of roles and relationships in which two or more public and private entities coordinate/combine complementary resources to achieve their separate objectives through joint pursuit of one or more common objectives. Khoury (1993) used the term "partnership" to describe "a relationship involving two or more organizations that have agreed to work co-operatively with the common goal of addressing a human or community issue or set of issues. A partnership requires the sharing of power, work, support and information with others. Through mutual agreement and shared values, a partnership confers benefits on each partner as well as the community, while fostering an achievement of ends that are acceptable to all participants" (p. 26).

Referring to the book *When Giants Learn to Dance,* by Rosabeth Moss Kanter (1989), Khoury distinguishes three types of partnerships: stakeholder alliances, multiorganization service alliances, and opportunistic alliances. Although these alliances concern corporate relationships, they contain attributes that apply equally to community development partnerships.

1. Stakeholder alliances involve those groups upon which an organization depends: its customers, suppliers, and employees. Such an alliance produces the closest relationship among the partners and the most extensive overlap of activities. Corporate volunteer programs are stakeholder alliances. Within such a program, a corporation and its employees work together to satisfy a community need.
2. In multiorganization service alliances, several organizations with similar motivation band together to create a new entity—a jointly controlled consortium—to satisfy a common need. The National Food Drive proposed by Toronto's Daily Bread Food Bank was meant to create a consortium of Canadian food banks that would work together as a multiorganization service alliance.
3. In opportunistic alliances, organizations see an opportunity to gain an immediate, though perhaps temporary, advantage through an alliance or joint venture. Corporate sponsorships often fall into this category when they involve like-minded investors who seek to pool resources for a set period of time.

In essence, all these types are long-term concession arrangements between private firms and public organizations. A wider partnership format that includes third sector parties is also possible and will be discussed in chapter 4. In all cases, the private sector participates through donations, involvement, or spreading of knowledge. It may also be engaged through actual economic involvement, designing, building, financing, and operating infrastructures (Brown, 1999; Burnes and Coram, 1999). It delivers related services to the public sector and sometimes, for example, in transport projects, to consumers. The public sector brings in legitimization, handling of bureaucratic procedures, or payments for services over the life of the concession. It defines the services to be purchased or obtained (in case of voluntary involvement) and usually pays for them, unless the private firm has decided to cover expenses for the project in advance. Thus, privatization techniques and other arrangements such as Buy-Operate-Transfer and Public Finance Initiative are only one side of the collaborative process. A purer model is built on voluntary action, community involvement strategies, and engagements in projects where the financial profit is secondary to the social one.

The value of public-private partnership and a wider collaboration doctrine has been recognized and developed enormously in recent years. These relationships are frequently an effective means of improving public outcomes, outputs, and general performances by implementing technologies, methods, and experiences previously tested and evaluated in business firms. Such relationships have flourished in recent decades in various forms, where central and local governance administration as well as manifold private organizations have started to explore the immense potential of partnership and collaboration for citizens, bureaucracies, and the economy.

For example, pressures to expand in the face of dwindling public financial support have led the higher education system in the United Kingdom and elsewhere to look increasingly to the private sector for support. Moreover, as Huxham (1994) notes, every left-wing local authority has looked to collaborate with the private sector. Another example of PPP comes from Canada (Grant, 1996), where the government of New Brunswick became a leader in responding to the need to reengineer social service systems. It chose public-private sector cooperation as a key element in its strategy and policymaking. The human resource department in government worked closely with private consultants to redesign business processes in a way that improved service to citizens and saved money. As part of this mutual effort several key elements of the meaning of "partnership" have emerged:

1. Shared authority and responsibility. If the private sector partner has a financial stake in the project's success, it will insist on a say in how it is implemented. Still, government's prerogative to set public policy needs to be acknowledged, understood, and respected by the private partner(s).
2. Joint investment. Private investment will be matched by a government's investment of time, creditability, and political capital.
3. Shared liability or risk-taking. Private partners usually shoulder the financial risk. Governments, however, carry the social and political responsibilities and the risks that they hold.
4. Mutual benefit. This is perhaps the essence of partnership. Projects must be built in such a way as to provide opportunities and clear advantages for both parties.

Therefore, governments and businesses are expected to enrich the process with several inputs. First, governments bring into the process four major elements:

1. Strong but responsive leadership
2. Vision and a clear view of success
3. Broad agreement on the general need for a partner and a specific agreement on the partner as chosen
4. Strong commitment to a long-lasting effort.

The private firm is expected to contribute four other essentials:

1. Full understanding of various constraints involved in a government-based process
2. Strong organizational and financial stability
3. Willingness to commit its best human resources to the project; to build a team of managerial experts that is best attached to the partnership theme and essence, and that is socially oriented toward working together with public officials
4. Ensuring that the partnership project is beneficial in business terms. The private firm must answer "yes" to the question "Is it worth it?"

Nonetheless, another element is crucial for a successful partnership. As noted by Khoury (1993), each partner must have a real desire to compromise, cooperate, and add value to the relationship. These orientations require that responsibility and accountability be clarified from the beginning and that they be led by wise managerial executives.

Other examples of PPP come from the United States. For instance, Kennedy and Rosentraub (1999) discussed the issue of public-private partnership in professional sports teams. According to their study, the period since the early 1990s has given rise to an almost unprecedented building boom involving new stadiums and arenas for such teams. They expected that by 2002 at least 60 percent of the 121 major sports franchises would play their home games in a facility built or remodeled since 1991. Construction costs were in excess of $175 million for arenas and $300 million for stadiums. Thus, these projects could increase the demand for labor, and many of the newer facilities were built in aging downtown areas to attract visitors to the core areas of central cities. Building a new stadium or arena can enhance the quality of life and bring national attention to a community through the presence of a team.

However, although a relatively small group of team owners have paid for the stadiums and arenas their clubs use, the vast majority of facilities built since 1991 have involved public-private partnerships and subsidies. In these partnerships, it is quite common for the public sector to be responsible for more than half of the construction costs while the teams retain the preponderance of revenues from ticket sales, luxury seating fees, concessions, advertising, parking, and so on. In a few instances, the public sector has assumed responsibility for 100 percent of the cost of a new stadium or arena while allowing teams to retain virtually all of the revenues generated by the new facility (Rosentraub, 1999).

According to Kennedy and Rosentraub (1999), governments make these extraordinary investments for several reasons. One is that the public sector hopes either to stimulate or to redirect economic development and regional recreational patterns through the building of a new facility and a team's presence. Yet these writers note that most research indicates that teams and the facilities they use produce very little or no new economic development. Relatively few full-time jobs are created, and the service sector and construction jobs associated with a team or facility tend to be transfers from other communities in the region or from other sectors of the local economy.

Nonetheless, Kennedy and Rosentraub agree that teams produce a substantial level of intangible benefits. There is little debate over the extensive civic pride and community spirit generated by successful teams. Attracting or retaining a team also has been found to increase citizens' perceptions of the quality of life in their community and the value they place on living in their city (Swindell and Rosentraub, 1998). Many elected officials conclude that if a team's presence enhances residents' perceptions of the quality of life and the identity of a city, then the investment of tax dollars is indeed appropriate (Morgan, 1997; Rosentraub, 1999).

Another example of public-private partnership concerns cooperation between local governments in the United States and their private sector partners. This collaboration process was recognized and encouraged by the International City/County Management Association (ICMA) (*Public Management*, 1998). ICMA created the Corporate Partnership Program that fosters the idea that local governments are an appropriate laboratory for the exploration and development of effective PPP. The goal of the program is to open important lines of communication and creativity and to provide a vehicle for sharing the expertise, resources, and experiences of professionals and organizations in both the public and the private sector.

The Corporate Partnership Program is distinguished from similar programs in that it is based on the same high standards of honor and integrity as those set for professional local government managers through ICMA's code of ethics. A corporate partner's code of ethics, adopted by the ICMA executive board, ensures that all activities of the partners continually improve local government management and reaffirm the dignity and worth of the profession.

At the heart of public-private partnership and collaboration is the need to hold mangers of both sectors accountable for their actions, performance, efficiency, and cost savings. These managers must be able to show the highest levels of flexibility and creativity in order to operate successfully in a competitive and highly demanding environment. However, while private sector managers are inherently familiar with and experienced in market-oriented management, public sector managers as well as local government administrators need to go through a much more radical mind transition. They are required to abandon old-style knowledge and practices relevant to traditional bureaucracies in favor of a new managerial style, where innovation and continuous renewal take the lead. According to this new style they play diverse roles, including those of entrepreneur, facilitator, teacher-coach, partner, and gatekeeper. In the local government arena there are several illustrations of these roles:

Public Managers as Entrepreneurs: Managers are called on to explore new, innovative ways to address challenges and needs within their states and communities. For example, the city of Dallas, Texas, worked with Fannie Mae and other partners to develop the "homes for Dallas" initiative, a program that assists thousands of families in obtaining affordable housing.

Public Managers as Facilitators: Managers engage government officials, private sector representatives, and citizens in the communities. For example, the city of Hopewell, Virginia, developed a unique partnership among local government, citizens, and industry, resulting in a healthier environment, a more prosperous economy, and an improved quality of life.

Public Managers as Teachers and Coaches: Managers share their experiences by leading through example. For instance, Orange County, Florida, partnered several private and public agencies to establish a community recycling program and distribution center, including the creation of vocational training programs for eligible criminal offenders.

Public Managers as Partners: Managers generate new processes and alliances in partnership. For example, the city of Sunnyvale, California, developed a neighborhood center providing educational programs and social and health services for neighborhood children and their families. This partnership offers services that no one organization could provide alone.

Public Managers as Gatekeepers: Managers oversee the ethical standards of partnership prescribed in ICMA's code of ethics. In turn, ICMA oversees the ethical principles of its corporate partners. In both cases, it is critical that the partnership be based on a level of trust that can be measured by and held accountable for, both ethically and financially, a common interest and a clear vision for the overall benefit of a community.

Actual Examples of Public-Private Partnership and Collaboration

As noted above, ideas for public-private partnership and collaboration are countless. They involve mutual ventures in the fields of general management and organization, as well as in more specific arenas such as health services, environmental affairs, education, culture, and child care. Some of these ven-

Figure 3.1
Public-Private Partnership for the Urban Environment (1)

---

www.undp.org/pppue/index.htm

At the beginning of the twenty-first century, more people live in cities and towns than in rural areas. While this trend is likely to continue, it has been accompanied by an alarming growth in the incidence of poverty, especially in developing countries. In particular, the provision of basic urban services like water, sanitation, and energy represents a major urban environmental challenge.

Private-public partnerships (PPP) are an effective means of establishing cooperation between public and private actors, and bundling financial resources, know-how, and expertise to address these urban environmental needs. PPPs offer alternatives to full privatization, combining the advantages of both the public and the private sector.

UNDP's (United Nations Development Program) Public-Private Partnerships for the Urban Environment (PPPUE) facility supports the development of such innovative partnerships at the local level. Focusing on assisting small and medium-sized cities, PPPUE works with all potential stakeholders, including investors, providers, regulators, users, and experts to meet the challenge of providing basic urban environmental services.

Participation, local ownership, and shared responsibility are important aspects of PPPUE's innovative approach. This complementary approach with a unique international network, flexible design and a constant feedback mechanism contributes to the success of PPPs.

The management structure reflects PPPUE's arrangement as a multipartner and multidonor facility. While the PPPUE Consultative Group, consisting of contributing donors, UNDP senior managers, and a Public-Private Infrastructure Advisory Facility (PPIAF) representative, provides strategic leadership, the PPPUE national programs are implemented by the UNDP country office in selected program countries. The PPPUE Trust Fund allows donors to contribute to PPPUE's general activities or to specific projects. PPPUE is designed as a complementary facility to the many existing initiatives and institutions, and works with a variety of partners at global, regional, and country levels. PPPUE offers numerous opportunities for partners, and invites interested parties to join the facility.

---

tures are also fostered through the Internet. I present an exemplary collection of these ventures, but others undoubtedly will accumulate with time. Figures 3.1–3.10 provide some useful information from the home pages of several such projects. This information well demonstrates the creativity and rationality behind these initiatives.

Building a Successful Public-Private Partnership

As Grant (1996) notes, PPPs are now widely accepted in many states as a viable strategic alternative to traditional methods of designing and man-

Figure 3.2
Public and Private School Collaboration

www.ed.gov/pubs/EPTW/eptw3/eptw3j.html

Public and Private School Collaboration is a program for students in grades 10 and 11 also known as the Connecticut Scholars Program. It is a collaboration for the purpose of providing an opportunity for advanced residential study for academically promising urban students.

Public Private School Collaboration makes connections and makes connections work. Where public and private schools have not traditionally joined forces, they do so within a collaborative framework. This allows them to apply their finest resources to meet significant needs. It also allows them to gain the support of leading corporations and foundations, as well as research institutions and museums, as they seek to respond to those needs.

The developer demonstrator has engaged in this work for over ten years. In Connecticut, Choate Rosemary Hall (a private boarding school) and the Connecticut Association of Urban Superintendents sponsor a five-week program of advanced residential study for students from Connecticut's thirteen urban school districts. They have been joined by distinguished corporations (from AT&T to Xerox) and noted research institutions (from Brown University to the federal Star Schools Program). Students study topics ranging from advanced astronomy to vectors and matrices. They return to their schools encouraged by their accomplishments. Many other collaborative activities have flowed from this initiative, including programs for students and teachers alike.

Importantly, a collaboration does not have to involve a boarding school, urban schools, or huge foundation grants. It does require the full participation of public and private school partners, definition of genuine need, and the commitment to work together to find and apply resources to meet that need. After three and a half years, adoptions are now under way from Maine to California. They can be found in boarding schools, urban public high schools, day schools, elementary schools, and more. Winston Churchill once said that opportunity seeks not a "seat but a springboard." That is just what this program supplies.

Figure 3.3
Partnership for Public Service

www.ourpublicservice.org/Main_Site/Frameset_IE.html

The Partnership for Public Service is a newly formed nonpartisan organization dedicated to revitalizing the public service. Through an aggressive campaign of public-private partnerships, focused research, and educational efforts, the Partnership seeks to restore public confidence in and prestige to the federal civil service.

Figure 3.4
Public-Private Collaboration in Pollution Management

---

www2.worldbank.org/hm/pollmgt/0000.html

Industrial pollution has become a serious problem in many developing countries since the 1980s. Policy instruments used for pollution control are limited, and a combination of federal, state, and local environmental regulations have created a highly complex system of requirements that are not systematically implemented and enforced. There is an urgent need to develop new ways of thinking and new approaches to governance: locally, nationally, and internationally. This calls for a more open and market-oriented approach including budgetary discipline and more private sector participation. Governments are discovering that working with the private sector to manage industrial pollution can be more cost-effective than a traditional command and control approach.

At the same time, the recent opening up of many economies through liberalization of trade and capital flows has created new opportunities for many businesses, which are beginning to recognize the need for improving both their economic and their environmental performance. Many of the international and domestic firms are interested in meeting the requirement of ISO 14000 and use environmental audits to identify areas for further improvements. Companies are learning that collaborative approaches can trim costs, improve quality, enhance their public image—and increase profits.

As a contribution to greater knowledge-sharing and coordination among the various initiatives focused on these issues, the World Bank is hosting long electronic discussions which will bring together the views of government, private sector, and community representatives on successful collaborative approaches to managing pollution around the world. The discussion will explore government and business experiences in

1. Enhancing profitability through responsible environmental management
2. Designing environmental information disclosure programs
3. Managing environmental liability and related issues
4. Removing barriers to and promoting incentives for environmental innovation.

---

aging government services. However, partnering with the private sector represents much more than an interesting new way for governments to increase their efficiency and effectiveness in economic terms. A survey by Andersen Consulting in Canada tried to examine attitudes toward partnership and collaboration across a variety of public and private organizations. More than 90 percent of those surveyed reported their sense that "most" or "many" organizations will need to partner in some way to achieve their business objectives. In many cases, the same forces that create increased

Figure 3.5
Public-Private Partnerships for the Urban Environment (2)

---

www.yale.edu/envirocenter/research/pubpriv.html

This program, undertaken in collaboration with the United Nations Development Program (UNDP), supports UNDP's efforts to bring the public and private sectors together to address urban environmental issues. It distributes information, provides training, develops networks, and sponsors events to help reinforce environmental cooperation between government and business.

---

business-to-business alliances in the private sector drive governments to pursue partnership as well. These forces usually include the following:

1. A need for increased operating efficiencies to attract investors and reduce the high cost of capital. For governments, this force is expressed by efforts to bring about balanced budgets and decrease external and internal debt.
2. Growing pressure by taxpayers as well as the investment community to find new ways to deliver services and reduce spending.
3. The increase of market alternatives for investments and the high-level competition among many organizations that seek to survive and succeed.
4. A cultural change of values and aspirations in modern societies. Here, various types of continuous organizational improvements (e.g., benchmarking and the power of mutual action) take the place of older managerial strategies. This change is accompanied by the use of high-speed and sophisticated media and communication channels that set new frontiers for governmental activities.

Hence, Khoury (1993) suggests that the current interest in partnerships, spanning both public and private sectors, is fueled by a growing perception that acting in collaboration with like-minded partners is more effective than acting alone. Increasingly, corporations are adopting partnerships as essential strategies. Partnerships, by developing linkages and pooling resources, can facilitate the appropriate efficient and effective allocation of scarce resources, increase the effectiveness of a group or organization, and enhance the organization's impact on the community. In the 1950s, the United Way came into being in many cities through the efforts of Canadian corporations. In some cases, a Community Chest was first established, later evolving into a United Way. This was a strategic response to community need and to the growing competition for corporate support. Continued corporate support of United Way/Centraide demonstrates the effectiveness and endurance of good partnerships.

Furthermore, Khoury argues that partnerships make good business sense, offering individuals and organizations the opportunity to extend their reach. Working with like-minded, compatible partners can maximize visibility, im-

Figure 3.6
Minnesota Department of Health: Collaboration Plans

---

www.health.state.mn.us/divs/chs/hsd/colplans.htm

The purpose of the Collaboration Plans is twofold:

1. To promote an exchange of information that allows the public and private sectors to begin to identify areas of mutual interest
2. To focus the collective efforts of the public and private sectors on a few, high-priority health problems in a community. (For additional information, see the Collaboration Plan legislation and Collaboration Plan guidelines.)

Private organizations, especially health plan companies and health systems, can play a strong role in working with public health officials to achieve the goals published in the Healthy Minnesotans Public Health Improvement Goals. Collaboration Plans, coupled with the Community Health Services (CHS) Plans prepared by Community Health Boards, provide an opportunity to exchange information about the specific goals each entity is pursuing and its activities to achieve them.

In 1995, the first legislatively mandated Collaboration Plan formalized a dialogue between public health and organized systems of health care. As a result, these groups started to develop a common language, and to identify and undertake common efforts to achieve goals that prevent disease and improve the health of the people of the state. They began to build collaborative relationships, and learned to appreciate and understand each other's language, strengths, and positions. The State Community Health Services Advisory Committee established a Collaboration Work Group during 1996 to develop guidelines for use in collaborative planning and in efforts to contribute to the achievement of public health goals. Their 1997 report, *Developing Partnerships to Improve Public Health: Information for Health Plans, Providers and Public Health Agencies*, describes seven reporting elements for the 1998–1999 Collaboration Plans and recommends that the Minnesota Department of Health undertake a variety of activities to foster public/private collaboration.

---

prove credibility, and contribute to community investment. In addition, cost-sharing makes start-up and maintenance less burdensome, and some resources may be more readily available to a team than to individual members. The partnership also reduces risk to individual members, and the resulting security encourages bold and innovative initiatives that might not be attempted by one player alone.

Partnerships are thus seen as a way to complement existing strengths and avoid high development costs by taking advantage of the acknowledged capabilities of (an)other organization(s). They allow businesses and governments quickly to overcome the competence and capability gaps that stand between where they are and where they want, need, or are forced to be.

Figure 3.7
A Model for Public and Private Child Welfare Partnership Collaboration for Change

www.aecf.org/familytofamily/tools/model.htm

What Is "a Model for Public and Private Child Welfare Partnership"?

Reconstructing the family foster care system requires a new role for child welfare agencies that is family-focused and neighborhood-based, relies less on institutional and congregate care, and responds effectively and flexibly to the needs of each child and family served. Making this shift requires that both government and voluntary agencies work very differently—with families, neighborhoods, and each other.

How Was the Tool Applied in Family to Family?

The tool makes references to valuable work being implemented in Family to Family sites throughout the United States. Specific examples of efforts in Ohio are used to help the reader understand how public/private partnership works. The two case examples of communities working to develop public/private partnerships are Cuyahoga County (Cleveland and the surrounding area) and Hamilton County (the Cincinnati area). These sites reflect developments in other jurisdictions. While both sites are in the midst of fluid change processes, neither is free of problems. That is not the reality for child welfare systems. Each site illustrates some elements of a new model relationship. Both communities are working to conduct business differently and to forge new public/private partnerships. Key stakeholders of both sectors are working together to try to effect change.

What Did We Learn from These Applications?

We learned that this tool can serve as a guide for forming new public/private relationships that achieve better outcomes for children who need foster care. It builds on the experiences of communities that are working together to care for their children differently, on other collaborative initiatives aimed at improved child and family well-being, and on the best thinking of outstanding public and private child welfare professionals working to change the foster care system.

What You Need to Get Started

This tool serves as a model of the way public human service agencies can work with contract agencies. First, it describes a vision and goals of public/private partnerships to redesign foster care, as well as issues, barriers, and challenges that must be acknowledged. It suggests strategies for partners to use in identifying, articulating, and reaching consensus on the outcomes they seek and the issues they must address. Second, it provides a toolbox of strategies for building a partnership. Together, these strategies provide a range of collaborative planning, implementation, and monitoring approaches.

What You Need for Full Implementation

Partnerships can take many forms, varying in emphasis and strategies. We urge public and private agency representatives to select the strategies most appropriate and useful in your circumstances, to adapt the approaches to fit your needs and capacities, and to use these ideas to develop new methods for building partnership. It is our hope

Figure 3.7 (*Continued*)

that this tool and the examples presented will allay fears that come with radical alteration of roles and relationships. We hope the tool will help public and private agencies integrate new experiences and lessons into practice, build upon a strong foundation of common goals, and develop new strengths and skills for working collaboratively.

BRIDGING BUSINESSES AND COMMUNITIES: CONCEPTIONS AND MISCONCEPTIONS

The Example of the British Health Care System

In the field of health care, and especially the treatment of aging population, there has been a call for increased partnership and collaboration between public sector agencies and private organizations. As Nicholson (1998) suggests, "The public and private sectors should be sinking their perceived differences and working to combine their separate strengths to meet changing—and ultimately infinite—public demand" (p. 5). Further on, Nicholson analyzes three misconceptions commonly held about the relationship between the public and the private sectors, as manifested in the British National Health Service (NHS).

1. The NHS set public provision apart from preexisting private health care, much of which was provided through charitable or mutual foundations. Therefore, a myth was developed that the two sectors were in competition and that private health care was a threat to the publicly funded health services. However, the private and third/voluntary sectors actually share a common objective with the public sector, which could be pursued more effectively in partnership.
2. Doctors and other medical staff frequently practice in both public and private sectors. This has created a belief that the private sector leeches on the public sector for its medical professionals. The truth is that consultants have practiced privately in addition to their NHS work for as long as the service has existed. By doing this, the professional staff supplement their income, which allows them to continue to work within the NHS at salary levels that the public purse can afford. Naturally, other implications of quality of work and social fairness also need to be taken into consideration here. However, in terms of collaboration and partnership the private sector actually sponsors the public health system, and more citizens benefit.
3. The charge of queue-jumping is leveled against those who use private medicine. Even when the NHS was established, it was clear that it would not be able to meet the demand for free services at the point of use, and waiting lists developed. Therefore, patients who choose to be treated in the private sector should not be criticized. By not taking up a place in the NHS queue, they allow the next patient in line to benefit from earlier treatment.

Figure 3.8
Key Issues in Public-Private Partnerships for Cultural Landscapes (by Alice Ingerson)

www.arboretum.harvard.edu/ICLS/PPP/KEY.HTM

Why Form Public-Private Partnerships for Cultural Landscapes?

1. To combine complementary resources or contrasting perspectives. Cultural landscapes involve multiple resources and interests, almost by definition. A single organization rarely has equal access to all of these resources, or can represent or understand all these interests equally well. Funders increasingly recognize this, and encourage groups with different resources or interests in the same landscape to submit cooperative rather than competing proposals.

2. To make the geographical scale of decision-making match the scale of the landscape itself. Regional cultural landscapes, such as those involved in heritage areas or heritage corridors, often cross ownership or political boundaries. Public parks may include private inholdings. Even landscapes in full public ownership are often surrounded by private land that is very much affected by park management decisions, or that could be used in ways incompatible with the goals of park managers.

3. Landscapes are dynamic, and partnerships may be more flexible in managing change than single-purpose organizations. Advocates often argue that public-private partnerships add private sector creativity and flexibility to public sector accountability and credibility. Short-term or strategic partnerships, focused on specific projects rather than long-term relationships, may help to train previously reactive organizations, including government regulatory or land stewardship agencies, to be more proactive and manage higher risks.

4. On the other hand, consistency is sometimes a more important goal than flexibility in managing cultural landscapes. Nonprofit partners may be in a better position to enforce consistency than are either for-profit organizations or elected governments.

5. During economic downturns, both for-profit businesses and governments may assign a low priority to maintaining shared landscapes, along with other kinds of "infrastructure." At such times, the best interests of the landscapes may be well served by nonprofit organizations with narrow, inflexible charters. Such organizations can often swim "against the tide" precisely because they have dedicated endowments and focused memberships.

Why Be Skeptical of Public-Private Partnerships?

1. Partnerships have sometimes been a euphemism for privatization or "load shifting." Public agencies may use the rhetoric of partnership to delegate controversial or difficult tasks to the private sector. Programs once evaluated by public policy and supported by taxes may become dependent on private initiatives and philanthropy. Shifting tasks that generate revenue to the private sector, while leaving tasks that require subsidies to the public sector, can unfairly reinforce stereotypes of private efficiency and public waste.

2. Equality among partners is often more rhetorical than real. The public sector has been the net loser in some partnerships because private benefits, such as com-

Figure 3.8 (*Continued*)

munity goodwill, and public costs, such as forgone revenue, are not measured with equal care. On the other hand, public participants sometimes hope to gain resources from private partners without sharing their own resources or authority. Such partnerships may produce mostly verbal cooperation at meetings, rather than concrete collaboration "in the field."

3. Public-private partnerships may be more efficient but less accountable and representative than other kinds of organizations, such as legislatures. Many partnerships aim to offer each participating interest an equal voice, regardless of how many people actually share that interest. The longer and more smoothly a partnership operates, the more likely it is to lose its capacity to represent genuinely conflicting interests, or to have some partners act as watchdogs or gadflies for other partners.

What Are the Primary Practical Challenges in Managing Public-Private Partnerships?

1. Simultaneously achieving accountability, confidentiality, and fairness. For example, procedures to ensure broad accountability make the public sector relatively slow-moving and rigid. In contrast, private organizations, both for-profit and nonprofit, can be flexible and efficient because their decision-making processes are not subject to public comment. They answer to relatively narrow "niche markets" or "special interests" rather than to all consumers or all voters. To work together, each side must adjust its expectations. For example, private partners must submit plans for public review, and public partners risk losing some political support when they are responsive to their private partners. Partnership agreements should balance the distribution of risks and rewards carefully in advance, for each partner and among partners.

2. Moving from fund-raising or short-term projects to long-term land management: Many arrangements now called "public-private partnerships" are in fact strictly financial and would once have been called grants, subsidies, donations, or contracts. In such partnerships, the participant contributing the largest share of funding usually expects, and often has, the largest say in decisions. This may not be problematic in the short term. However, long-term cooperation may require building equal respect among the partners for all contributions, both financial and nonfinancial.

What Are the Broad Implications of Public-Private Partnerships?

1. Advocates claim that partnerships fundamentally change the relationship between government and the private sector for the better, promoting collaboration rather than conflict.

2 Some critics respond that the term "public-private partnership" is essentially meaningless political rhetoric, because it is applied to such a wide range of arrangements.

3. Even some analysts who agree that partnerships promote change think that change is for the worse, away from representative government based on "one

Figure 3.8 (*Continued*)

person, one vote" to decisions based on "one interest, one vote" (regardless of how many people share each interest).

All these views have some truth in them. Seen against the background history of shifting relations between the public and private sectors in the United States, the most recent wave of partnerships seems neither innovative nor sinister:

1. Sometimes the public sector has provided the physical and social infrastructure for the private economy, while leaving any activity that can be financially self-supporting to the private sector.
2. Sometimes private organizations have been required to accomplish broad public purposes, such as building public infrastructure or providing public services, in return for privileges such as limited monopoly, limited liability, or exemption from certain taxes.
3. Sometimes the public-private relationship has been seen not as a division of labor but as a system of checks and balances. The private sector is expected to create and distribute most goods and services, but the public sector regulates private actions and redistributes resources to stabilize markets, or to maintain the credibility of private philanthropy.

This history suggests that public-private partnerships should be evaluated strategically, against concrete, short-term goals, rather than ideologically, against supposedly permanent definitions of each sector's "proper" role.

How Can Partnerships from Other Land-Related Fields Be Adapted to Cultural Landscapes?

1. Partnership arrangements developed to manage natural resources and ecosystems must be adapted to include all the human beings who live on or use the land. In contrast to natural resources, "human resources" not only respond to or resist management decisions but also can take managers to court or vote them out of office. Management decisions for cultural or working landscapes must therefore be sustainable, not just biologically, but economically and politically as well.
2. Partnerships for community and urban development must be adapted to recognize and value such landscape qualities as character, continuity, and design. In a sense, the real estate maxim that property values depend on "location, location, location" already recognizes these values implicitly—for example, in a historic neighborhood or near a well-maintained park. But cultural values must be included more explicitly in systems for making land use decisions, and for allocating the costs and benefits of those decisions between the public and private sectors.

   Ultimately, whether critical analyses of partnerships for urban or community development apply to cultural landscapes depends in part on whether cultural landscapes are seen as current services toward which partners make donations, or as assets in which partners invest, and from which they can expect some sort of return. The first perspective is often adopted implicitly in writing about conservation and historic preservation. In this context, both public and private partnership contributions are assumed to be needed indefinitely.

Figure 3.8 (*Continued*)

From the second perspective, more often adopted in writing on community and urban development, the public sector may be required to "prime the pump" for private investment, but wise management of land is expected to increase the land's value, whether that value is measured by markets or by some ecological or cultural standard. In this context, the public contribution may eventually be eliminated, and the project may become financially self-sustaining and entirely private, or the project may even become a source of public revenue. Seeing landscapes as assets often requires valuing them not only for their direct use in housing, farming, or tourism but also as part of the overall "quality of life" that draws or retains residents and businesses to an area, and as enhancing the local tax base.

It is possible that these three issues, and perhaps other misconceptions as well, have obstructed sensible discussion about an effective partnership between the NHS and the private sector. They both share one prime objective: to improve people's health. Talk about the profitability goal of private organizations proves less significant with time, when public agencies also look to the economic data and budgetary savings. However, both public and private health care bodies serve our modern society with better than ever medicines and treatment. In Britain, 11 percent of the population is covered by private medical insurance and the private sector carries out 20 percent of heart surgery, 30 percent of hip replacements, and a total of 500,000 operations each year. All these treatments, and others, would otherwise be added to NHS waiting lists. Moreover, the private sector provides and pays for a range of services that fall outside NHS provision, such as preventive health care and alternative homeopathic treatments as supplementary to mainstream/conventional medicine.

While no national strategy for public-private sector cooperation has ever been suggested and developed, several examples exist on the local level. Joint ventures between public agencies and private sector firms have benefited the whole community in Cambridge, where private firms bought a heart laser machine that provides alternative treatment for people who are unable to undergo conventional heart surgery. In Hastings private firms have worked with the local NHS trust to build a new hospital. In both cases the facilities are available to NHS and private patients alike.

As Nicholson predicts, if the United Kingdom is to continue to improve health and reduce illness, there must be a significant shift in opinion about private care. There will always be constraints on the amount of public money available to fund health care. There are other ways to maximize the limited pool of public resources. The for-profit sector and the third sector already play a major role in the provision of nursing home, residential, and domiciliary care services. In density, there is increasingly a mixed economy in

Figure 3.9
Institute for Public-Private Partnerships

---

www.ip3.org/

The Institute for Public-Private Partnerships, Inc. (IP3) is an international training and consulting firm that focuses on fostering public-private partnership opportunities in the environmental (water/sanitation and solid waste), energy, transportation, technology, and social sectors. IP3 provides training and consulting services on the requisite legal, regulatory, financial, technical, and institutional enabling environments for successful partnership arrangements. Its clients include national/state/local government agencies, multi- and bilateral development organizations, nongovernmental organizations, and private businesses.

---

which public and private provisions exist comfortably side-by-side. Even in pensions, unemployment benefits, and long-term care, the government is exploring how private and mutual insurance might be used to relieve the burden on existing state coverage.

Thus, according to Brown (1999), PPPs facilitate efficient long-term procurement of public services in various fields. Since the market in the United Kingdom extends beyond central government to hospitals, trusts, and local authorities, standardization of concession contracts is occurring. The use of PPPs can extend, and is extending, to other jurisdictions, for example, mass transit systems in India and prison projects in South Africa. The market in Europe has only just awoken to the potential, and in the United States it is also in its infancy. The scope for growth is therefore considerable, especially since the techniques and instruments for PPPs have been tried and tested successfully.

BUSINESSES FOR THE COMMUNITY

In recent years it has become clear that neither the public sector nor private firms can continue to carry sole responsibility for supporting social pro-

Figure 3.10
International Journal of Public-Private Partnership

---

www.shu.ac.uk/schools/sbf/events/conferences/ijppp/index.htm

A peer-reviewed journal with three issues per year, this is unique in affording an understanding of the current issues facing organizations crossing the public-private divide, an ever-growing phenomenon in world politics.

---

grams and advancing quality of life in modern nations. Governments at all levels are reassessing their role in many areas. The result is that citizens, community organizations, and the growing nonprofit/third sector bodies are assuming more of the burden. As will be explained later, these players have a major role in the process of collaboration with public administration. However, as noted by Khoury (1993), these groups, faced with growing demand, are increasingly less able to respond as the economic situation in many countries worsens and core funders freeze or reduce their contributions. In addition, the growing number of charitable organizations competing for available funding has cut into the budgets of many established organizations.

Nonprofit and charitable organizations are therefore turning to the private sector for funding: more fund-raisers are knocking on corporate doors at a time when corporate donations managers have less to dispense. For example, a 1992 survey by the Conference Board of Canada's Institute of Donations and Public Affairs Research revealed that while the corporate sector makes substantial contributions to the community, these contributions are not likely to narrow the widening gap between demand and available resources. As Khoury (1993) argued, major corporations are reassessing their corporate contributions strategy. In light of increased demand and shrinking budgets, many corporations are becoming more proactive in their support and more focused in their community investment. A trend in this direction has been apparent for some years, as corporate donations have evolved from straightforward cash contributions to a concentration on areas where the company has a natural interest.

Here lies the potential of Businesses for the Community (BFC) for businesses, communities, citizens, and the public sector. The idea of BFC is based on voluntary contributions by private firms to the welfare and prosperity of communities they operate in. This contribution can be donations of money or goods, spreading relevant knowledge, or offering services that otherwise would not be available at all or could be available only at a high price. By getting involved in BFCs, businesses earn public legitimacy, improve their public relations and image in the eyes of citizens and state leaders, and even expect to increase profits due to high exploration by various media channels. Businesses involved in BFCs also build good reputations in the eyes of politicians, who in turn may be more receptive to future requests and needs of these business firms. Citizens and communities enjoy some free-of-charge services or goods and, even more important, become involved in projects of high technology or leading knowledge. Those in the society who are defined as "less able" to consume such goods or services at their full cost are the most benefited of all. The public sector may thus free some of its resources for other tasks, leaving some responsibility in the hands of the private sector and causing it to increase its attachment to the community.

Still, criticism against BFCs may suggest that these ventures are self-interest-derived, and are launched only in cases where the private firm has a clear and sustainable profit. Even in cases where voluntarism by businesses occurs with no expectation of reward or profit, an indirect benefit for the firm exists by free advertisement of its activity, which frequently is worth more than the basic investment in the community. Nonetheless, many BFCs exemplify a higher level of collaboration between businesses, public organizations, and citizens and communities. These ventures are mostly a clear type of win-win game rather than a zero-sum game, where all parties involved have something substantial "in the pot."

Otterbourg (1999) describes two exemplary ventures of BFC in the field of education. One is a project of E-mentoring by Hewlett-Packard, and the other is the Virtual Trade Mission by United Airlines. These projects are aimed at fulfilling private sector firms' role as good corporate citizens.

Hewlett-Packard (H-P) has developed an E-mail mentor program, a structured, project-based program through which H-P employees worldwide volunteer to telementor fifth-to-twelfth-grade students in unique one-to-one relationships. The program focuses on helping students excel in math, science, and professional communication skills, and developing education and career plans for life beyond high school. E-mail mentoring is one of many opportunities the company provides for H-P people to give of their time and talents to meeting the difficult challenges facing education today.

As Otterbourg sees it, participation in the program is a collaboration among teacher, mentor, and student. The teacher, who defines the project on which the student and mentor will work, is the key to successful participation. Basically, all training and technical assistance for mentors is online. The program allows employees to balance their desire to contribute to their communities with the time and place constraints imposed by their jobs. To participate, they do not have to leave the H-P site. The E-mail mentoring permits participation by employees who have never had an opportunity to become involved with schools and students, such as those who work the third shift or are salespersons on the road. Time zones and geography mean nothing in this program: students on one side of the continent can be connected to H-P employees on the other side or to those who work across the ocean. In 1999 the program matched more than 1,000 students in the United States, Canada, Australia, and France with H-P mentors. H-P has committed more than $400,000 in direct support to this program, in addition to the thousands of hours contributed by the volunteer mentors. Program expansion plans include the launch of the International Telementor Center, with H-P transferring the program to Colorado State University to enable other companies to encourage their employees to become involved.

United Airlines launched a similar investment in education that reflects the company's vision that the future depends on well-informed people who understand the impact of world events. The company seeks to bring the issues of international business and the global economy into classrooms in a variety of ways. One such way is the Virtual Trade Mission (VTM) project. The VTM is an educational partnership developed by the federal government, educators, and private enterprise to teach high school and middle-school students the importance of the U.S. export economy. The program was piloted in five cities in 1996 and was rolled out to thirty cities in 1997–1998.

United Airlines team members helped design and develop the student materials for the VTM, which include world geography, economics, cross-cultural communication, and technical research, and they continue to serve as expert consultants on these issues. The United Airlines Foundation provided funding for ongoing program development and outreach.

What are the advantages for students and for society in general? By participating in a VTM, students acquire the skills and tools they need to participate, compete, and succeed in today's global marketplace. Students get to know experts in industry, technology, and business, as well as CEOs of leading firms, members of Congress, ambassadors, and diplomats. In fact, their engagement in world trade business affairs guides them to becoming productive members of society and illustrates an effective collaboration of business firms, public agencies, and individual citizens.

A REVISED MODEL OF "NEW PUBLIC MANAGEMENT": LEARNING FROM THE PRIVATE SECTOR WHILE CHANGING IT IN RETURN

Public-private partnership (PPP) is basically favored and praised by the new public management doctrine. Business for Communities is less a much less studied field. As argued by Brown (1999), one of the great conundrums of neoclassical economics has been to procure public goods or services efficiently. These goods and services have to be procured by the state for political purposes, but they are also a cultural-human aim of social institutions and citizens alike. For many years conventional wisdom held that only the state could be trusted to provide them. However, with fiscal constraints and economic restriction of the 1970s and 1980s, governments started to explore the potential of collaboration with business firms. Scholars and professionals agree today that a whole range of goods and services in health care, education, welfare, infrastructures, and other fields can be supplied more effectively either by the private sector alone or by a private-public alliance. For example, the total capital expenditure on PPPs between 1992 and 1999 in the United Kingdom came to almost $15.4 billion, a figure that continues to rise and accounts for about 13 percent of what would otherwise be solely government-monitored.

According to Nicholson (1998), it is time to stop regarding the private sector as a separate entity. In fact, when analyzing the various PPP and BFC ventures, one will readily observe how the private sector is becoming increasingly involved in governmental/administrative activities both in an organized and in a voluntary manner. Closer working between public and private sectors in no way challenges the fundamental fairness precept of modern health care, education, or welfare services. People should have equal access to these "public goods" regardless of their ability to pay. However, in a free society and an open market system, there will always be a group of people who can afford a higher level of services. These individuals, like others, will increasingly need to provide for their own welfare needs, and the government should encourage them to do so. Some argue that this will lead to a two-tier system. Yet it may encourage a wiser usage of public resources where the state is focused on those who really need help and support, society's least advantaged. The private sector hence contributes to a better modern society, and is seen as a partner rather than a competitor with the public system.

CHAPTER 4

Collaboration with Citizens and the Third Sector: A Community-Focused Analysis*

BRINGING THE SPIRIT OF COMMUNITY BACK IN

Following the events of September 11, 2001, a column was published on the web site of the American Society for Public Administration by Bob and Janet Denhardt of the School of Public Affairs at Arizona State University. The title was "Citizens and Public Service," and it argued that the spirit of public service extends beyond those formally working for government, those we think of as public servants. Ordinary citizens have also wished to contribute since the tragic events of September 11. In addition to contrasting "customers" with "citizens," the Denhardts called on governments to encourage and support efforts to extend a sense of community in neighborhoods, in workplaces, and throughout society (www.aspanet.org/publications/COLUMNS/archives/1101/denhardts1109.html).

According to this view, the terrorist events of mid-September reinforced trust and faith in America's public sector. The public service was displayed at its best by the work of law enforcement personnel, public health officials, postal workers, and members of the armed forces. The public sector again found itself doing what it was trained to do for many years: helping people in trouble, making the world safer and cleaner, helping children learn and prosper, and literally going where others could not or would not go.

However, the Denhardts continued, the spirit of public service extends beyond those formally working for government, those we think of as public servants. Ordinary citizens also wish to contribute. Despite this welcome motivation, the avenues through which they might bring their many talents

*Some sections of this chapter are based on E. Vigoda and R. T. Golembiewski, "Citizenship Behavior and the Spirit of New Managerialism: A Theoretical Framework and Challenge for Governance," *American Review of Public Administration* (2001).

to bear are somewhat limited in scope. The main reason is that over the past several decades we have severely constrained the citizenship role, preferring to think of people as customers or consumers rather than citizens. Certainly, this tendency has been seen in the way we talk about and interact with those people served by public agencies. The Denhardts suggest that, following the admonition that "government should be run like a business," we have come to characterize our clients as "customers" rather than "citizens." But that idea doesn't fully ring true with respect to the public service. Should government first or exclusively respond to the selfish, short-term interests of "customers"? In some ways, the idea just doesn't fit.

In this chapter I follow the logic and rationality suggested in this inspiring column by the Denhardts. Their argument that "customers" of government are much harder to define than the customers of the local hamburger stand is strong. As they mention, it is often because the interests of various "customers" are in opposition to one another that government is called upon to act in the first place. And of course, there are some instances in which "customers" of government simply don't want the service government provides—like traffic citations. Most important, in the private sector, those customers with the most money and most influence are accorded special treatment by the market, and that would be ludicrous as public policy. As citizens we expect government to act in a way that not only promotes services but also promotes a set of principles and ideals that are inherent in the public sphere. My view, which perfectly matches this column's logic, is that citizens cannot be reduced to customers without grave consequences for the notion of democratic citizenship.

COLLABORATION AMONG NONPROFIT AGENCIES

Collaboration by public and nonprofit organizations has become a key issue in public administration across the globe. In a special issue of the *International Journal of Public Administration* dedicated to the topic, it was argued that "government collaboration with third-sector organizations offers opportunities for solving problems of critical concern in contemporary governance" (Schwartz, 2001:1172). Some of these opportunities include (1) decreasing the size of government, (2) financing part of the cost of public service delivery through charitable donations, (3) infusing more orientation of service to citizens, and (4) increasing the efficiency, effectiveness, and thus also the performance of government. In addition, the greater involvement of citizens as individuals or, by proxy, of third sector agencies attracts voluntary activity and allows flexibility in dealing with the growing needs of citizens in general, and of those who are underprivileged in particular.

However, beyond the obvious advantages of collaboration lie some risks and potential disadvantages. As with collaboration between private and public sector organizations, the integration of citizens and third sector parties in governmental activity is not without difficulties. Several reports show that such collaboration may entail significant problems for local, state, and federal government agencies. First, third sector organizations are not necessarily more effective or flexible than government or private sector agencies. They sometimes suffer similar problems of bureaucracy, control mechanism, and coordination among units, which substantially harm their efficiency and performance. Moreover, in recent years many collaborative ventures between public administration bodies and citizens or voluntary organizations have been used as "convenient avenues for channeling funds and favor to political allies, family members and friends" (Schwartz, 2001:1182).

According to Grubbs (2000), relationships between diverse groups certainly are not new phenomena. However, in recent years we have come to recognize that a public agency's capacity to achieve better performance and desired public outcomes depends on its ability to establish meaningful, effective relationships with other institutions. As shown in the previous chapter, this can be done on the public-private level. However, it also has a primary meaning on the public-voluntary stage. Practical experience, however, makes it clear that although collaboration within and among organizations continues to be a stepping-stone to success, it never should be taken as a small step. "Agencies involved in, or searching for, partnerships in the governmental and non-governmental sectors face a myriad of challenges along their respective paths to collaboration" (Grubbs, 2000:275).

CITIZENS, CITIZENSHIP, AND THE THIRD SECTOR: THE PROFILE OF A COMPLEX PLAYER

Citizens, citizenship, and the emerging third sector are powerful concepts that may prove useful for our understanding of the idea of collaboration. The very basic nature of democracy includes, at least to a certain degree, the idea of citizens' self-government. Democracy encourages citizens to participate in new forms of governance, put in effort and knowledge, raise a profile of issues and interests that can change the course of public affairs, and become engaged in public activity personally, through interest groups or by other organizational forms that are mostly volunteer-oriented. According to Schwartz (2001), these nonprofit bodies, which are also called third sector organizations, may be considered a "vehicle for active citizen participation" that is vital for a healthy and prosperous democratic culture (p. 1172). Still, to better understand the interactions among nonprofit/third sector organizations and nonprofit/public sector agencies, one should clearly define each, and demarcate the borders between them. In addition, it is important to determine who are the citizens who are requested to hold leadership positions in taking progressive initiatives for the public good.

Box (1998:73–74) identified three types of citizens, classified along a continuum of a wish to affect rulers' actions and public policy processes:

(1) "freeriders," consumers of public services who receive those goods gratis and let others do the work of citizenship; (2) "activists," who are deeply involved in public life and in citizenship actions for the community; (3) "watchdogs," in the middle of the continuum, who are involved only in key issues of relevance to themselves personally. According to this classification, Box further suggests that public administration of our time denotes partnership with citizens. Practically and theoretically, governments and public administration mostly encourage the "freeriders" and perhaps some of the "watchdogs." They do not, however, elaborate on the significance of "activists," who are the most natural partners in launching high-quality administrative endeavors. Nonetheless, activists are few in modern societies. Even the most optimistic estimates by scholars in the field of participatory democracy place their proportion at less than 10 percent of the population (Almond and Verba, 1963; Verba et al., 1995). Still, the political and social influence of this relatively small group is immense, and must not be underestimated. This vanguard practically and ideologically paves the way to potential social changes, whatever these may be. Collaboration of governments and public administration with these people, as individuals or as groups, may lead others to join. The growing activity of the third sector is perhaps only one positive signal in this direction. According to O'Connell (1989), voluntary organizations and the third sector constituted about 10 percent of the economic volume of all governmental activities in the United States, and these numbers (including numbers of volunteers) are growing continually.

Citizenship may be defined by the core constructs of human activity, mentioned by T. H. Marshall (1950): obedience, loyalty, and participation. Beyond the basic constructs of obedience and loyalty, constructive citizenship behavior in modern societies encompasses active participation, involvement, and voluntary actions of the people in managing their lives. Nonetheless, and as we stated in a previous work (Vigoda and Golembiewski, 2001), this idea has so far received scant consideration in modern public administration thinking. Until the 1980s only a few attempts had been made to develop a comprehensive analysis of citizenship behavior that could be related to general management science, and especially to images of public administration theory and action. Studies concerned with exploring the citizenship-management connection took a relatively narrow perspective. One line of research focused on citizens' involvement, participation, and empowerment in the national and local environments (e.g., Pateman, 1970; Barber, 1984). More recent studies have fostered the notion that voluntarism and spontaneous actions of individuals are useful tools for governments in their efforts to overcome budgetary difficulties, advance stability, and promote effectiveness in public arenas (Box, 1998, 1999; Brudney, 1990; Fredrickson, 1997; Rimmerman, 1997). Other studies, mainly in management and organizational psychology, have emphasized a valuable self-derived contribution by employees that can lead to greater efficacy and success inside the workplace. Prosocial/altruistic behaviors (e.g., Brief and Motowidlo, 1986) and organizational citizenship behavior (e.g., Morrison, 1996; Organ, 1988; C. A. Smith et al., 1983) were mentioned as necessary for the creation of a healthy organizational atmosphere, and particularly for promoting service quality and general outcomes of public organizations (Podsakoff and MacKenzie, 1997).

In addition, a budding interdisciplinary approach elaborated on the possibility that higher levels of citizens' involvement on the state or community level are related to more involvement in the job and to enhanced organizational democracy that improves organizational outcomes (Peterson, 1990; Putnam, 1993; Sobel, 1993). Organizational democracy and participatory climate were found to be good predictors of employees' performance in private and public systems, and thus have received increased attention in recent years (Cohen and Vigoda, 1999, 2000; Cotton et al., 1988). All the above studies pointed to the added value of citizenship behavior, in its many forms and settings, to management in general, and to public organizations in particular. Regrettably, these efforts have not matured into a broader perspective on the overall relationships between characteristics of citizenship behavior and new trends in modern managerialism. Knowledge about different aspects of the citizenship-management connection have not been combined in an effective way that could lead to better understanding of both fields. Hence, the advantages of such mutual enrichment have been overlooked and left incomplete.

In this light several questions should be asked about the potential interrelationships among citizens, citizenship behavior, and the nature of modern public administration: What is so important about the relationship between multidimensional citizenship and new public managerialism? What are the variants of citizenship behavior in and around organizations that can be used to enhance public management goals? And, most important, is it realistic to see citizenship behavior by the people as a reliable construct of collaboration with the public sector? If so, who should be involved in fostering citizens' involvement and participation that may promote what I define as "a spirit of collaboration," and what duties and responsibilities should each participant carry? Answers to these questions may contribute to the development of higher levels of collaboration between citizens and the administrative state. They will enhance responsiveness in public administration and contribute to the creation of healthier democratic societies. My theoretical discussion also leads to a model for understanding the territory. It suggests that planned, strategic cooperation and genuine collaboration among players in the political, administrative, and social arenas are crucial and possible. In my view it is a prime managerial challenge for the future.

DIMENSIONALITY OF CITIZENSHIP BEHAVIOR

Foundations and Settings

Previous research has pointed to three core elements of general citizenship behavior: *obedience* of the people to social rules, *loyalty* to social institutions, and *participation* in social life (T. H. Marshall, 1950). While obedience and loyalty naturally belong to a worldwide definition of citizenship, the essence of citizenship behavior is participation. Participation concerns active involvement of citizens in three main settings: governance (a national arena), local lives (a communal arena), and the workplace (an organizational arena).

The National and Communal Arenas

In *The Spirit of the Laws,* Montesquieu argued that a state based on popular participation, as distinct from other forms of government (e.g., those based on obedience or loyalty), depends for its stability on the civic virtue of its good citizens. Rousseau emphasized the importance of citizens' freedom, political participation, and the "general will," which calls for contribution to the governing and administrative process without gaining any personal advantages, only the common interest. Active citizens assist in safeguarding and supporting sound governance (e.g., by holding or electing others to executive positions) and in adjudicating violations (e.g., by serving on juries). They also participate (directly or through representatives) in changing laws in response to new needs and in evolving an understanding of the common interest. Consequently, citizenship behavior includes devoting time and effort to the responsibilities of governance and administration, keeping well informed, sharing information and ideas with others, engaging in discussions about controversial issues, voting in whatever manner is provided under the law, and encouraging others to do likewise (Graham, 1991; Putnam, 1993; Van Dyne et al., 1994).

Community involvement and participation in local administrative processes constitute another unique aspect of participatory citizenship. Communal citizenship represents more informal participation than national activity (Sobel, 1993). Some people may decline to participate in citizenship behavior at the national level through disinclination or indifference. They may prefer a closer, perhaps more personal domain, such as the community. While much research has been conducted to uncover the mechanisms of individual voluntary action at the national level (e.g., Almond and Verba, 1963; Milbrath, 1965; Verba and Nie, 1972), recent studies have emphasized the importance of citizen participation and voluntary action at the communal level (Barber, 1984; Etzioni, 1994, 1995; Hurd, 1989; King and Stivers, 1998; Putnam, 1993). For example, Barber (1984:303) argued that "political participation in common action is more easily achieved at the neighborhood level, where there are a variety of opportunities for engagement," and Hurd (1989) noted that "[t]he need to foster responsible citizenship is obvious. Freedom can only flourish within a community where shared values, common loyalties and mutual obligations provide a framework of order and self-discipline, otherwise, liberty can quickly degenerate into narrow self-interest and license." King and Stivers (1998:195–196) suggested that "active citizenship is different from voting, paying taxes, or using government services . . . in active citizenship citizens rule and are ruled in turn." Putnam (1993) concluded that communities with higher levels of voluntarism and civic engagement become better places to live, characterized by more trust in government, better government performance, and positive relations between citizens and the state.

The Organizational Arena

Beyond the national and communal spheres, active citizenship participation has an organizational aspect. Studies in organizational behavior have long argued that more participation in the workplace, high job involvement, and opportunities to use an effective voice may lead to high job satisfaction, low turnover and absenteeism, and better performances of organizations (Keller, 1997; Lum et al., 1998). Other studies found that public organizations that promote values of employees' empowerment and participation in decision-making are more likely to enhance communication throughout units, increase commitment to stakeholders, and improve productivity as well as quality of services (Berman, 1995; Young et al., 1998). Hence, an analysis of citizenship behavior in modern societies entails a broader conceptual discussion, applicable not only to nations, states, and communities but also to organizations, bureaucracies, and public agencies. In a rapidly changing environment, organizations and the workplace have an important task. Organizations' productivity leads to significant improvement in quality of life. Citizens' demands and needs grow faster and reach farther than ever before. The expansion of welfare services provided by the state to its citizens, directly or by proxy, must meet such demands and satisfy more people more frequently and more extensively. In practice, organizational change in these agencies only partly follows the rapid transformation of the environment, and it needs better support of quasi-public and nonpublic organizations (the third sector). Therefore, the idea that self-derived citizenship activity should be related to management and organizational sciences, as well as to public administration operation, has attracted growing attention in recent decades (Katz and Kahn, 1966; Organ, 1988).

Two basic patterns of relationship between citizenship behavior and the organizational arena should be mentioned in this regard. First, enhanced involvement of citizens in the administrative process (e.g., becoming members or supporters of public or third sector agencies) generates commitment to a healthy public service, proper understanding of what is right and what is wrong in managing public organizations, and education toward constructive participatory democracy. Second, improved intraorganizational citizenship behavior by public employees improves performance by public and third sector agencies. The advantages of self-inspired contributions of employees reach far beyond the merits of formal authority and bureaucratic mechanisms. Rimmerman (1997:19) suggested that increased citizens' participation in workplace decision-making processes is important if people are to recognize their roles and responsibilities as citizens within the larger community. This idea is consistent with an earlier work of Pateman (1970), who argued that through participation in decision-making (on the state, community, and organization levels), the individual learns to be a public as well as a private citizen.

We thus suggest that participation in multiple settings, such as the national or communal arena, as well as participation inside organizations, should be borne in mind when New Public Management (NPM) strategies are developed. The involvement in and contribution of citizens to the state, community, workplace, and society in general are valuable. Citizens' involvement has the advantage of being the lowest-cost input in the administrative process. Participation also enhances individuals' commitment to their environment and approval of public administration's legitimacy. Also, the increase in political participation carries improvement of political stability and accountability of the public sector (King and Stivers, 1998). Stability and accountability create proper responsiveness and effectiveness of services to the people.

Levels of Analysis

Citizens' participation is manifested in two major ways: personal initiatives and organized action. McKevitt (1998:42) suggests that participation and active citizenship are frequently portrayed as an individual quality, but at the same time they have strong overtones of collective responsibility. Box (1998:71–74) also emphasizes the centrality and current trends in individualism and collectivism, especially in communities. Like McKevitt, Box identifies a struggle for "a point of balance" between individualism and collectivism that largely influences the nature of citizenship in America. The tension between the individualistic and the collectivist ideas of citizenship is real, and disagreement exists over its boundaries. Following this, I identify two levels of active citizenship behavior that are discussed in the psychological, sociological, managerial, and administrative literature: (1) individual—altruism and voluntarism of persons in the national, communal, and organizational settings; (2) collective—organized or semiorganized citizenship behavior as represented by interest groups, volunteers' associations, volunteers' programs, nonprofit organizations, and the third sector. Together, these levels comprise the citizenship behavior hierarchy of modern societies.

Collaborating with Citizens as Individuals

Individual citizenship behavior refers to the very basic construct of personal actions and reactions by individual citizens. These are spontaneous, altruistic deeds of unorganized persons aimed at enhancing the prosperity and development of their environment. Citizens may show compassion for other citizens; contribute time, money, and other resources to help the incapable; and provide assistance for others whenever the situation requires it, without seeking any personal advantage or compensation (e.g., Conover et al., 1993; Monroe, 1994; Piliavin and Charng, 1990). Moreover, inside public organizations, citizen-employees may exert additional effort to help fellow employees in fulfilling their duties and in serving the public without seeking any personal rewards. General management literature has defined these enterprises as organizational citizenship behavior, which reflects an informal contribution that participants can choose to make or withhold without regard to sanctions or formal incentives. As noted in previous studies (e.g., Organ, 1988; Organ and Konovsky, 1989; Podsakoff and MacKenzie, 1997), many of these contributions, aggregated over time and persons, considerably enhance organizational efficiency and effectiveness. Further studies concluded that working under multiple pressures, public organizations should better understand the relationship of citizenship behavior inside and outside the workplace, management, and organizational outcomes (Cohen and Vigoda, 1999, 2000; Graham, 1991). Encouragement of citizenship behavior in and around public agencies may contribute to these organizations' productivity, competence, and success, and hence to society in general.

Collaborating with Citizens as Groups

This level of citizenship behavior comprises semiorganized and fully organized actions initiated by groups of individuals. Usually, citizenship behavior at this level emerges when a group shares mutual interests and all members are willing to be actively involved in collective voluntary endeavors. The group's ambition is high and there is recognition that it will be almost impossible to achieve and secure most of the joint goals as individuals. Among these groups one finds neighborhood associations, ad hoc groups that seek limited ecological goals, volunteer programs inside organizations, and even altruistic support groups offering help to those in need from others who have experienced similar needs (e.g., quitting smoking, avoiding drugs or alcohol, supporting families in distress, etc.). Previous research has demonstrated that the emergence, growth, and decline of voluntary groups can be explained by human capital variables, emergence of leadership, socioeconomic status, and competition with other groups (Janoski and Wilson, 1995; McPherson and Rotolo, 1996). It was also found that membership in voluntary groups increased forms of political expression and participation (Michael, 1981), and membership in volunteer programs in the public sector had economic merit for public organizations as well as symbolic effects of citizen participation (Brudney, 1990; Brudney and Duncombe, 1992).

Collaboration with the "Third Sector"

In November 1999, during a short official visit to the United States in connection with the Middle East peace process, Israeli Prime Minister Ehud Barak had to face a massive media offensive from an unexpected quarter. Reporters were anxious to hear his reaction to some unflattering formal figures published in Israel about hundreds of thousands of hungry people who were far below the poverty line and who needed immediate support and help simply to stay alive. This astonishing information caught Barak unaware. Despite its problematic geopolitical status, Israel is considered a developed country with a Western economy and an advanced social structure, in which quality of life is fair and welfare services are modern, highly evolved, and available to the entire population. The leaders of the state have never imagined that considerable numbers of ordinary citizens will have to deal with elementary problems such as having enough food to eat—concerns typical of undeveloped countries in Africa, Asia, or even eastern Europe. However, reality was otherwise. It was surprising and shocking, and won wide media coverage as well as extensive public attention. In response, Barak acted unconventionally. During an emotional TV interview, he did not announce that the state was taking full responsibility and firm actions to solve the problem. Instead, he called for immediate voluntary action by citizens and citizens' associations to help those who needed immediate support. He called for a self-driven initiative, and urged individuals as well as nonprofit groups to support their fellow-citizens. In this, Barak indirectly admitted that the state does not have adequate solutions for the public's needs, and that it depends considerably on the quality, intensity, and general performance of third sector agencies.

So apart from the semiorganized citizenship actions, the collective level of analysis includes highly organized and fully institutional collective endeavors. The most obvious representative of this subcategory is the organized third sector, elsewhere defined as nonprofit or voluntary organizations. Collective institutional citizenship derives from ambitious interests of large groups that have undergone a relatively complicated process of institutionalization and formalization. Management and public administration sciences have devoted considerable attention to this field (Brinton, 1994; Coble, 1999; O'Connell, 1989; S. R. Smith and Lipsky, 1993). In many ways these organizations represent increased public involvement aimed at providing services in which the state is unable or unwilling to play a significant role.

Organized voluntary activity in modern nations has rapidly expanded in recent decades. With the years, people, organizations, and governments have become aware that the state cannot, or will not, be involved in every field of human life. They have discovered that no bureaucracy is capable of being everywhere, all the time, and with optimal resources and remedies for all social problems. This "third sector" is distinct from the traditional public and private sectors (Gidron et al., 1992). In recent years voluntary organizations and the third sector have constituted about 10 percent of the economic size of all governmental activities in the United States (O'Connell, 1989), and their relative size continues to grow. Such figures may indicate that citizens of modern societies have more needs/demands and that they are disappointed with governments' operation and inability to provide satisfactory welfare services. Hence, it seems that today, more than ever before, citizens are willing to engage in collective voluntary actions (both semi-organized and fully organized) to support their needs (King et al., 1998).

Therefore, initiatives have been taken to do things better than governments and to provide quality services and goods which otherwise could not be delivered. Consequently, better understanding has become essential on how to run third sector bodies, how to manage their human resources better, and, most important, how to enhance their performance. High performance of third sector bodies is important not only for maintaining general organizational survival, but first and foremost for the healthy development of society and for the prosperity of citizens who derive primary benefit from third sector services. However, it seems that some straightforward managerial questions on how to run the business of voluntary and nonprofit organizations better have so far not enjoyed adequate scholarly attention (Batsleer, 1995).

If the third sector is present to respond consistently to challenges set by the prime minister of Israel, or by other leaders of modern democracies, a much more detailed and inclusive theory, as well as practical frameworks of managerial actions, are required that can guide voluntary organizations to better performances. For the third sector to enhance its knowledge and practices, it needs to establish a more profound relationship and greater collaboration with both the private and the public sectors. The best and most effective means is to absorb existing knowledge available from other disciplines of the social sciences, mainly organizational studies, psychology, and human resource management. For example, I agree with Forbes (1998) and with Kanter and Summers (1987), who argue that today effectiveness, outcomes, and performances of third sector organizations are problematic concepts in that they can mean different things to different people. In line with this, an inclusive analysis of employees' outcomes, as studied in the business sector, is vital because it is an indispensable dimension of overall organizational performance and effectiveness, and it carries unique advantages that so far have not been fully cultivated. Along with this, collaboration with the public and private sectors means setting mutual targets, agreeing on social priorities, and conducting an effective separation of work and tasks among these three sectors. Since the performance of one sector affects the others, it is crucial to increase coordination, share information, and better handle financial, physical, and human resources.

A MULTIDIMENSIONAL PERSPECTIVE OF COLLABORATION: AMONG CITIZENS, GOVERNMENTS, AND PUBLIC ADMINISTRATION

The complex construct of modern citizenship behavior and its limited employment in NPM theory calls for a revised conceptual framework that can unite this "odd couple." This framework should advocate the coexistence as well as solidarity of the public as represented by citizens, on the one hand, and the administration as reflected in NPM, on the other. Figure 4.1 presents a suggested model of multidimensional citizenship behavior and its effect on public service systems as stemming from the NPM approach. Based on the settings of citizenry action (communal and national versus organizational) and on the levels of analysis (individual versus collective action), I distinguish four types of citizenship behavior: micro-citizenship (MC1), midi-citizenship (MC2), macro-citizenship (MC3), and meta-citizenship (MC4). Each type is then related to the relevant construct of managerial operation and outcomes. Together they are intended to provide a synthesis of the fields.

Micro-Citizenship

Micro-citizenship (MC1) is the very basic image of citizenship actions as taken by individuals in the limited sphere of the workplace. Employees may present high levels of participation in workplace activities and greater willingness to support others even when not asked or ordered to do so. These employees may be defined as good organizational citizens (Organ, 1988). They differ from individuals who show lower levels of citizenship behavior or withhold such positive behaviors entirely. Some of these employees may even engage in organizational misbehaviors, such as stealing organizational property or sabotaging the work itself (Vardi and Wiener, 1996). Micro-citizenship of individuals inside the workplace has been shown to have a direct and significant impact on employees' performance (Cohen and Vigoda, 2000). Findings suggest that organizations benefit from using measures of organizational citizenship behavior as an integral part of their routine performance evaluation strategy because of the valuable information they provide on employees' informal contributions (Morrison, 1996).

Hence, a challenge for management theory in general, and for (new) public management in particular, is the development of highly valid and

Figure 4.1
Multiple Dimensions of Citizenship Behavior and Its Effect on Public Service Systems

Setting / Level	Organizational	Communal & National
Individual	**MC1** Micro-citizenship → Employees' Performance	**MC3** Macro-citizenship → Personal Welfare
Collective	**MC2** Midi-citizenship → Organizational Performance	**MC4** Meta-citizenship → Social Welfare

highly reliable research tools that can distinguish different types of public employees or "organizational citizens" in public agencies. Such indicators are expected to increase the explanatory power and predictability of organizational behavior models. In the public sector, it is extremely important that good organizational citizens be those who interact with the public to create a responsive environment and, as highlighted in NPM theory, serve citizens as clients. Enriching the public sector with employees who are better organizational citizens may also have an educative spillover effect on the public, improve the image of public administration, and make the contact with the citizens more fruitful and efficient both economically and socially.

Midi-Citizenship

Midi-citizenship (MC2) also refers to actions taken inside organizations, but they arise from the collective voice of groups of individuals rather than from independent individual actions. Whereas micro-citizenship has the greatest effect on other individuals, the midi-citizenship pattern is fashioned by groups for the sake of other groups or units, or for the sake of the organization as a whole. Midi-citizenship focuses on better attainment of wider objectives and goals in the workplace, not only personal targets and interests. The involvement and general voice of groups in the manufacturing process are valuable. Studies have demonstrated that more involvement of organized individuals in decision-making processes contributes to better operation in private as well as in public organizations (Erez et al., 1985). Methods such as quality circles, team-building strategies, and management by objectives emphasize the general encouragement of work groups to become more active as well as entrepreneurial in the various stages of production (Drucker, 1966; Hirschman, 1970).

Midi-citizenship is accordingly built on micro-citizenship, but is far more ambitious in its effort to increase and improve general performance of public organizations. Furthermore, groups are more powerful than detached individuals and set more challenging goals, which are later translated into massive improvement of goods and services. The collective action also enhances the feeling of communitarianism and the sense of cooperation that can spill over into the extraorganizational environment (Peterson, 1990; Sobel, 1993). In this way, organizations generally, and especially public agencies, serve as habitats for the growth of citizenship awareness and the development of sensitivity toward others, be it other work units or social groups.

Macro-Citizenship

Macro-citizenship (MC3) is defined as altruistic endeavors of individuals in the national and communal settings, those that express self-initiated contribution for the sake of others in the wider society. Moving beyond the narrow organizational arena, individuals use similar tendencies of altruism and willingness to help fellow citizens in the national and communal spheres. As elucidated earlier, active citizenship of individuals outside the workplace is characterized by independent enterprises focused on assisting others who may need help. Such spontaneous actions of unorganized people aim at enhancing the prosperity and development of the environment in general, thereby increasing the welfare of their fellow citizens. This is why macrocitizenship is related, in this model, to personal welfare in the national and communal arenas.

Citizens may help other citizens by showing tenderness, kindness, and generosity. They can contribute a variety of resources, such as time or money, to help the handicapped. They may also provide assistance for the elderly, for children in need, for minorities, or for other less capable groups. In so doing, they seek no personal advantage or compensation in return (Monroe, 1994; Piliavin and Charng, 1990). Studies have also suggested that some practices and skills gained in intraorganizational experiences may be useful for these initiatives. Citizens in the intimate workplace may learn how to use their personal resources more effectively, and then transfer them to the wider society (Peterson, 1990). Macro-citizenship is also characterized by people engaging only in one-on-one or one-on-group activities, avoiding (intentionally or not) any relationship with organized groups of volunteer associations.

Meta-Citizenship

Meta-citizenship (MC4) is the term I decided to use for collective citizenry action in the wider society. With the exception of ideas like universal citizenship (Oliver and Heater, 1994), this is perhaps the highest level of participatory and constructive citizenship behavior identifiable. Meta-citizenship is representative of collective actions at the communal and national levels that stem from deep altruistic dispositions, conscientiousness, and extensive acceptability of the constructive citizenship duties and responsibilities.

As noted by Fredrickson (1997), collective actions by interest groups, by political parties, or by citizenship lobbies are the most acceptable and widely studied aspects of citizenship behavior in contemporary political science literature. However, during the nineteenth century, citizens (especially in America) functioned in a more direct way, through town meetings, raising a militia for defense, and engaging in barn raisings (p. 12). Citizens' associations had been the most powerful image of American society in earlier centuries, but became less popular from the late 1800s to the mid-1900s with the emergence of the reform movement in public administration. The founding fathers of modern public administration, such as Woodrow Wilson and Dwight Waldo, urged that the discipline become a formal field of knowledge and an independent science among all other social sciences.

The reform movement introduced specialization, professionalism, and merit-based appointment and promotion into government, and the application of management sciences. Similarly, citizens continued to play a role, but a less direct one. They continued to organize, albeit less and less, to solve problems or provide services, and increasingly formed interest groups to influence government. As Fredrickson (1997) indicates, in the 1950s "pluralism" emerged as the best term to describe the connection between citizens and governments. Thus the indirect relationship between the public and the administrators became ever more widespread. The tradition of citizenship as involving an energized and self-directed public had essentially been lost.

Citizenship behavior was reconstructed only in the 1970s, and citizens resumed their functions in associations and nonprofit organizations, later known as the emerging "third sector." Hence, patterns of meta-citizenship were transformed over the years, but they continued to represent the overt, pure, and massive connection between organized citizens and governments. More specifically, meta-citizenship has had a major impact on public sector services through a creation of awareness of social welfare. Today, more and more organized citizens take action when the state is unable or unwilling to do what it ought to do for the public. Meta-citizenship is advanced as supplementary to governmental policy, and in some cases as an accelerator of processes already in progress.

CITIZENSHIP AND COLLABORATION IN PUBLIC ADMINISTRATION

It is suggested that better incorporation of the idea of citizenship into NPM thinking can be acquired through a multidimensional model, such as the one presented here. The model provides a classification that may better map voluntary enterprises in modern society and better explain them theoretically. Another theoretical contribution of this model may be the examination of the relationship among different dimensions of citizenship behavior in and around public organizations. Here one may follow some literature in political theory and management science which argues that citizenship behaviors at the state, community, and organizational levels are related (Graham, 1991; Peterson, 1990; Sobel, 1993). An alternative theory may suggest that such a relationship is not possible, and further studies should subject the three perspectives to comprehensive empirical evaluation. The results of this effort may expose the nature of a good and constructive "citizenship syndrome" and the wide basis of voluntary action in society.

So far, I have demonstrated that citizenship behavior has many faces. However, it has only one source: the people and their willingness to engage in the citizenry's constructive action. Building a spirit of new managerialism means bringing the citizens closer to their original role as equal participants in the administrative process. An added value is necessary for turning simple bureaucracies and stagnated public service into a more flexible, responsive, and vital entity with broad shoulders on which modern societies can safely rest. The final sections of this chapter elaborate on the nature of this spirit and the challenges it sets for the future.

CITIZENSHIP AND "NEW PUBLIC MANAGEMENT": A CRITIQUE

This section criticizes new public management for not doing enough to usher in the idea of citizenship behavior through the main entrance to the halls of modern management. Unlike traditional public management approaches, the NPM movement focuses on citizens as sophisticated clients in complex environments. Relying heavily on private sector management, the proponents of NPM perceive citizens of modern democracies more and more as clients with multiple alternatives for consuming high-level services. Public authorities must treat the public well, not only because of their presumed administrative responsibility for quality in action but also because of their obligation to democratic rules, to accountability demands, and transparency criteria—and sometimes even because of their fear of losing clients in an increasingly competitive, businesslike arena. Hence NPM opposes the more classical approach to governance and public administration that used to see citizens as simple constituents or voters. However, NPM creates a different obstacle to productive citizenship behavior that must be recognized and isolated. I argue that NPM encourages passivity among the citizenry whereby citizens acquire a power of exit (which was virtually unavailable in the past), but at the same time discourages use of the original power of voice by citizens who may have much to contribute to their communities.

To better explain the arguments and criticism on the current status of NPM, I focus on two major groups of players that are involved in governmental and administrative processes in democracies. Each of these has a special function and a unique set of duties. One group comprises rulers and public administrators who are responsible for the proper management of large organizations and bureaucratic agencies. The other is the public, the "citizens," especially authentic citizen-leaders who agree to be managed by "others" and must develop and sustain the appropriate control, involvement, and participation in the administrative process. Hobbes argued that these groups are tightly bound in a kind of mutual agreement. According to Hobbes, the people and their government have a hidden social contract, which calls for the people's obedience and loyalty to the government in return for government's commitment to provide some of their basic "natural" rights. In its elementary configuration, this contract advocates bidirectional transactions of human resources promoting the mutual interests of citizens, states, and society.

While recent developments in the study of NPM have focused on the responsibilities of the first group (rulers and administrators), they have paid much less attention to the second (citizens). NPM favors a massive socialization of business management practices in the public sector to provide rulers with better tools for policy implementation (e.g., Lynn, 1998; Pollitt, 1988). The only problem is that these orientations and practices have, thus far, not been integrated with another key construct of healthy democratic systems. That construct is the active role of the public, its participation and involvement in running its own life more effectively, and the responsibility of administrators to encourage such a welcome public contribution. This underestimation of active and constructive citizenship behavior is a weakness in contemporary NPM theory.

For example, Box (1998:73–74) asserts that NPM takes a very clear and unfavorable approach to active citizenship involvement in the administrative process. As was suggested earlier in this chapter, Box identified three types of citizens classified along a continuum of desire to affect the public policy process: (1) "freeriders," (2) "activists," and (3) "watchdogs." Thus, practically and theoretically, NPM mostly encourages the "freeriders" and perhaps some of the "watchdogs." So far, NPM has not emphasized the need for better reciprocal linkage between rulers and citizens. At most it has concentrated only on one direction of flow of influence, from rulers to citizens. In many respects this position does not adequately consider the positive effect of citizens' action on (new) public systems.

Why and how has such a tendency occurred? Several answers can be identified within the evolutionary development of modern public administration. During the 1960s and 1970s a growing number of observers perceived public administration as an old and declining discipline that no longer could provide the public with satisfactory answers to its needs and demands. The contract between rulers and citizens, once a fundamental principle of democratic societies, seemed to have lost its glory. Governments and governors in Europe and in America became unpopular in the eyes of many citizens as well as elites (Rainey, 1990:157), and public administration seemed to have no adequate answers for problems in education, transportation, employment, crime, natural resources, and other salient social issues. All these evinced a declining image of public administration. Theoreticians and practitioners were left with an epidemic of social dilemmas waiting for new solutions.

In the search for alternative answers, business management theory was proposed as a source for new and invigorating ideas (Bozeman, 1993). It was suggested that public management, rather than public administration, could manifest a new understanding of how to run governments more efficiently, how to improve their relationships with citizens as clients, and thereby to surmount some of society's pandemic ills. This process of "liberalization" in public administration, which is recognized today as "New Public Management," was elegantly defined by Garson and Overman (1983:278) as "an interdisciplinary study of the generic aspects of administration . . . a blend of the planning, organizing, and controlling functions of management with the management of human, financial, physical, information and political resources." Focusing on different resources that may contribute to better performance of public organizations, NPM has emphasized strategies successfully applied in private sector firms. Drawing on the business sector's experience, scholars expressed a more "demanding" attitude to dynamics, activities, and productivity of public organizations (e.g., Thomas, 1999). Demands for more consideration of proper managerial tools and principles were directed mainly at policy makers and public administrators. The public sector was urged to treat citizens as clients, and to provide competitive as well as high-quality services. Indeed, these were appropriate goals for a public service which prior to the 1980s paid scant attention to the economy of bureaucracies.

Today, despite the popularity in America and Europe of the theme of running government like a business, it also carries an unexpected difficulty. NPM has taken the lead in the study and practice of public systems, highlighting the main direction of flow of responsibilities: the commitment and obligation of public institutions to citizens as passive clients. Conversely, however, the idealized relationship between citizens and governments has been described more in terms of a unidirectional treaty rather than the bidirectional relationship consistent with representative democracy. Administrators are encouraged to assume greater responsibility toward citizens, while citizens' participation and involvement in the administrative process are perceived by politicians and by public servants as problematic. As King et al. (1998) argued, many public administrators view close relationships with citizens as both necessary and desirable. However, most of them also do not actively seek public involvement. If they do seek it, they do not use public input in making administrative decisions and, in fact, believe that greater citizen participation increases inefficiency, delays, and red tape.

Hence, NPM tends to overlook the importance of self-derived, spontaneous, and voluntary actions that are both vital and economic for prosperous societies (Etzioni, 1994, 1995), as well as for successful organizations (Katz and Kahn, 1966). Ironically, this behavior has enjoyed considerable attention in the business management literature, which served as a role model for NPM but has never been properly utilized in its original form. For example, since the early 1980s many studies of organizational behavior have elaborated on the importance of prosocial and extra-role activities later known as organizational citizenship behavior (OCB). Organ (1988) defined this behavior as the "good soldier syndrome," and other scholars sought to relate it to a broader concept of citizenship on the national and community levels. A progressive definition of citizenship behavior refers to voluntary actions inside and outside the workplace that can be beneficial for private or public organizations (e.g., Graham, 1991; Organ, 1988; Van Dyne et al.,

1994). Still, many issues have been overlooked in NPM literature, including engaging the public in administrative processes, encouraging citizens to take an active part in managing local governance, OCB, spontaneous involvement of public employees inside the workplace, and the general promotion of citizenship and altruistic behavior at all social levels.

Consequently, NPM traditionally does not elaborate on the advantages of citizenship behavior within or around the public system. Most of the writing in the field focuses on simplistic businesslike orientations; these are necessary and important, but they fail effectively to cultivate the many dimensions of human enterprise. The conventional perspective of NPM calls for a massive implementation of business standards in the public sector by strategies of privatization, outsourcing, performance indicators, and orientation to quality service. It does call for improved communication channels with citizens, but only as passive clients (Pollitt, 1988). It also views rulers and administrators as the major agents of managerial change. In this view, public administration assumes a "patronage" position toward citizens, who are left with only minor responsibilities, such as becoming "good customers" or "sensible clients." It does not, however, encourage more voluntary active effort and participation by citizens in the administrative process.

An advance across ground broken by Fredrickson (1997) in *The Spirit of Public Administration* suggests that a revitalized spirit of new public administration is necessary. In line with this idea I further argue that a balanced reciprocal relationship between citizens and rulers may lead to the creation of "a spirit of new managerialism." This spirit is relevant to the twenty-first century and may flourish only in a soil rich in mutual contributions by different parties. There is a need to develop the theory of the advantages of multidimensional citizenship behavior and to elaborate on its contribution to modern societies via NPM. My argument is that citizenship behavior is vital for any public system and administrative bureaucracy in quest of effectiveness, efficiency, fairness, social justice, and overall healthy growth and development. Citizenship behavior, whatever form it takes, carries significant values for the environment.

A more comprehensive inclusion of citizenship behavior in the study of new managerialism is also in line with the contemporary business management approach because of the relatively low costs of voluntary action (Brudney, 1990; Brudney and Duncombe, 1992). From an economics viewpoint, the NPM approach does not take advantage of its most powerful, valuable, and inexpensive resources: goodwill, civic virtue, spontaneous initiatives, and innovation by individuals. Even in its own business-oriented terminology, contemporary NPM theory is limited and incomplete. It needs a much more sound understanding of how to relate citizenship behavior to the management of public systems. In the following sections I try to portray this multidimensionality of citizenship behavior and to prepare the ground for a model of integration between citizenship and NPM. Such a discussion is vital to understand better how to incorporate manifold voluntary enterprises into modern public management.

INTERACTING WITH CITIZENS: AN EVOLUTIONARY CONTINUUM

Figure 4.2 presents an evolutionary continuum of the role of citizens, governments, and public administration authorities, and their reciprocal interaction as it advances with the years. Along this line citizens may be seen as subjects, voters, client-customers, partners, or owners. Moving along the

Figure 4.2
An Evolutionary Continuum of Public Administration–Citizen Interaction

Continuum 1: The role of citizens

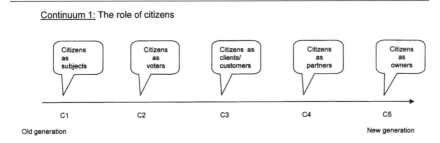

Continuum 2: The role of governance and public administration (G&PA)

Continuum 3: Type of interaction

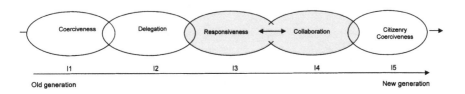

continuum, we also observe governments and public administration as rulers, trustees, managers, partners, or subjects. Stemming from these are five types of interactions between governments and public administration, and citizens. These profiles form a cycle from coerciveness through delegation, responsiveness, collaboration, and back to coerciveness, but this time of a different type: citizenry coerciveness. The profiles also overlap, to indicate that the progress and development of interactions are frequently characterized by coexistence of profiles and a gradual decline of the former before the latter (e.g., Weikart, 2001:362).

Coerciveness

The old generation of public administration used to treat citizens as subjects, with leaders and administrators holding almost absolute power and control over the people. Citizens, for their part, accepted the unlimited tyranny of the state and made only a minimal effort to sound their voices in such an unreceptive environment. The kinds of services delivered to the people were limited and in any case absolutely dependent on the government's will and decisions. This type of coercive interaction existed for ages, until the mid- or late eighteenth century (Fredrickson, 1997; T. H. Marshall, 1950). In many respects it still predominates in the "popular democracies" or dictatorial states of the second and third world. In both cases centralized power in governance is accompanied by rigorous bureaucratic structures and is mostly a result of nondemocratic culture. Such a culture imposes a government and public administration monopoly on national resources through armed force and dominance of education and socialization systems. The old-orthodox public administration controlled and monitored many, if not all, aspects of citizens' daily lives to create a pattern of coerciveness in the citizen-ruler relationship.

Delegation

The first institutional option for citizens' inputs into the process of government and society building was through the installation of the voter-electoral system, better defined as democratic governments and public administration or an interaction of delegation. Without doubt, democracy has created a more equal, fair, open, and flexible coexistence of citizens and rulers, and has enabled the former to become active in framing the nature of governance. This is how a citizens-as-voters style emerged, and made a tremendous conceptual and practical change in the understanding of citizen-government relationships. Since the end of the eighteenth century, and more robustly toward the late nineteenth century, developing representative democracies of the Western world fostered the idea of delegation. In a representative democracy, it was argued, citizens cannot manage their lives but count on the wisdom, experience, and civic goodwill of their representatives. Woodrow Wilson and Dwight Waldo called for a reform of government and public administration and for an emphasis on specialization, professionalism, merit-based appointment and promotion, and the application of management sciences in local, state, and federal agencies.

Following this, citizens were given the option of voice, but only via representatives and at wide intervals of time (between elections), with no sufficient instruments for an effective in-between influence. Nonetheless, citizens in America and in Europe initiated self-derived attempts to become more involved in administrative actions by interest groups and by political parties. Fredrickson (1997) argued that in the 1950s "pluralism" emerged as the best term to describe the indirect connection between citizens and governments. Yet with the passage of time it also became clear that such attempts were too few, too vague, and too slight in impact on government and on public administration. The formal "open gate" for citizen involvement did not mean that a widespread atmosphere of original participation by individual citizens or groups actually matured.

As scientific knowledge has accumulated, the theory of political participation has clarified that there are people who are unable or unwilling to participate in governmental or political processes, while others are simply not aware of the importance and contribution of this involvement (Verba et al., 1995). In fact, representative democracy highly contradicted the promise of vast spontaneous citizen involvement. Being remote from decision-making centers, by choice or not, citizens developed increased cynicism toward government and toward public administration systems. As argued by Eisinger (2000), "Over the past decades, scholars, political pundits and elected officials have professed that cynicism has spiraled up and down . . . to the point that it has become an endemic part of the psyche in the 1980s [when] a fog of cynicism surrounds American politics, and that the 1990s are a time of unparalleled public cynicism about politics, which has continued and accelerated to this day" (p. 55). Hence, this simple delegation type of relationship between rulers and citizens drew heavy fire from academics, professionals, public servants, and even politicians. In many respects, the need for an additional change in the nature of state-citizen interaction drove the NPM movement in the following years.

Responsiveness

Citizens-as-voters was only one step toward the development of a citizens-as-clients/customers model. As suggested by Rainey (1990), the 1960s and the 1970s were characterized by the initiation of unsuccessful public policies in Europe and in America. Over the years, efforts by governments to create extensive changes in education, welfare systems, health programs, internal security, and crime control were widely criticized for being ineffective and low-performing, and for misusing public budgets, while responsiveness to the real needs and demands of citizens was paltry. The crisis in practical public policy implementation, together with intensified citizens' cynicism regarding government and public administration, generated rich scholarly activity aimed at creating useful alternatives for improved policy in various social fields as well as in the administrative processes in general (Peters, 1999). Voters expressed their dissatisfaction with governors, and hand in hand with the academic community called for extensive reforms in government.

This call produced a large number of working papers, articles, and books that portrayed and targeted extensive administrative changes. One of the most inspiring works, Osborne and Gaebler's *Reinventing Government* (1992), is frequently mentioned as the unofficial starting point of such reforms, later known as NPM. According to Peters (1996a), Terry (1998), and Weikart (2001), NPM is presently increasing in popularity in North America and across the world, and many governments adopt ideas and recommendations that have proven beneficial in the continuous implementation of this strategy.

True enough, the NPM approach suggested a different type of interaction between citizens and rulers in democracies. However, the roots of such interactions can be found around a century ago. For example, Weikart (2001) asserted that "the ideas behind NPM are not new" and that "NPM builds on a long history of using business practices in government and reflects a resurgence of old ideas about the form and functions of government" (p. 362). During the first years of the twentieth century, reformers and business leaders demanded greater accountability in local government, and many politicians as well as public officials turned to business principles to improve governmental activities, invigorate performance, and decrease corruption.

However, the vision of NPM is far different from the old business-guided governance due to its aspiration to decrease government size and lower its involvement in citizens' lives. NPM relies on the theory of the marketplace and on a businesslike culture in public organizations. For example, in an extensive review of NPM literature, Hays and Kearney (1997) found five core principles of this approach: (1) downsizing—reducing the size and scope of government, (2) managerialism—using business protocols in government, (3) decentralization—moving decision-making closer to the service recipients, (4) debureaucratization—restructuring government to emphasize results rather than processes, and (5) privatization—directing the allocation of governmental goods and services to outside firms (Weikart, 2001). All these principles are mutually related, relying heavily on theory of the private sector and on business philosophy, but aimed at minimizing the size and scope of governmental activities. Integrated with ideas rooted in political economy, they became applicable for public sector institutions (Farnham and Horton, 1995).

Stemming from the above principles, a major belief of NPM advocates is that governments and public administration encourage a view whereby citizens are clients/customers of the public sector while governments and public administration are perceived as managers of large bureaucracies. According to this outlook (Aucoin, 1995; Garson and Overman, 1983; Pollitt and Bouckaert, 2000), the state and its bureaucratic subsystems are equivalent to a large private organization operating in an economic environment of supply and demand. In this spirit a major goal of government is to satisfy the needs or demands of citizens, to show higher responsiveness to the public as clients. In line with this, Savas (1994) argued that modern states must rely more on private institutions and less on government to satisfy societal needs of vast populations. Hence, the goal of satisfying citizens' needs became central to NPM.

Nevertheless, NPM may be criticized for not doing enough to encourage and infuse the idea of collaboration or partnership between citizens, governments, and public administration, and for failing to apply these themes in modern managerial thinking (Vigoda and Golembiewski, 2001). Unlike traditional public administration, the NPM movement focuses on citizens as sophisticated clients in complex environments. The principles of NPM cohere with theories of political economy such as regulative policy by governments or the trend of transferring responsibilities from the state sector to the third sector. As suggested by Farnham and Horton (1995), "these ideas, and the governmental policies deriving from them, challenged the social democratic principles and values" (p. 3) in Britain, America, and many other Western democracies. Public authorities were urged to treat the public well not only because of their presumed administrative responsibility for quality in action but also because of their obligation to marketplace rules and to economic demands, and above all because of their fear of losing clients in a increasingly competitive businesslike arena. In fact, while NPM has proved to be an advance over more classic views of public administration that saw citizens as subjects or voters, it is still very limited in fostering the idea of vital collaboration between citizens, government, and public administration, which is the essence of democratic civil society.

In line with this, "neo-managerialism" (Terry, 1998) places an additional obstacle before productive partnership that must also be recognized and isolated. According to Terry, neo-managerialism fosters the idea that administrative leaders should assume the role of public entrepreneurs. However, "Public entrepreneurs of the neo-managerialist persuasion are oblivious to other values highly prized in the U.S. constitutional democracy. Values such as fairness, justice, representation, or participation are not on the radar screen [and] this is indeed, troublesome" (p. 200). In many respects neo/new managerialism and NPM encourage passivity among the citizenry. They impart to citizens the power of exit (which was virtually unavailable in the past), but at the same time they discourage use of the original power of voice by citizens who may have much to contribute to their communities (Vigoda and Golembiewski, 2001). Hirschman (1970) suggested that exit is an economic choice, while voice is more of a political selection by individuals in and around organizational systems. Exit is also classified as a general destructive behavior, while voice is a productive one. According to this rationality, NPM restricts and discourages productive political voices of the people.

Hence, recent developments in the study of NPM have focused on the responsibilities of governments and public administration in their interaction with citizens, but similarly have paid far less attention to the active roles of citizens and to their obligations in the community. Most of the up-to-date NPM literature favors massive socialization of business management practices in the public sector to provide governments with better tools for policy implementation (e.g., Lynn, 1998; Pollitt, 1988; Pollitt and Bouckaert, 2000; Rosenbloom et al., 1994). But on the other hand, these orientations and practices have so far not been integrated with another core construct of healthy democracies: genuine collaboration and partnership with citizens founded on equal opportunities for participation and massive involvement in running public life more effectively (Peters, 1999). This underevaluation of the idea of partnership and collaboration, at the expense of well-responding management, may be deemed a flaw in contemporary NPM theory.

EMPOWERING CITIZENS FOR COLLABORATION

The four types of citizenship behavior suggested here may be viewed as one alternative typology of human activism and voluntary actions that are revitalizing administration in modern society. As Joyce (1994) and Box (1998) argued, people in America and other developed democracies are ready for "a new citizenship" that will liberate and empower them. The new citizenship calls for a revived relationship with governance, or "citizen-centered governance." Citizens should be encouraged to become part of governance, taking on more responsibilities for running their lives rather than treating the administrative process as something separate, with themselves as customers to be "served" or antagonists to be opposed (Ostrom, 1993). According to Schachter (1997), "a new citizenship" must be related to the process of reinventing government, which is a way of creating change through managerial techniques (Box, 1998).

Referring to the Clinton administration's National Performance Review, Schachter (1997) describes a situation in which "current reform proposals do not include a wake-up call to the public to assume its obligations since customers have no obligations to the enterprise from which they buy products and services. . . . Citizens can sit back comfortably in their rocking chairs and watch government improve to meet their expectations" (p. 90). Schachter criticizes this view because it encourages passive citizenship, equivalent to Box's "freeriders," instead of yielding productive involvement and participation. He then suggests a model of "citizen owners" and "active citizenship" that may be the ground for "new citizenship." In all, these perspectives and models lead to considerable citizen reliance on public management's commitment to increasing agency effectiveness and responsiveness. Active citizenship behavior on the individual or collective level that emerges in national, communal, and organizational arenas represents people engaged in deliberation to influence public sector decision-making. It shapes the political agenda and ponders the ends that governments should pursue, as well as evaluating how well particular public sector programs work (Box, 1998:73).

Nowadays NPM literature tries to recognize and define new criteria that may help determine the extent to which public agencies succeed in keeping pace with the growing needs of the citizens (Pollitt, 1988; P. Smith, 1993). Nevertheless, it has not fully considered the potential advantage of multidimensional models or "new citizenship" involvement (Box, 1999). The prime advantage of such citizenship involvement is its long-term effect and continuity. More involvement, participation, and voluntarism by citizens (as individuals or collectively as groups and organized institutions) in different settings (state, community, or organization) is a valuable resource that new managerialism should not ignore.

P. Smith (1993) provides reasoning and support for this notion, arguing that citizens' participation in, involvement in, and awareness of the performance of public services should be a core element of NPM. It can increase the political pressure placed on elected and appointed public servants, thereby enhancing both managerial and allocative efficiency in the public sector. This process of public accountability to stakeholders/citizens is comparable to the role adopted by financial reporting in the private/corporate sector. As in the private sector, externally related outcomes (e.g., citizens' satisfaction, perceptions of public administration's responsiveness, perceptions of public personnel's morality and fairness, etc.) have a more profound impact on internal control mechanisms. Managers and public servants become more sensitive to their duties and more deeply committed to serving their public customers. Higher citizenship involvement, altruistic and voluntary activity, and participation and engagement in national or local managerial processes may breed internal organizational involvement, commitment, and innovation by public servants. Furthermore, public employees may become more willing to exert extra-role behavior, prosocial behavior, and OCB (Brief and Motowidlo, 1986; Organ, 1988; Podsakoff and MacKenzie, 1997) to support the common goals of citizens, governments, and the public service. In return it is expected that citizens will further develop loyalty, commitment, and participation. They will exert additional effort and contribute to the general good of their environment.

A multidimensional analysis of citizenship behavior and its relationship with NPM creates a momentous challenge for governance. As suggested by

Lynn (1998:231), NPM of the late 1990s had three constructive legacies for the field of public administration and for democratic theory and practice. First, stronger emphasis on performance-motivated administration and inclusion in the administrative canon of performance-oriented institutional arrangements, structural forms, and managerial doctrines fitted to the particular context. This may be considered a real advance in the state of the public management art. Second, international dialogue on, and a stronger comparative dimension in the study of, state design and administrative reform. Third, integrated use of economic, sociological, social-psychological, and other advanced conceptual models and heuristics in the study of public institutions and management.

These models have the potential to strengthen scholarship in the field and the possibilities for theory-grounded practice. While the first two legacies are widely discussed in contemporary NPM literature, the third is scarcely studied and needs further theoretical development, empirical research, and practical implementation. I argue that the present multidimensional and interdisciplinary conceptual model conforms to the third legacy of Lynn. A study by McKevitt (1998) supports this perspective. Criticizing public administration reforms in several European countries, McKevitt (1998:169) argued that "[t]he reforms do not allow for any interest, except self-interest; the measure of success is financial rather than community-based . . . and the reform programs do not take adequate account of citizens." In my opinion, the incorporation of multidimensional analysis of citizenship behavior in the study of new public administration is vital. The voice of citizens (as opposed to the option of exit) and their spontaneous actions must be viewed as a strategic tool for new managerialism in its attempt to improve the public service.

Supported by rapidly growing academic interest and practical ventures, the promising potential of reciprocal linkage and collaboration between governments, public administration, and citizens can be further developed. In this linkage, citizens have several roles. The most elementary is active participation in running their lives and managing their communities. This role is momentous, so it should not be left solely in the hands of politicians or even professional public servants. It can be accomplished on several levels: individual, group, or institutional (Vigoda and Golembiewski, 2001). Participation in neighborhood associations or voluntary groups to aid the young, the elderly, or other sections of the population; active involvement in citizens' committees as presented earlier in this chapter; involvement in parents' committees at schools; donating money, time, or effort for charity or equivalent social goals; development of community services in various manners; and encouraging others to take part in such activities—all are worthy missions that allow continuous partnership of the people in administrative processes.

In addition, citizens have the duty to voice constructive criticism of the public system to encourage a culture of accountability, and to provide feedback for politicians and public servants, thereby increasing their responsiveness and sense of responsibility. This can be achieved through original civic journalism; letters to newspapers, public officials, and politicians; calling radio and television stations; and using the computerized media to spread knowledge and attitudes. The education system has the power of teaching the youngest to become more involved and to use these methods more extensively. This way civic involvement may resound when children grow up and become adult citizens with formal rights and duties. Thus, citizens, like other social players, serve as socialization agents of partnership. They have an educational mission to contribute increased motivation and furnish values of involvement in future generations. It is well within their power to promote understanding of shared responsibilities within social life.

Last, it would be naive to seek large-scale political participation (e.g., Almond and Verba, 1963; Verba et al., 1995) and vast self-derived mobilization by citizens without creating the necessary conditions for such involvement. People have the duty to become engaged in collaborative activities with governments and public administration. However, as mentioned earlier, governments and public administration have the greater duty to create conditions for such involvement by all available means. Moreover, and as I describe later, the voyage to increased collaboration between citizens, governments, and public administration can become calmer and much more effective when media and academe join in the effort.

THE ONGOING STUDY OF THIRD SECTOR AND PUBLIC SECTOR COLLABORATION

A critique by Grubbs (2000) holds that the field of collaboration between citizens, third sector bodies, and the public sector suffers a serious lack of knowledge. Recent inquiry has explicated some of the notions associated with networks (O'Toole, 1997; Milward and Provan, 1998; Milward, 1996), but the scope of the research has been limited. One of the reasons is the rational concerns-treating approach adopted by many scholars. In line with my arguments earlier in this book, such issues focus on the economic and social costs of collaboration, mechanisms for administrative control, or applications of public-choice models and game theory for the purpose of predicting behavior (O'Toole, 1997). Therefore, public administration theory has failed to adequately inform practice on important managerial concepts that are tightly related to an effective process of collaboration such as coordinating systems of governance, sharing resources and accountability, and integrating organizational cultures. As presented in the first chapters of this book, Grubbs's critique closely coheres with my perspective, which draws upon the need for collaboration among disciplines and banks of knowledge, and not merely among sectors, organizations, and field-acting agencies.

Grubbs's (2000) criticism of the ongoing study of collaboration between the third sector and the public sector relies on three recent books on the topic: (1) Jane Arsenault's *Forging Nonprofit Alliances* (1998); (2) Eugene Bardach's *Getting Agencies to Work Together: The Practice and Theory of Managerial Craftsmanship* (1999); (3) Seymour B. Sarason and Elizabeth M. Lorentz's *Crossing Boundaries: Collaboration, Coordination, and the Redefinition of Resources* (1998). I agree with Grubbs that the three books contribute to our collective knowledge by illuminating the conundrums faced by public and nonprofit organizations as they engage in strategic alliances. All of the books express concern for the ways in which agencies find common ground, the diverse strengths each brings to an alliance, and how these strengths may be joined together in the pursuit of common outcomes. However, the books differ on what they believe promotes successful collaboration. Such differences reflect the complexity public administrators face as they attempt to build and sustain interagency relationships.

Grubbs's analysis makes several interesting distinctions among these related but different books. According to Arsenault (1998), there are many forms of interorganizational alliances. At the "more loosely integrated" end of the spectrum there are joint ventures and management service organizations, and at the "more consolidated" end she considers parent corporations and mergers. She discusses optimal conditions for each option, and follows this with step-by-step coaching for the negotiation, design, and implementation of the emerging partnerships. This approach is highly in line with the presentation of the strategic map for collaboration, as presented here in earlier chapters. Arsenault thus also elaborates on emotional and normative considerations underlying alliances, communicating valuable information relating to the integration of organizational cultures. Her focus is on the nonprofit sector, but this is highly relevant for public agencies as well.

Bardach (1999), on the other hand, makes an attempt to identify key success factors in the collaborative process. He measures the level of integration achieved in a variety of partnerships, based on an analytical framework he refers to as interagency collaborative capacity (ICC), a calculation of the integration, discounted by the social costs of the interaction. He concentrates the ICC measurement on collaboration in the fields of social services, fire prevention, military base reuse, and environmental protection. A process of "reverse engineering" is then used to compile the "smart practices" from the analysis to a leadership approach that he calls "managerial craftsmanship," geared toward achieving effective, value-adding collaboration.

Sarason and Lorentz (1998) apply a different thinking than the other two books. Rather than concentrating on the process of collaboration, they examine the role of an individual facilitator, or a network coordinator, in creating a sense of community and shared commitment across organizations. They frame the discourse in a denouncement of the public sector, which they consider hopelessly bounded by an "organizational chart mentality." They then turn to the private sector for models of successful resource exchange. As I demonstrated in chapter 4, the partnership between private sector firms and public sector organization is perceived to be indispensable to other processes that denote the general idea of collaboration. To aid potential collaborators, Sarason and Lorentz describe the ideal traits of a network coordinator, which include a capacity for appreciating organizations in their broader social context, for scanning the environment to build connections across organizational systems, and for focusing on strengths rather than seeing only weaknesses in individuals and groups (Grubbs, 2000).

CHAPTER 5

The Promise of Cross-Sectoral Alliances: Surveying Managers on the Challenge of Collaboration

AN EMPIRICAL APPROACH TO THE STUDY OF COLLABORATION

If collaboration is here to stay, it deserves more than merely theoretical justification and practical illustrations. It may step forward only with careful and comprehensive scientific study of its basic fabric as viewed from the bridge by those involved in the daily routine of serving the people. These individuals have already experienced the promises and barriers of collaboration in daily public work. Hence, they are ideal participants in an empirical effort that can enhance knowledge as well as explore some of the hidden domains of collaboration.

Furthermore, an empirical approach to the study of collaboration must rely on current knowledge of various disciplines in the social sciences. Most important, it may benefit from the experience in organizational studies, management, politics, sociology, and psychology. An empirical approach relies on original data sets that can be collected by extensive examination of the field through case study analyses, interviews, or surveys. Populations may comprise members of public, private, and third sector organizations that interact with plans or programs of collaboration. These are mostly managers and executives at various levels; in the public sector they may also involve politicians and other policy makers who participate in making collaboration work. In this chapter I focus on the managerial level of organization members. I assume that managers in both the private and the nonprofit sector have the advantage of facing collaborative ventures, becoming entrepreneurs of such activities, and evaluating their present level of success as well as future development. Hence, I describe and develop one strategy based on one survey of Israeli managers. Since collaboration necessitates and breeds higher levels of data processing from different sources, I have tried to obtain information on collaboration by assessing senior managers' views and beliefs from various angles. Managers were expected to share their opinions on the current state of the field and on its potential advancement in the future. They were asked to report their lessons and vision on what may prove to be a vital trend for tomorrow's bureaucracies.

THE MANAGERS' SURVEY

Participants in this survey were 244 managers. Of these, 144 were from the public and nonprofit sector (PBS) and 100 from the private sector (PRS). Of the PBS managers, 48.5 percent were women and 51.5 percent were men. Average age was 42.2 (S.D. = 8.7), and average tenure with the organization was 14.5 years (S.D. = 8.3). The PBS managers were highly educated, with 95.2 percent of the total sample having an academic degree of some kind: 54.4 percent having a bachelor's degree, and 40.8 percent having a graduate degree or higher. Jews accounted for 86.5 percent of the respondents, and 13.5 percent were non-Jews (Muslims, Christians, and Druze). By type of organization, 31.4 percent were in local government, 26.3 percent in education organizations, 11.9 percent in the security services (army, police, and other services), 8.5 percent in health care organizations, 6.8 percent in the Ministry of Finance and other economic-oriented authorities, 5.1 percent in government companies and authorities (aviation, transport, ports), and 10.0 percent in welfare services, the Labor Ministry, and environmental agencies.

Of the PRS managers, 41.9 percent were women and 58.1 percent were men. Average age was 33.4 (S.D. = 6.1), and average tenure with the organization was 4.9 years (S.D. = 3.8). The PRS managers also were highly educated, with 95.6 percent of the total sample having an academic degree of some kind: 57.8 percent having a bachelor's degree and 37.8 percent having a graduate degree or higher. Of the PRS respondents, 94.8 percent were Jews and 5.2 percent non-Jews (Muslims, Christians, and Druze). By type of organization, 61.7 percent were in industrial and marketing firms, 24.6 percent in high-technology firms, 8.2 percent in private law offices, and 5.5 percent in privately owned firms.

EVIDENCE ON CURRENT COLLABORATION
AND FUTURE VISIONS

Evidence on the state of current collaboration in and around the Israeli public sector was obtained through several questions targeted at distinguishing collaboration in numerous fields. I was primarily interested in managers' perceptions as to the level of collaboration in these arenas: (1) education, (2) health, (3) welfare, (4) culture and sports, (5) employment, and (6) other (e.g., transportation, environment, communication). Managers were asked to report separately on the level of collaboration between public administration and (a) private organizations and business firms, and (b) voluntary and nonprofit organizations, and citizens as individuals or groups.

Next, evidence on the future vision of collaboration among the public, private, and third sector organizations was obtained. Participants were asked to express their feelings and attitudes on various statements. Each statement presented a different view with which a manger might agree or disagree on a five-point scale. There were fourteen such statements:

1. Today, more than ever before, government offices collaborate with each other to improve services for citizens.
2. I think that the level of collaboration among public administration, private organizations, and voluntary and nonprofit bodies can greatly improve.
3. Senior managers in the public sector well understand the advantages of collaboration with other bodies and work to improve these relations.
4. Many problems on the state level could be solved if public organizations learned to collaborate with the private sector and with voluntary and nonprofit organizations.
5. The private sector is interested in collaborating with the public sector.
6. Voluntary and nonprofit organizations are interested in collaborating with the public sector.
7. Today, more than ever before, the public sector is searching for ways to increase collaboration with private firms and with voluntary organizations.
8. Personally, I am willing to become actively involved in public sector initiatives aimed at improving the quality of life in our nation.
9. I am willing to spend time in such activities (e.g., join citizens' committees).
10 I am willing to bring in knowledge and ideas (e.g., suggest new ways to improve quality of life).
11. I am willing to bring other people into the collaborative processes.
12. An advanced state must seek better collaboration between the public sector and private and voluntary bodies.
13. In the future, the public sector will be forced to increase collaboration with others in order to reach its goals.
14. Collaboration between the public sector and the private sector is more important than collaboration between the public sector and voluntary/nonprofit organizations.

EVIDENCE ON COLLABORATION WITH PRIVATE ORGANIZATIONS AND BUSINESS FIRMS

Figure 5.1 shows that managers perceived the level of collaboration between public and private sector organizations in the educational arena as average to low (mean PBS = 2.75, S.D. = 0.98; Mean PRS = 2.39, S.D. = 0.73). A percentage of 43.7 of the PBS managers and 58.7 percent of the PRS managers reported that, to the best of their knowledge, public-private collaboration in education took place never or only seldom. A percentage

Figure 5.1

How Much Collaboration Exists Between Public Sector and Private Sector Organizations in Education Services?

	Never or almost never		Seldom		Sometimes		Usually		Always or almost always	
	PBS	PRS	PBS	PRS	PBS	PRS	PBS	PRS	PBS	PRS
%	9.2	8.2	34.5	50.5	29.6	35.1	25.4	6.2	1.4	0.0

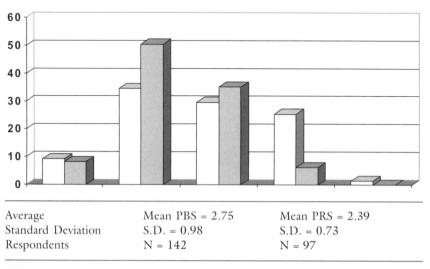

Average	Mean PBS = 2.75	Mean PRS = 2.39
Standard Deviation	S.D. = 0.98	S.D. = 0.73
Respondents	N = 142	N = 97

PBS = Public Sector Managers; PRS = Private Sector Managers.

of 26.8 of the PBS managers and only 6.2 percent of the PRS managers reported that such collaboration was more prevalent and took place usually, always, or almost always. Examples of collaborative programs in the educational arena included constant and long-term support by private firms of schools, kindergartens, and public day-care homes on a financial, technological, or other basis, and integration of students in business projects where specific professional skills and methods could be acquired and practiced.

Figure 5.2 shows managers' perceptions of the level of collaboration between public and private sector organizations in health services (e.g., mutual plans aimed at helping hospitals, clinics, or needy infirm citizens; rehabilitation plans supported by business firms; integration of handicapped into the workforce, etc.). Managers reported that according to their experience, the level of collaboration in this field was average to low (mean PBS = 2.73, S.D. = 1.98; mean PRS = 2.55, S.D. = 0.91). A percentage of 46.4 of the PBS managers and 45.4 percent of the PRS managers reported little or no collaboration. Similarly, 27.2 percent of the PBS managers and 13.4 per-

Figure 5.2
How Much Collaboration Exists Between Public Sector and Private Sector Organizations in Health Service?

	Never or almost never		Seldom		Sometimes		Usually		Always or almost always	
	PBS	PRS	PBS	PRS	PBS	PRS	PBS	PRS	PBS	PRS
%	12.1	13.4	34.3	32.0	26.4	41.2	22.9	12.4	4.3	1.0

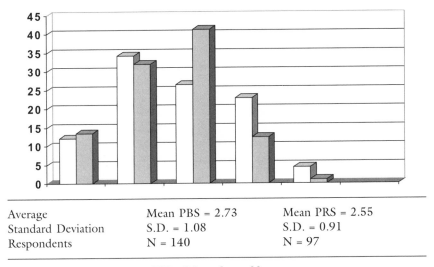

Average	Mean PBS = 2.73	Mean PRS = 2.55
Standard Deviation	S.D. = 1.08	S.D. = 0.91
Respondents	N = 140	N = 97

PBS = Public Sector Managers; PRS = Private Sector Managers.

cent of the PRS managers reported that, to the best of their knowledge, a relatively high level of collaboration existed.

Figure 5.3 shows managers' perceptions of the level of collaboration between public and private sector organizations in welfare services (e.g., mutual plans aimed at sponsoring, financially and spiritually, families in distress, children in need, or lonely people who would like once again to become part of the community). Managers reported that, according to their experience, the level of collaboration in this field was average to low (mean PBS = 2.88, S.D. = 1.05; and mean PRS = 2.50, S.D. = 0.85). A percentage of 40.3 of the PBS managers and 53.2 percent of the PRS managers reported little or no collaboration. Similarly, 33.1 percent of the PBS managers and 11.4 percent of the PRS managers reported that, to the best of their knowledge, a reasonable level of collaboration existed in providing welfare services to citizens.

Figure 5.4 portrays managers' perceptions of the level of collaboration between public and private sector organizations in culture services and sports

Figure 5.3
How Much Collaboration Exists Between Public Sector and Private Sector Organizations in Welfare Services?

	Never or almost never		Seldom		Sometimes		Usually		Always or almost always	
	PBS	PRS	PBS	PRS	PBS	PRS	PBS	PRS	PBS	PRS
%	8.6	9.4	31.7	43.8	26.6	35.4	29.5	10.4	3.6	1.0

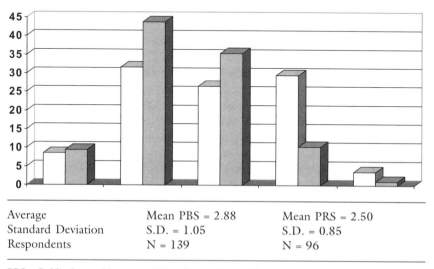

Average	Mean PBS = 2.88	Mean PRS = 2.50
Standard Deviation	S.D. = 1.05	S.D. = 0.85
Respondents	N = 139	N = 96

PBS = Public Sector Managers; PRS = Private Sector Managers.

(e.g., mutual long-range plans aimed at developing art clubs, theaters, and orchestras, and support for local sports clubs or other public sports activities). Managers reported in their experience, the level of collaboration in this field was average to high (mean PBS = 3.11, S.D. = 1.00; mean PRS = 2.89, S.D. = 1.06). A percentage of 25.1 of the PBS managers and 34.8 percent of the PRS managers reported little or no collaboration, while 10.8 percent of the PBS managers and 32.7 percent of the PRS managers reported that, to the best of their knowledge, a high level of collaboration existed in providing culture services or in sports.

Figure 5.5 portrays managers' perceptions of the level of collaboration between public and private sector organizations in employment services (e.g., allocating jobs for the unemployed or activating courses for professional development). Managers reported that, according to their experience, the level of collaboration in this field was average to low (mean PBS = 2.75, S.D. = 1.01; mean PRS = 2.67, S.D. = 0.98). A percentage of 42.1 of the PBS managers and 45.8 percent of the PRS managers reported little

Figure 5.4
How Much Collaboration Exists Between Public Sector and Private Sector Organizations in Culture Services and Sports?

	Never or almost never		Seldom		Sometimes		Usually		Always or almost always	
	PBS	PRS	PBS	PRS	PBS	PRS	PBS	PRS	PBS	PRS
%	8.1	11.6	17.0	23.2	34.1	32.6	7.8	29.5	3.0	3.2

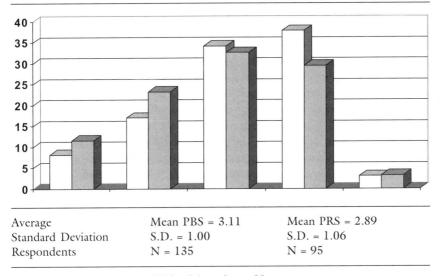

Average	Mean PBS = 3.11	Mean PRS = 2.89
Standard Deviation	S.D. = 1.00	S.D. = 1.06
Respondents	N = 135	N = 95

PBS = Public Sector Managers; PRS = Private Sector Managers.

or no collaboration. Similarly, 22.9 percent of the PBS managers and 19.8 percent of the PRS managers reported that, to the best of their knowledge, a relatively high level of collaboration existed in providing employment services to citizens.

Figure 5.6 portrays managers' perceptions of the level of collaboration between public and private sector organizations in various other services, such as environment, transportation, and communication. Managers reported that, according to their experience, the level of collaboration in these fields was average to low (mean PBS = 2.91, S.D. = 1.08; mean PRS = 2.33, S.D. = 1.03). A percentage of 30.4 of the PBS managers and 66.7 percent of the PRS managers reported little or no collaboration. Also, 30.4 percent of the PBS managers and 16.7 percent of the PRS managers reported that, to the best of their knowledge, a relatively high level of collaboration existed in providing these services to citizens. Note, however, that the number of respondents for this item was very low.

Figure 5.5
How Much Collaboration Exists Between Public Sector and Private Sector
Organizations in Employment Services?

	Never or almost never		Seldom		Sometimes		Usually		Always or almost always	
	PBS	PRS	PBS	PRS	PBS	PRS	PBS	PRS	PBS	PRS
%	10.0	10.4	32.1	35.4	35.0	34.4	18.6	16.7	4.3	3.1

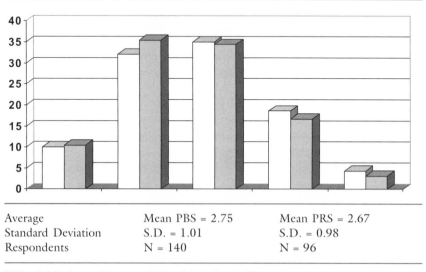

Average	Mean PBS = 2.75	Mean PRS = 2.67
Standard Deviation	S.D. = 1.01	S.D. = 0.98
Respondents	N = 140	N = 96

PBS = Public Sector Managers; PRS = Private Sector Managers.

EVIDENCE ON COLLABORATION WITH CITIZENS
AND THE THIRD SECTOR

Figure 5.7 portrays managers' perceptions of the level of collaboration
between public and third sector organizations in education services. Managers reported that, according to their experience, the level of collaboration
in this field was average (mean PBS = 3.00, S.D. = 1.04; mean PRS = 2.83,
S.D. = 1.05). A percentage of 33.1 of the PBS managers and 36.2 percent
of the PRS managers reported little or no collaboration. A percentage of 33.1
of the PBS managers and only 24.5 percent of the PRS managers reported
that, to the best of their knowledge, a reasonable level of collaboration existed in providing education services to citizens.

Figure 5.8 portrays managers' perceptions of the level of collaboration
between public and third sector organizations in health services. Managers
reported that, according to their experience, the level of collaboration in this
field was average to low (mean PBS = 2.86, S.D. = 1.09; mean PRS = 2.63,

Figure 5.6
How Much Collaboration Exists Between Public Sector and Private Sector Organizations in Other Services (e.g., Environment, Transportations, Communication)?

	Never or almost never		Seldom		Sometimes		Usually		Always or almost always	
	PBS	PRS	PBS	PRS	PBS	PRS	PBS	PRS	PBS	PRS
%	13.0	16.7	17.4	50.0	39.1	16.7	26.1	16.7	4.3	0.0

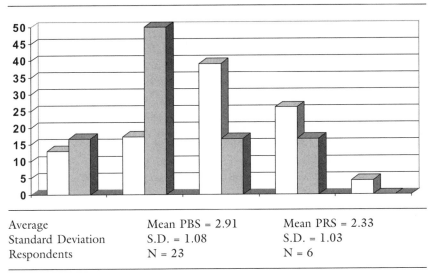

Average	Mean PBS = 2.91	Mean PRS = 2.33
Standard Deviation	S.D. = 1.08	S.D. = 1.03
Respondents	N = 23	N = 6

PBS = Public Sector Managers; PRS = Private Sector Managers.

S.D. = 0.89). A percentage of 37.2 of the PBS managers and 43.1 percent of the PRS managers reported little or no collaboration. Similarly, 27.7 percent of the PBS managers and 16.2 percent of the PRS managers reported that, to the best of their knowledge, a reasonable level of collaboration existed in providing health services to citizens.

Figure 5.9 portrays managers' perceptions of the level of collaboration between public and third sector organizations in welfare services. Managers reported that, according to their experience, the level of collaboration in this field was somewhat higher than average (mean PBS = 3.17, S.D. = 1.07; mean PRS = 2.75, S.D. = 0.98). A percentage of 28.3 of the PBS managers and 43.6 percent of the PRS managers reported little or no collaboration. Similarly, 41.8 percent of the PBS managers and 25.5 percent of the PRS managers reported that, to the best of their knowledge, a reasonable level of collaboration existed in providing welfare services to citizens.

Figure 5.7
How Much Collaboration Exists Between the Public Sector, Citizens, and Third
Sector Organizations in Education Services?

	Never or almost never		Seldom		Sometimes		Usually		Always or almost always	
	PBS	PRS	PBS	PRS	PBS	PRS	PBS	PRS	PBS	PRS
%	7.2	5.3	25.9	30.9	33.8	39.4	26.6	24.5	6.5	0.0

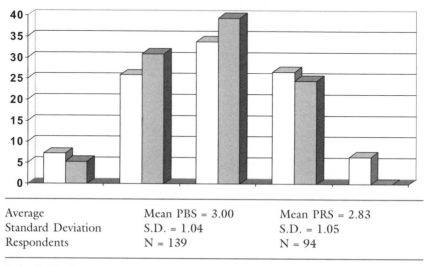

Average	Mean PBS = 3.00	Mean PRS = 2.83
Standard Deviation	S.D. = 1.04	S.D. = 1.05
Respondents	N = 139	N = 94

PBS = Public Sector Managers; PRS = Private Sector Managers.

Figure 5.10 presents managers' perceptions of the level of collaboration between public and third sector organizations in culture services and sports. Managers reported that, according to their experience, the level of collaboration in this field was somewhat higher than average (mean PBS = 3.18, S.D. = 1.07; mean PRS = 2.98, S.D. = 0.97). A percentage of 26.0 of the PBS managers and 34.0 percent of the PRS managers reported little or no collaboration. Similarly, 44.4 percent of the PBS managers and 34.1 percent of the PRS managers reported that, to the best of their knowledge, a relatively high level of collaboration existed in providing culture and sports services to citizens.

Figure 5.11 portrays managers' perceptions of the level of collaboration between public and third sector organizations in employment services. Managers reported that, according to their experience, the level of collaboration in this field was significantly lower than average (mean PBS = 2.48, S.D. =

Figure 5.8
How Much Collaboration Exists Between the Public Sector, Citizens, and Third Sector Organizations in Health Services?

	Never or almost never		Seldom		Sometimes		Usually		Always or almost always	
	PBS	PRS	PBS	PRS	PBS	PRS	PBS	PRS	PBS	PRS
%	11.7	9.7	25.5	34.4	35.0	39.8	20.4	15.1	7.3	1.1

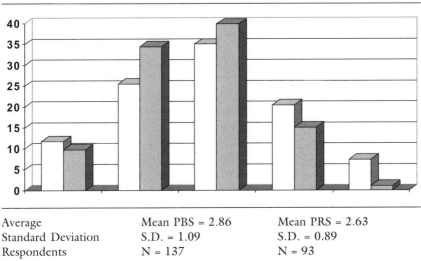

Average	Mean PBS = 2.86	Mean PRS = 2.63
Standard Deviation	S.D. = 1.09	S.D. = 0.89
Respondents	N = 137	N = 93

PBS = Public Sector Managers; PRS = Private Sector Managers.

0.97; mean PRS = 2.48, S.D. = 0.94). A percentage of 54.1 of the PBS managers and 57.0 percent of the PRS managers reported little or no collaboration. Similarly, only 15.1 percent of the PBS and PRS managers reported that, to the best of their knowledge, a relatively high level of collaboration existed in providing employment services to citizens.

Figure 5.12 presents managers' perceptions of the level of collaboration between public and third sector organizations in various other services, such as environment, transportation, and communication. Managers reported that, according to their experience, the level of collaboration in these fields was average (mean PBS = 3.10, S.D. = 0.94; mean PRS = 2.60, S.D. = 1.06). A percentage of 23.8 of the PBS managers and 46.6 percent of the PRS managers reported little or no collaboration. Similarly, 33.4 percent of the PBS managers and 13.4 percent of the PRS managers reported that, to the best of their knowledge, a relatively high level of collaboration existed in providing these services to citizens. Note, however that the number of respondents for this item was very low.

Figure 5.9
How Much Collaboration Exists Between the Public Sector, Citizens, and Third Sector Organizations in Welfare Services?

	Never or almost never		Seldom		Sometimes		Usually		Always or almost always	
	PBS	PRS	PBS	PRS	PBS	PRS	PBS	PRS	PBS	PRS
%	6.0	8.5	22.4	35.1	29.9	30.9	32.1	23.4	9.7	2.1

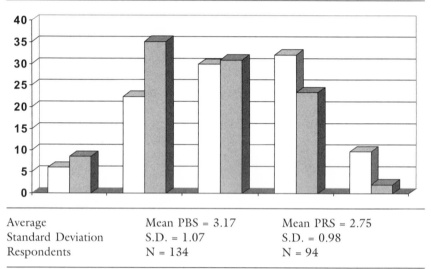

Average	Mean PBS = 3.17	Mean PRS = 2.75
Standard Deviation	S.D. = 1.07	S.D. = 0.98
Respondents	N = 134	N = 94

PBS = Public Sector Managers; PRS = Private Sector Managers.

A GENERAL ASSESSMENT OF THE OUTCOMES OF COLLABORATION

The following sections sketch respondents' general assessment of the initiation of the collaborative process, the advantages of this process for the parties involved, and the general level of success of such initiatives. While these are general views of the outcomes of collaboration, they are meaningful and important for obtaining an impression of what public sector officials see as the core results of the process.

According to figure 5.13, PBS managers and PRS managers disagreed on the sources of collaborative ventures. According to PBS managers, the public sector was a more frequent initiator of collaborative projects (56 percent) than the other sectors (44 percent). However, according to the opinions of PRS managers, the other sectors were more frequent initiators of collaborative projects (83.5 percent) than the public sector (16.5 percent).

Figure 5.10
How Much Collaboration Exists Between the Public Sector, Citizens, and Third Sector Organizations in Culture Services and Sports?

	Never or almost never		Seldom		Sometimes		Usually		Always or almost always	
	PBS	PRS	PBS	PRS	PBS	PRS	PBS	PRS	PBS	PRS
%	6.7	5.3	19.3	28.7	29.6	31.9	38.5	30.9	5.9	3.2

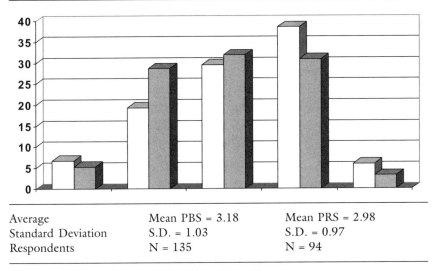

Average	Mean PBS = 3.18	Mean PRS = 2.98
Standard Deviation	S.D. = 1.03	S.D. = 0.97
Respondents	N = 135	N = 94

PBS = Public Sector Managers; PRS = Private Sector Managers.

A subsequent question to the previous one is presented in figure 5.14. Here I tried to better understand who gains the main benefits from the collaborative process. According to figure 5.14, the public as a whole (41.8 percent of the PBS managers and 31.2 percent of the PRS managers) and the organizations involved in the process (41.2 percent of the PBS managers and 34.4 percent of the PRS managers) were the main beneficiaries of this process. Only 9.9 percent of the PBS managers and 11.8 percent of the PRS managers believed that the public sector was the main beneficiary. In addition, only 7.1 percent of the PBS managers and 22.6 percent of the PRS managers thought that the other organization (private or voluntary) was the main beneficiary. These findings clearly indicate a positive attitude toward collaboration that is reflected by an overall view that many parties are likely to enjoy the benefits of this process. It is also possible that these findings reflect a realistic situation where there is no one party that needs the collaboration process more than others, and that citizens can become the biggest winners if such programs expand and become more ambitious.

Figure 5.11
How Much Collaboration Exists Between the Public Sector, Citizens, and Third
Sector Organizations in Employment Services?

	Never or almost never		Seldom		Sometimes		Usually		Always or almost always	
	PBS	PRS	PBS	PRS	PBS	PRS	PBS	PRS	PBS	PRS
%	15.0	11.8	39.1	45.2	30.8	28.0	12.8	12.9	2.3	2.2

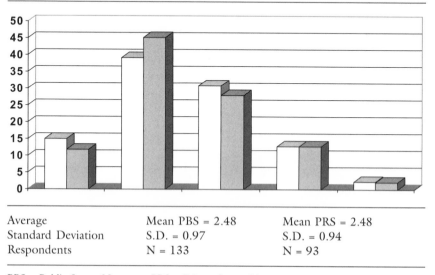

Average	Mean PBS = 2.48	Mean PRS = 2.48
Standard Deviation	S.D. = 0.97	S.D. = 0.94
Respondents	N = 133	N = 93

PBS = Public Sector Managers; PRS = Private Sector Managers.

Following the two preceding questions, I was interested to find out if the
respondents generally believed that collaborative programs end successfully.
While one should bear in mind that this is a general question, it still seems
worth asking so as to obtain a collective impression of the potential results
of collaboration. As demonstrated in figure 5.15, a four-point scale was used
to assess success in collaborative ventures. I found a relatively positive attitude toward these projects, reflected in the 2.87 average score for PBS managers (S.D. = 0.52) and the 2.52 average score for PRS managers (S.D. =
0.54). Among the PBS managers 73.4 percent believed that these initiatives,
in their experience, were quite successful, while 7.2 percent indicated that
these ventures were very successful. PRS mangers were rather less optimistic. Of them, 43.4 percent believed that these initiatives were quite unsuccessful and 54.4 percent believed that they were quite successful. Note also
that among the PBS managers a notable group of 19.4 percent had a negative evaluation of these collaborative projects. I thus believe that this group

Figure 5.12
How Much Collaboration Exists Between the Public Sector, Citizens, and Third Sector Organizations in Other Services (e.g., Environment, Transportation, Communication)?

	Never or almost never		Seldom		Sometimes		Usually		Always or almost always	
	PBS	PRS	PBS	PRS	PBS	PRS	PBS	PRS	PBS	PRS
%	4.8	13.3	19.0	33.3	42.9	40.0	28.6	6.7	4.8	6.7

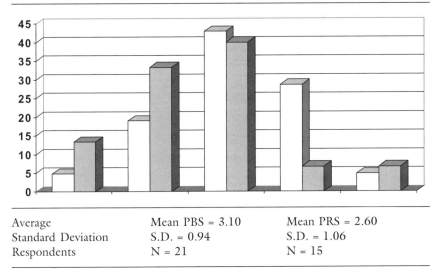

Average	Mean PBS = 3.10	Mean PRS = 2.60
Standard Deviation	S.D. = 0.94	S.D. = 1.06
Respondents	N = 21	N = 15

PBS = Public Sector Managers; PRS = Private Sector Managers.

needs to be studied more extensively so that we may better learn the reasons for such views.

ATTITUDES TO AND PERCEPTIONS OF COLLABORATION

Respondents were asked to react to a wide range of notions on the current situation of collaboration and its potential for the years to come. In the following sections I try to describe the views of the public officials' sample and what may be learned about the potential development of such projects, as viewed from the managerial bridge.

Figure 5.16 shows respondents' views on the level of internal collaboration in the public sector. In all, 44.8 percent of the PBS managers and 51.5 percent of the PRS managers agreed that such collaboration did not exist or existed on a very low level. Only 30.3 percent of the PBS managers and

Figure 5.13
Who Initiates the Collaborative Process?

	The public organization		The other organization (Private or Third sector)	
	PBS	PRS	PBS	PRS
%	56.0	16.5	44.0	83.5

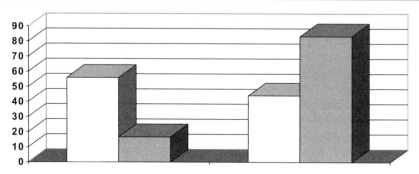

PBS = Public Sector Managers; PRS = Private Sector Managers.

Figure 5.14
Who Gets the Main Benefits from a Collaborative Process?

	The public organization		The other organization		Both oraganizations		The public as a whole	
	PBS	PRS	PBS	PRS	PBS	PRS	PBS	PRS
%	9.9	11.8	7.1	22.6	41.2	34.4	41.8	34.2

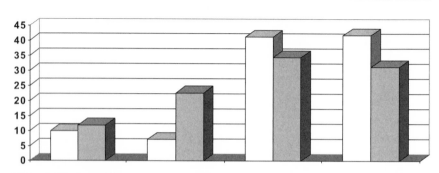

PBS = Public Sector Managers; PRS = Private Sector Managers.

Figure 5.15
Is This Collaboration Usually Successful?

	Not at all successful		Quite unsuccessful		Quite successful		Very successful	
	PBS	PRS	PBS	PRS	PBS	PRS	PBS	PRS
%	0.7	2.2	18.7	43.3	73.4	54.4	7.2	0.0

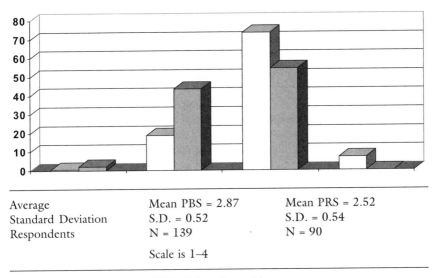

Average	Mean PBS = 2.87	Mean PRS = 2.52
Standard Deviation	S.D. = 0.52	S.D. = 0.54
Respondents	N = 139	N = 90
	Scale is 1–4	

PBS = Public Sector Managers; PRS = Private Sector Managers.

19.2 percent of the PRS managers believed that governmental agencies collaborated quite well in order to provide services to citizens. An additional 25.2 percent of the PBS managers and 29.3 percent of the PRS managers reported that this collaboration existed, but only to a limited extent. Thus, the level of agreement with this statement was low to average (mean PBS = 2.78, S.D. = 1.03; mean PRS = 2.53, S.D. = 1.03). It may reflect some disappointment with the current level of collaboration within the public sector and between its institutions.

Figure 5.17 shows respondents' expectations as to future collaboration among the three sectors. According to this figure, the vast majority (90.9 percent of the PBS managers and 80.8 percent of the PRS managers) agreed that collaboration among public organizations, private firms, and the voluntary sector needed to be improved. Only 9.1 percent of the PBS managers and 19.2 percent of the PRS managers expressed the position that there is little or no need for such enhancement of the level of collaboration—that

Figure 5.16
Today, More Than Ever Before, Governmental Agencies Collaborate with Each Other to Improve Services for Citizens

	Not at all true		A little true		Somewhat true		Generally true		Very true	
	PBS	PRS	PBS	PRS	PBS	PRS	PBS	PRS	PBS	PRS
%	9.4	17.2	35.3	34.3	25.2	29.3	28.1	17.2	2.2	2.0

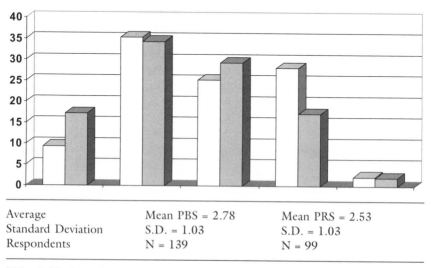

Average	Mean PBS = 2.78	Mean PRS = 2.53
Standard Deviation	S.D. = 1.03	S.D. = 1.03
Respondents	N = 139	N = 99

PBS = Public Sector Managers; PRS = Private Sector Managers.

the present separation in activities and responsibilities should be maintained. Accordingly, the average score for this item was high (mean PBS = 4.18, S.D. = 0.64; mean PRS = 4.08, S.D. = 0.85).

Figure 5.18 presents respondents' views on senior managers' perceptions of the option of collaboration and on their willingness to promote it. A percentage of 41 of the PBS managers and 21.4 percent of the PRS managers agreed that senior managers in the public sector understand the advantages of collaboration with private and voluntary organizations well, and advance it accordingly. However, 28.5 percent of the PBS managers and 40.9 percent of the PRS managers expressed some skepticism regarding this statement. An additional 30.6 percent of the PBS managers and 37.8 percent of the PRS managers believed that it was true, but only to a limited degree. Similarly, the score for this item was higher than average (mean PBS = 3.16, S.D. = 0.94; mean PRS = 2.79, S.D. = 0.84).

Figure 5.17
Collaboration Among Public Organizations, Private Firms, and the Voluntary Sector Needs to Be Improved

	Not at all true		A little true		Somewhat true		Generally true		Very true	
	PBS	PRS	PBS	PRS	PBS	PRS	PBS	PRS	PBS	PRS
%	0.0	1.0	2.1	4.0	7.0	14.1	62.2	47.5	28.7	33.3

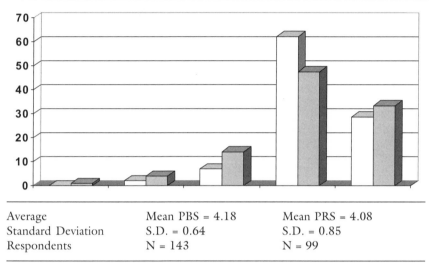

Average	Mean PBS = 4.18	Mean PRS = 4.08
Standard Deviation	S.D. = 0.64	S.D. = 0.85
Respondents	N = 143	N = 99

PBS = Public Sector Managers; PRS = Private Sector Managers.

Figure 5.19 presents respondents' views on collaboration among the three sectors as a major tool for solving major national ills. Here again, senior managers from private and nonprofit organizations expressed their belief that collaboration may well serve the state's objectives and become a strategic tool for the remedy of national ills. A percentage of 83.9 of the PBS managers and 81.0 percent of the PRS managers agreed that the public, private, and third sectors had to learn to collaborate in order to cure governmental ailments. Similarly, only 4.2 percent of the PBS managers and 4.0 percent of the PRS managers believed that collaboration was not a satisfactory solution for such problems. A further 11.9 percent of the PBS managers and 15.0 percent of the PRS managers believed that this statement was somewhat true. Thus, the mean score for this item was high (mean PBS = 4.06, S.D. = 0.77; mean PRS = 4.04, S.D. = 0.76).

Figure 5.20 presents respondents' views on the level of interest by the private sector in joining mutual collaboration projects with the public sector.

Figure 5.18
Senior Managers in the Public Sector Understand the Advantages of
Collaboration with Private and Voluntary Organizations Well and
Promote It Accordingly

	Not at all true		A little true		Somewhat true		Generally true		Very true	
	PBS	PRS	PBS	PRS	PBS	PRS	PBS	PRS	PBS	PRS
%	2.1	3.1	26.4	37.8	30.6	37.8	35.4	20.4	5.6	1.0

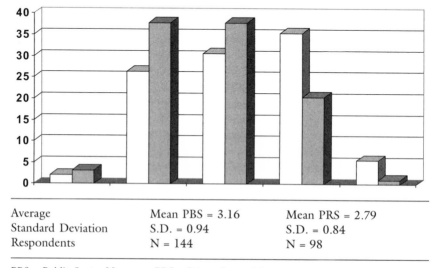

Average	Mean PBS = 3.16	Mean PRS = 2.79
Standard Deviation	S.D. = 0.94	S.D. = 0.84
Respondents	N = 144	N = 98

PBS = Public Sector Managers; PRS = Private Sector Managers.

A percentage of 64.4 of the PBS managers and 50.1 percent of the PRS managers believed that the private sector was greatly interested in such collaboration for various reasons. Only 16.1 percent of the PBS managers and 13.2 percent of the PRS managers were highly skeptical about this interest. Finally, 19.6 percent of the PBS managers and 35.7 percent of the PRS managers thought that this interest existed at a reasonable level. Thus, the mean value for this item was relatively high (mean PBS = 3.71, S.D. = 1.02; mean PRS = 3.49, S.D. = 0.93).

Figure 5.21 presents respondents' views on the level of interest by the citizens and third sector organizations in joining mutual collaboration projects with the public sector. A percentage of 82.4 of the PBS managers and 75.2 percent of the PRS managers believed that the citizens and the third sector were highly interested in such collaboration for various reasons. Only 2.1 percent of the PBS managers and 11.4 percent of the PRS managers were

Figure 5.19
Many National Ills Would Be Solved If Public Organizations Learned to Collaborate with Private and Voluntary Organizations and with Citizens

	Not at all true		A little true		Somewhat true		Generally true		Very true	
	PBS	PRS	PBS	PRS	PBS	PRS	PBS	PRS	PBS	PRS
%	0.7	0	3.5	4.0	11.9	15.0	56.6	54.0	27.3	27.0

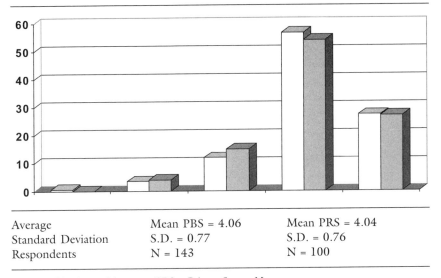

Average	Mean PBS = 4.06	Mean PRS = 4.04
Standard Deviation	S.D. = 0.77	S.D. = 0.76
Respondents	N = 143	N = 100

PBS = Public Sector Managers; PRS = Private Sector Managers.

highly skeptical about this interest. An additional 15.5 percent of the PBS managers and 13.4 percent of the PRS managers held that this interest existed to a reasonable level. Thus, the mean value for this item was high (mean PBS = 4.09, S.D. = 0.72; mean PRS = 3.87, S.D. = 0.96).

Figure 5.22 presents respondents' agreement with the notion that today, more than ever before, the public sector is looking for better ways of collaboration with private and voluntary organizations to improve services for citizens. A percentage of 56 of the PBS managers and 19.6 percent of the PRS managers believed that this notion was true: that today the public sector is seeking more collaboration with the other sectors and with citizens. A percentage of 4.9 of the PBS managers and 41.3 percent of the PRS managers thought that this notion was not true. A further 29.1 percent of the PBS managers and 39.2 percent of the PRS managers—a relatively high proportion of the respondents—believed that this notion was somewhat true. The mean value for this item was average to high (mean PBS = 3.47, S.D. = 0.84; mean PRS = 2.77, S.D. = 0.81).

Figure 5.20
The Private Sector Is Interested in Collaboration with the Public Sector

	Not at all true		A little true		Somewhat true		Generally true		Very true	
	PBS	PRS	PBS	PRS	PBS	PRS	PBS	PRS	PBS	PRS
%	0.7	2.0	15.4	11.2	19.6	35.7	40.6	37.8	23.8	13.3

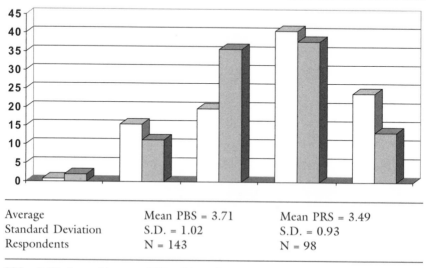

Average	Mean PBS = 3.71	Mean PRS = 3.49
Standard Deviation	S.D. = 1.02	S.D. = 0.93
Respondents	N = 143	N = 98

PBS = Public Sector Managers; PRS = Private Sector Managers.

Figure 5.23 depicts the willingness of PBS managers to become involved in collaborative ventures. This table is divided into four subdiagrams, each referring to a different type of activity, as follows: (1) general willingness to become involved in collaborative ventures in order to improve quality of life, (2) willingness to invest time (e.g., participate in committees), (3) willingness to invest knowledge (e.g., bring new ideas and gather information), (4) willingness to bring in other people. As figure 5.23 shows, the majority of the participating managers reported a high level of willingness to become involved in collaborative ventures by various methods and means, and mean values ranged between 3.93 and 4.24.

Figure 5.24 presents the willingness of PRS managers to become involved in collaborative ventures. Like figure 5.23, this is divided into four sub-diagrams, each showing a different type of activity, as follows: (1) general willingness to become involved in collaborative ventures in order to improve quality of life, (2) willingness to invest time (e.g., participate in committees), (3) willingness to invest knowledge (e.g., bring new ideas and gather infor-

Figure 5.21
Citizens and the Third Sector Are Interested in Collaboration with the
Public Sector

	Not at all true		A little true		Somewhat true		Generally true		Very true	
	PBS	PRS	PBS	PRS	PBS	PRS	PBS	PRS	PBS	PRS
%	0.0	2.1	2.1	9.3	15.5	13.4	53.5	50.5	28.9	24.7

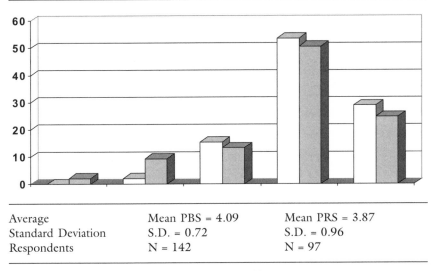

Average	Mean PBS = 4.09	Mean PRS = 3.87
Standard Deviation	S.D. = 0.72	S.D. = 0.96
Respondents	N = 142	N = 97

PBS = Public Sector Managers; PRS = Private Sector Managers.

mation), (4) willingness to bring in other people. As figure 5.24 shows, a majority of the participating managers reported a high level of willingness to become involved in collaborative ventures by various methods and means, and mean values ranged between 3.36 and 3.78. Note, however, that these behavioral intentions were somehow lower than those of PBS managers, indicating again some skepticism toward collaboration among the PRS managers.

Figure 5.25 presents the extent of respondents' agreement with the notion that advanced states encourage collaboration among public sector agencies and other organizations. A percentage of 88.7 of the PBS managers and 79.8 percent of the PRS managers believed that this notion was true, while only a small minority of 0.7 percent of PBS managers and 4.0 percent of PRS managers thought that this notion was not true. An additional 10.6 percent of the PBS managers and 16.2 percent of the PRS managers believed that this notion was somewhat true. The mean value for this item was thus high (mean PBS = 4.27, S.D. = 0.65; mean PRS = 4.06, S.D. = 0.83).

Figure 5.22
Today, More Than Ever Before, the Public Sector Is Looking for Better Ways of Collaboration with Private and Voluntary Organizations to Improve Services for Citizens

	Not at all true		A little true		Somewhat true		Generally true		Very true	
	PBS	PRS	PBS	PRS	PBS	PRS	PBS	PRS	PBS	PRS
%	0.7	2.1	4.2	39.2	29.1	39.2	49.6	18.6	6.4	1.0

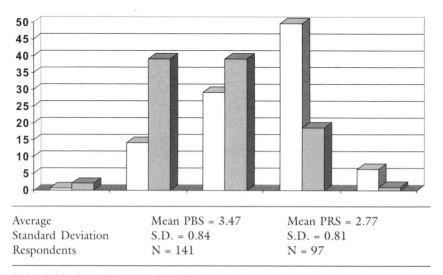

Average	Mean PBS = 3.47	Mean PRS = 2.77
Standard Deviation	S.D. = 0.84	S.D. = 0.81
Respondents	N = 141	N = 97

PBS = Public Sector Managers; PRS = Private Sector Managers.

Figure 5.26 presents the extent of respondents' agreement with the notion that in the future the public sector will have to increase collaboration with private voluntary organizations in order to achieve its goals. A majority of 85.6 percent of the PBS managers and 63.7 percent of the PRS managers believed that this notion was true: that collaboration had to become a strategic tool for the public sector. Similarly, only 3.6 percent of the PBS managers and 5.0 percent of the PRS managers thought that this notion was not true. A percentage of 10.8 of the PBS managers and 31.3 percent of the PRS managers believed that this notion was somewhat true. The mean value for this item was high (mean = 4.12, S.D. = 0.74; mean PRS = 3.73, S.D. = 0.82).

Finally, figure 5.27 presents the extent of respondents' agreement with the notion that collaboration between public and private organizations was more important than collaboration between public and voluntary organiza-

Figure 5.23
Public Sector Managers' Willingness to Become Involved in Collaborative
Ventures

%	Not at all willing	A little willing	Somewhat willing	Generally willing	Very willing
General*	0.0	1.4	11.3	49.3	38.0
Time	2.8	2.8	16.7	54.2	23.6
Knowledge	0.7	2.8	8.4	62.2	25.9
Social	0.7	2.1	15.5	55.6	26.1

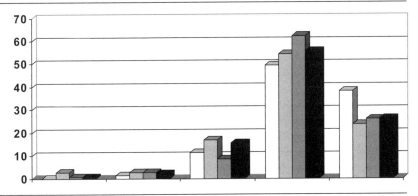

Average Standard Deviation

General	Mean PRS = 4.24	S.D. = 0.70
Time	Mean PRS = 3.93	S.D. = 0.87
Knowledge	Mean PRS = 4.10	S.D. = 0.71
Social	Mean PRS = 4.04	S.D. = 0.75
Respondents	N1 = 142, N2 = 144, N3 = 142, N4 = 142	

PBS = Public Sector Managers.
*General = general willingness; Time = willingness to invest time; Knowledge = willingness to invest knowledge; Social = willingness to bring in other people.

tions. Here the results were distributed across the various possible answers. A percentage of 30.8 of the PBS managers and 24.0 percent of the PRS managers believed that this notion was not true, while a very similar 34.3 percent (PBS managers) and 39.0 percent (PRS managers) thought that it was true. An additional 35.0 percent of the PBS managers and 37.0 percent of the PRS managers, which is a relatively high proportion of the respondents, believed that this notion was somewhat true. The mean value for this item was therefore average (mean PBS = 3.05, S.D. = 0.99; mean PRS = 3.22, S.D. = 0.99).

Figure 5.24
Private Sector Managers' Willingness to Become Involved in Collaborative Ventures

%	Not at all willing	A little willing	Somewhat willing	Generally willing	Very willing
General*	3.0	7.0	23.0	56.0	11.0
Time	6.0	17.0	25.0	39.0	13.0
Knowledge	4.0	4.0	20.0	54.0	18.0
Social	6.1	10.1	23.2	46.5	14.1

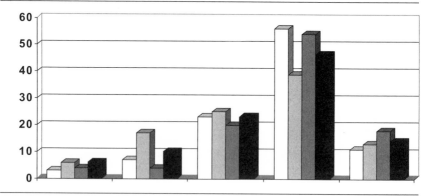

Average Standard Deviation

General	Mean PRS = 3.65	S.D. = 0.88
Time	Mean PRS = 3.36	S.D. = 1.09
Knowledge	Mean PRS = 3.78	S.D. = 0.93
Social	Mean PRS = 3.52	S.D. = 1.05
Respondents	N1 = 100, N2 = 100, N3 = 100, N4 = 99	

PRS = Private Sector Managers.
*General = general willingness; Time = willingness to invest time; Knowledge = willingness to invest knowledge; Social = willingness to bring in other people.

BEYOND SIMPLE STATISTICS: SOME IMPLICATIONS OF THE FINDINGS

Chapter 5 has focused on managers' perceptions of collaboration in and around the public sector. The exploratory study was based on a survey conducted among 244 Israeli managers primarily from the public and private sectors. Naturally, this was only a first step in better studying the nature of collaboration by empirical methods borrowed from the behavioral sciences. In fact, the study and its findings should be treated as a pilot effort aimed

Figure 5.25
Advanced States Encourage Collaboration Among Public Sector Agencies and Other Organizations

	Not at all true		A little true		Somewhat true		Generally true		Very true	
	PBS	PRS	PBS	PRS	PBS	PRS	PBS	PRS	PBS	PRS
%	0.0	1.0	0.7	3.0	10.6	16.2	49.3	48.5	39.4	31.3

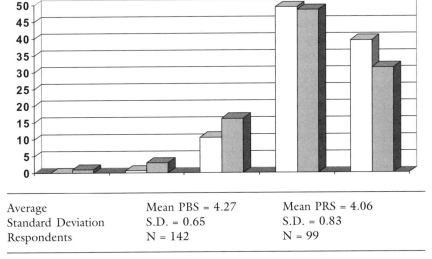

Average	Mean PBS = 4.27	Mean PRS = 4.06
Standard Deviation	S.D. = 0.65	S.D. = 0.83
Respondents	N = 142	N = 99

PBS = Public Sector Managers; PRS = Private-Sector Managers.

at better mapping collaborative ventures and managers' views on the option of working with extraorganizational parties rather than acting independently. Therefore, the study was not intended as an in-depth examination of case studies but as a sketch of the general landscape of managers' attitudes toward this expanding phenomenon that is growing in scale. Nonetheless, I believe that the study carries several meaningful implications that deserve closer attention.

First, we found that managers were aware of collaborative ventures in their organizations and their surroundings. The level of existing collaboration in fields such as education services, health services, welfare, cultural activities, employment, and other areas was considered average to low. Most of the participants indicated that collaboration occurred more intensively in the fields of culture and sports, welfare, and education. However, almost all participants believed that the level of collaboration was not satisfactory and needed to be improved dramatically. Averages across fields ranged from 2.33

Figure 5.26
In the Future, the Public Sector Will Have to Increase Collaboration with Private and Voluntary Organizations in Order to Achieve Its Goals

	Not at all true		A little true		Somewhat true		Generally true		Very true	
	PBS	PRS	PBS	PRS	PBS	PRS	PBS	PRS	PBS	PRS
%	0.0	1.0	3.6	4.0	10.8	31.3	55.4	47.5	30.2	16.2

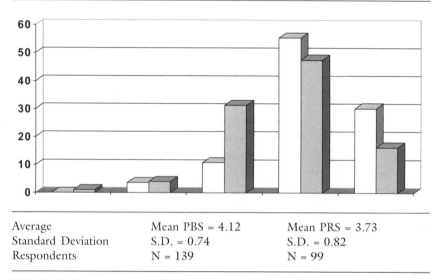

Average	Mean PBS = 4.12	Mean PRS = 3.73
Standard Deviation	S.D. = 0.74	S.D. = 0.82
Respondents	N = 139	N = 99

PBS = Public Sector Managers; PRS = Private Sector Managers.

(attitudes of PRS managers toward collaboration in environment, transportation, and communication) to 3.18 (attitudes of PBS managers toward collaboration in culture services). These figures imply that a general perception of all managers of the various types and intensity of collaboration was not very high, even if it was also not very low. Thus, while there is some good indication that today the public sector does collaborate with private firms and with citizens in various fields, managers expressed a desire for more activism in this direction.

In addition, a comparison of views on the current state of cross-sectoral collaboration between PRS managers and PBS managers revealed the existence of some meaningful differences. PRS mangers were more skeptical about the current state of collaboration than PBS managers, who expressed a higher level of optimism. This can be found in the constant discrepancies in average scores in figures 5.1–5.12. A comprehensive statistical analysis based on

Figure 5.27
Collaboration Between Public and Private Organizations Is More Important Than Collaboration Between Public and Voluntary Organizations

	Not at all true		A little true		Somewhat true		Generally true		Very true	
	PBS	PRS	PBS	PRS	PBS	PRS	PBS	PRS	PBS	PRS
%	4.9	3.0	25.9	21.0	35.0	37.0	28.0	29.0	6.3	10.0

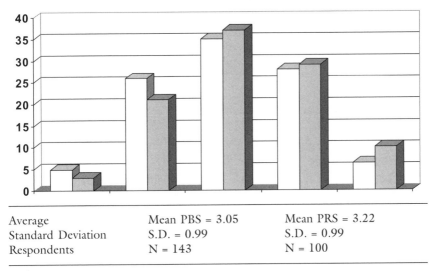

Average	Mean PBS = 3.05	Mean PRS = 3.22
Standard Deviation	S.D. = 0.99	S.D. = 0.99
Respondents	N = 143	N = 100

PBS = Public Sector Managers; PRS = Private Sector Managers.

t tests supported the conjecture that these differences were significant. Therefore, an interesting question that will need to be discussed in the future is the reason for such differences. A possible explanation is higher sensitivity among PBS managers to the presence of collaboration and the need to implement it more effectively. However, the relatively small sample size and the unicultural orientation of this study limited the possibility of generalization, and further studies need to replicate this one and test the differences among populations more closely.

It was interesting to find that PBS managers and PRS managers also differed substantially in other perceptions. For example, PRS managers believed that the public sector was not doing enough to push collaboration forward and that most of the initiatives for collaboration come from the private or the third sector. PBS managers, however, perceived the current state differently, assuming that the public sector enjoyed little advantage over the private sector in the field of innovative collaboration projects. Still, PBS managers and PRS managers generally agreed that the contribution of collective/mutual action was to the benefit of the public as a whole, as well as the communities and the organizations involved. Thus, my interpretation is that managers view collaboration in a generally favorable manner that can contribute to as many stakeholders as possible. The alternative option of working "alone" or "independently" under the rough conditions of competing parties in a free market is balanced by a strong desire to share knowledge and resources in favor of valuable social targets. In support of this, PBS managers and (to a lesser degree) PRS managers described their general understanding and experiences of collaboration as successful and fruitful.

A further examination of the findings as presented in figures 5.16–5.27 revealed mixed attitudes toward collaboration. Respondents generally believed that government agencies collaborate with each other, yet there is much to be improved in this arena. There is also much to improve in cross-sectoral collaboration, and public managers need to enhance their understanding of the advantages of collaboration. Respondents generally agreed that many national ailments would be solved if the public sector could infuse a better culture of collaboration and use it as a strategic tool for policy implementation. They thought that the private sector, as well as citizens and the third sector, were really interested in such a move toward collaboration with public organizations. However, they were also quite critical of the effort invested by public officials in order to achieve a satisfactory level of collaboration. Moreover, PBS managers and PRS managers expressed their personal willingness to become involved in collaborative ventures and invest time, knowledge, and social effort to promote them. Note, however, that PBS managers expressed a somewhat higher level of such participatory trends, perhaps due to the potential benefits that such ventures can bring to the public sector and to its leading cadre. Finally, all mangers agreed that advanced states are characterized by higher levels of collaboration among public, private, and third sector bodies. According to their views, which closely conform to my general perception in this book, the future requires more activism in this direction. They thus see no real difference as to where this collaboration should take place. In their opinion, it needs to increase in all possible directions and by all possible means.

CHAPTER 6

Conclusion: The Challenge of Collaboration—New Managerial Frontiers for Public Administration

THE CHALLENGE OF COLLABORATION

The concept of collaboration is not new but, as demonstrated so far, it has lately become more relevant for public, private, and third sector organizations. Today, collaboration is perceived by managers of all sectors as a promising way to meet growing demands in our modern societies. My view seeks to contribute to this process and expand on future possible trends in public administration scholarship by renewing the values of collaboration and partnership. Throughout this book it has been argued that civic society is almost unthinkable in purely rational-economic patterns. Thus, following the dimensions of new governance as suggested by John et al. (1994), and somewhat enlarging them for my purposes, the discussion now elaborates on several questions: (1) What is the integrative meaning of collaboration for governments, public administration agencies, businesses, and citizens? (2) Where on the continuum of public administration evolution do we stand today? (3) Whose responsibility is it to make the collaboration and partnership ventures possible, and with what tools? Consequently, and most important, (4) How can we practically apply our strategic managerial wisdom to the greater need for collaboration in order to help modern society fulfill its productive promises?

AN INTEGRATIVE VIEW OF THE MANAGEMENT OF COLLABORATION

As I have indicated, collaboration is founded on responsiveness. However, it also reaches decidedly beyond. Moreover, while greater collaboration is not a very new idea in public administration, it has never fulfilled its promising potential, partly due the informal competition with businesslike strategies such as New Public Management (NPM). An economic interaction between managers and customers carries some basic deficiencies for modern states. The term client, or customer, which is so applicable in the private sector (i.e., rational choice theory or agency theory), contradicts the very basic notions of belonging, altruism, contribution to society, and self-derived participation in citizenry actions. When someone is defined as a client, he/ she is not actively engaged in social initiatives, but is merely a passive service (or product) consumer, dependent on the goodwill and interest of the owner. While direct democracy suggests that citizens themselves "own" the state, representative democracy adds an interface to this ownership of politicians and administrators. Citizens run their lives through representatives only because they need a "board of directors" that is professional and capable of making wise decisions for huge communities. An absolute democracy, where every citizen is equally responsible for every single decision of the state, cannot practically survive and function in expanding and fast-moving societies (as opposed to the limited nature of the Greek polis).

The evolutionary process of interaction among governments, public administration, citizens in communities, and businesses must thus be followed by a rational and applicable level of integration across all social players. As figure 6.1 demonstrates, interrelationships among these and other social players are becoming strategic goals of modern democracies on their way to a new administrative spirit (Fredrickson, 1997). The old orthodox type of public administration was characterized by a triple structure of transactions: (1) a legitimacy-services transaction between governments and public administration and citizens; (2) a socialization-information and human resources transaction between citizens and businesses; and (3) an authorization-criticism, knowledge, and economic goods transaction between governments and public administration and businesses. The new, cooperative hat of public administration, however, will be dominated by higher levels of collaboration and partnership that exceed the nature of simple transactions presented above. In fact, this is one core challenge for future generations. Governments and public administration must take a step forward, going beyond elementary exchange relationships and responsiveness to demands. The useful adaptability of knowledge on strategies of collaboration may become a key issue in this dynamic process.

Each of the players has its own uniqueness and field of responsibility. Governments and public administration will always take the leading part in the effort at collaboration, but they must be supported by both the private and third sector allies. Partnership among governments, public administration, and citizens similarly implies that the first two have core responsibilities in this process. Contrary to the perception of responsiveness, where governments and public administration hold almost exclusive power and authority and are expected to navigate among various public demands, the collaborative approach asks for extensive responsibilities and involvement on the part of the public. A process of citizen empowerment and greater in-

Figure 6.1
Collaboration Among Social Players: An Insight into the Next Generation

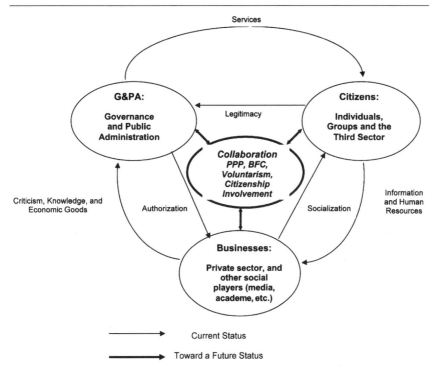

volvement in the community may bring vitality into old democratic patterns of governability. This can take the form of individual initiatives that seek greater participation in administrative decisions and actions or, alternatively, various kinds of organized citizenry actions (e.g., as represented by semi-organized groups or as formed by the third sector). An interesting example of broader collaboration among citizens, businesses, and governments can be found in the solid initiatives of the United Way movement, as presented in figures 6.2 and 6.3.

The United Way movement, through its national branches (e.g., the United Way of America and the United Way of Canada), is dedicated to making a measurable impact in communities across North America and elsewhere. It encompasses approximately 1,400 community-based United Way organizations. Each is independent, separately incorporated, and governed by local volunteers. Its governance and structure are based on a volunteer board consisting of forty-five members. The national center, established in 1918, does not raise or distribute funds. The strategic goals of the United Way movement are threefold: creating national leadership of citizens,

Figure 6.2
The United Way Movement

http://national.unitedway.org/

Mission

The mission of United Way is to improve people's lives by mobilizing the caring power of communities.

A Community-Based National Movement

United Ways across the country activate community resources to make the greatest possible human impact. The United Way system includes approximately 1,400 community-based United Way organizations. Each is independent, separately incorporated, and governed by local volunteers. As community leaders, United Ways address the most critical local issues and mobilize resources beyond the dollars that are pledged through their fund-raising efforts. Community partners often include schools, government policy makers, businesses, organized labor, financial institutions, voluntary and neighborhood associations, community development corporations, and the faith community.

Mobilizing the Caring Power of Communities

United Ways bring communities together to focus on the most important human needs—building partnerships, forging consensus and leveraging resources to make a measurable difference. Focus areas are identified at the local level and vary from community to community. Common focus areas include helping children and youth succeed, strengthening and supporting families, promoting self-sufficiency, building vital and safe neighborhoods, and supporting vulnerable and aging populations. In 2000/2001, United Way annual campaigns reached a new high of $3.91 billion. United Ways also leveraged almost $1 billion in additional resources—for a total of $4.7 billion—to build stronger communities. A vast network of volunteers keeps administrative expenses low, averaging 13 percent of all funds raised at the largest United Ways. This figure compares favorably with Better Business Bureau guidelines of up to 35 percent.

United Way Initiatives

A United Way–led partnership is currently working with the White House and Congress in support of 211, the national abbreviated dialing code for free access to health and human services. United Way's children's initiatives, Success By 6®, Bridges to Success®, Young America Cares!™, and 100% Access/Zero Health Disparities, build upon community strengths, fund programs, advocate for public policy changes, and collaborate with others to improve the lives of children, youths, and their families. The United Way State of Caring Index™ is a dynamic approach to measuring the health and well-being of the nation. It analyzes thirty-two social and economic indicators at the state and national levels to create a dynamic approach to measuring the health and well-being of the nation. It also analyzes thirty-two social and economic indicators at the state and national levels to create a summary measure of Americans' capacity to care for one another.

Figure 6.2 (*Continued*)

National Leadership

United Way of America (UWA) is a national leadership organization for the United Way movement. UWA speaks as the voice for the uniqueness of American philanthropy. UWA leads the movement through public relations, national brand advertising, the NFL partnership, and the management of relationships with national corporate and philanthropic partners and the federal government. UWA provides world-class support services to local United Ways, including training, consultation, mediation, conferencing, national research, and assessment tools.

The Community Impact Agenda

United Ways across the country bring diverse people and resources together to address the most urgent issues their communities face. Through unique partnerships and approaches, United Ways mobilize resources beyond the dollars that are pledged through their fund-raising efforts. Community partners often include schools, government policy makers, businesses, organized labor, financial institutions, voluntary and neighborhood associations, community development corporations, and the faith community. United Ways' Community Impact Agendas focus their work in communities. Agendas are set by a broad range of caring individuals, including those directly affected by the agenda, and community-based organizations, all dedicated to making a difference in the lives of children, families, and neighborhoods. Because Community Impact Agendas are determined at the local level, they vary from community to community, and are often referred to as focus, impact, or goal areas. Impact areas that are most universal across the United Way system are helping children and youth succeed, strengthening and supporting families, promoting self-sufficiency, building vital and safe neighborhoods, and supporting vulnerable and aging populations. United Ways' strategies include identifying and building on community strengths and assets, funding programs and initiatives, advocating for public policy changes, and collaborating with others in support of these and related issues every day.

promoting modern and advanced public policy in various fields, and providing support for members.

National leadership: United Way of America invests in the programs and services that strengthen the ability of local United Ways to identify and build a coalition around a set of community priorities and measure success based on community impact.

Public policy: United Way of America works with Congress and the administration to promote policies and programs that activate national resources to address local priorities.

Membership support: United Way of America supports its members with services that include national brand advertising, the NFL partnership, training, public relations, research, and management of relationships with national corporate and philanthropic partners.

Figure 6.3
Collaborative Strategies and Vision of the United Way

UNITED WAYS' COMMUNITY IMPACT AREAS	COMMON UNITED WAY IMPACT STRATEGIES	TARGETED RESULTS
Helping Children and Youth Succeed Successful children and youth: • Enjoy healthy social, emotional, cognitive, and physical development. • Have opportunities to grow and achieve their full potential. • Have nurturing and supportive caretakers and providers. • Have access to affordable, quality early care and education. • Experience safe, quality learning environments.	• Promoting mobilizations like Success By 6® that help children prepare for school. • Enhancing the quality of child care services. • Increasing children's enrollment in health insurance plans. • Establishing comprehensive school-based resources offering health care, education and enrichment opportunities. • Expanding youth involvement in community service and leadership.	• Enhanced academic performance. • Increased school attendance. • Reduced incidents of gang activity. • More youth are active in safe and productive after-school activities. • More children have health insurance.

UNITED WAYS' COMMUNITY IMPACT AREAS	COMMON UNITED WAY IMPACT STRATEGIES	TARGETED RESULTS
Strengthening and Supporting Families Strong families: • Have the knowledge and skills to thrive. • Live in a safe and healthy environment. • Have access to affordable, quality services and supports. • Have strong family and community ties.	• Coordinating and making accessible a comprehensive range of health, human services, and other programs through family resource centers. • Conducting outreach on immunizations, child care/after-school programs and other community services. • Promoting family-friendly workplace policies and practices.	• Reduction of family violence/abuse. • Lower incidence of health-related issues. • Parents have more time to participate in their children's extracurricular activities and to spend at home. • Parents are actively involved in schools.

UNITED WAYS' COMMUNITY IMPACT AREAS	COMMON UNITED WAY IMPACT STRATEGIES	TARGETED RESULTS
Promoting Self-Sufficiency Self-sufficient people: • Receive quality education and have life and work skills. • Have access to quality jobs, work supports, and career opportunities. • Are supported in entrepreneurial efforts. • Can build savings and access capital.	• Supporting job training, literacy and career development programs that enhance long-term employment opportunities. • Coordinating child care, financial counseling, transportation, and other services that support economic self-sufficiency. • Establishing individual development account (IDA) programs to help lower-income individuals save for education and training, homeownership, and business development.	• Increased levels of technical and educational skills. • Reduced rates of adult illiteracy. • Lower unemployment. • Higher average wage earnings. • Increased home ownership. • Increased savings and assets. • Reduced rates of homelessness.

Figure 6.3 (*Continued*)

UNITED WAYS' COMMUNITY IMPACT AREAS	COMMON UNITED WAY IMPACT STRATEGIES	TARGETED RESULTS
Building Vital and Safe Neighborhoods In vital and safe neighborhoods, residents: • Have access to affordable housing and economic opportunities. • Are active in civic life and have strong networks. • Lead community-building efforts. • Trust, respect, and cooperate with each other.	• Supporting neighborhood-led public-private partnerships that are working to increase the supply of affordable housing. • Supporting resident-led efforts to strengthen schools, create new community facilities, increase neighborhood safety, and expand access to jobs. • Building the leadership and financial capacity of minority-led organizations.	• Lower crime rate. • Increased participation in neighborhood-based associations. • Wider diversity in home and business ownership. • Increased neighborhood retail and commercial activity. • Improved public transportation.
UNITED WAYS' COMMUNITY IMPACT AREAS	**COMMON UNITED WAY IMPACT STRATEGIES**	**TARGETED RESULTS**
Supporting Vulnerable and Aging Populations Vulnerable and aging individuals need: • A nurturing support system. • Access to comprehensive health care services. • Services that support independence and minimize institutionalization. • Access to emergency and transitional services that foster long-term independence. • To be involved in decisions regarding their own care.	• Coordinating efforts enabling individuals to get to medical and other appointments. • Providing home maintenance and meals, case management, counseling, and outreach. • Coordinating mental, emotional, physical health and terminal-illness services. • Supporting health care access to un- and underinsured individuals • Organizing comprehensive health and human services for individuals facing crises.	• Seniors enjoy greater quality of life. • People with disabilities have access to all opportunities. • Uninsured and underserved individuals have increased access to health care. • People in crisis regain stability. • Emergency room visits for basic health care needs decrease.

As demonstrated by the example of the United Way, all parties (citizens, government, and public administration) must be actively engaged in the process of administrative change and reforms; otherwise, the very essence of collaboration is flawed. Still, in addition to these central players there is vast room for the operation of other social units. Among these I have chosen to expand on the role of the media and academe, but other players are relevant here as well (e.g., political parties, interest groups, constitutional and electoral institutions, and other bodies of the private sector and the third sector). As will be explained below, the role of these institutions is mostly educative and is directed at enhancing socialization for citizen-government/administrative collaboration.

BRINGING OTHER SOCIAL PLAYERS BACK IN: THE MEDIA AND ACADEME

The Role of the Media

Fox and Miller (1997) suggested that "public policy discourse has entered an era of media-driven hyperreality, becoming detached from the lived experience of the polity" (p. 64). The media in free democracies bear responsibility for promoting accountability to citizens. To achieve this goal, the media seek increased transparency of governmental institutions. This important task advances a legitimate debate between citizens and government on how public resources are spent and whether responsibilities are properly shared to increase the public good. Despite its considerable limitations, the positive elements of "loop democracy" (Fox and Miller, 1995) cannot be realistic without active, independent, and responsible media.

However, the media have other roles as well. Their primary responsibility is to serve as an effective and reliable communication channel between citizens and governments, one that promotes collaboration and partnership. The media are a powerful tool exercising immense influence over people's attitudes and opinions. This power can be used to encourage citizenship involvement and participation in a variety of ways, but also to extend administrative willingness to consult citizens on relevant policy decisions. The promotion of this goal on public television and radio channels as well as computerized networks is subject to policy makers' decisions. Citizens who are aware of their power may demand greater involvement by the public media in covering entrepreneurial actions and in generating favorable public opinion about supportive community activities. The media may also encourage public recruitment to collaborative activities by means of educational programs. Regarding private media, newspapers, and computer networks, citizens' power may be aimed directly at the business-telecommunication firms, using the collective strength of consumer groups and general public opinion. This is an important way in which responsiveness can work in the service of collaboration.

The Role of Academe

Another important player in these processes is academe. The contribution of the management and administration sciences to citizen-government/administrative collaboration and partnership is twofold. First, by pointing out theoretical considerations, conceptual grounding, and practical means for

cooperation, managerial science promotes the understanding of mutual social efforts. This knowledge is crucial for isolating and cultivating the benefits of partnership. It also highlights its advantages over a simple state of
competition, which is a major construct of economics-based systems or a
responsiveness-based interaction. Second, when reconfirmed by the power
of science, the discussion on collaboration acquires priority over other issues
in social affairs. The public agenda becomes more sensitive to issues of partnership and their growth value. This way the managerial and administrative
sciences also promote legitimization of cooperation and encourage more
individuals to participate in public management enterprises. Scientific con-
firmation of the actual benefits of collaborative actions fosters their acceptance in the eyes of both citizens and rulers, which in the long run may
establish them more solidly in state culture.

THE ISRAELI EXPERIENCE: FOSTERING
COLLABORATION IN THE CARMELITE PROJECT

We have chosen to conclude with a focus on one promising example that
exhibits some of the potential of collaborative innovation on the local-gov-
ernment and on the national-government levels. This example illustrates how
bureaucracy, citizens, and the private sector may eventually contribute to the
development of collaborative culture in a modern state.

Public Involvement Process in the Carmelite Project

Background

The idea of urging higher and more intensive involvement by citizens has
taken an interesting course in the Carmelite project as planned in the city
of Haifa. Originally this project was similar to many other local government/
urban development programs in the sense that it was a private venture asking for the approval of the city authorities. Like other plans, the Carmelite
project was suggested by private entrepreneurs and by the owners of a piece
of land on the top of Mount Carmel in the city of Haifa. This area with its
breathtaking view, which for many years was held by the Israel Defense Forces
for military reasons of air control, was released and returned to its original
owners in the mid-1990s. The legal owners, the Catholic Church and the
Carmelite Order, resolved to develop the area and suggested a comprehensive plan targeted at building commercial centers, hotels, and residential
neighborhoods, as well as gardens and green areas, and they sought the formal approval of the city authorities. In an exceptional decision, supported
by professionals and academics, the mayor of Haifa appointed a twelve-mem-
ber committee whose task was to initiate a unique public involvement process intended to probe residents' opinions of the project.

Moreover, the committee was authorized to suggest changes in the plan in keeping with the opinions of citizens and professionals. The entrepreneurs had to agree to this condition in order to move ahead with the formal request for approval by the city authorities. In any case, the entire public involvement process was designed to be activated and completed prior to the discussion in the regional Planning and Building Committee, whose duty is to examine and formally approve or reject such plans. Note, however, that the public involvement process was not intended to replace or adversely affect the right of vested opposition by the public as enforced by the Israeli planning and building law (*The Carmelite Plan*, 2001:7). Thus, the process was aimed at bringing city residents closer to decision-making centers on the local community level, providing them with the opportunity of an organized voice, and stimulating a collaborative process among private, public, and third sector organizations as well as individual citizens.

Steering Committee and Process

As noted, the committee consisted of twelve members who directed, supervised, and accompanied the public involvement process. Of these members five were municipality representatives from various relevant departments, such as the city engineering branch, the mayor's office, and the ombudsman's branch; two represented the forum of environmental organizations, which are basically third sector bodies; three were academic professionals in the field of urban planning; one was an independent architect; and one was a lawyer representing the entrepreneurs. In addition, two academic experts were involved in the active process of analyzing public opinion regarding the project. The committee worked for a year and submitted its recommendations to the mayor and the entrepreneurs, and also published its conclusions for the citizens of Haifa. All in all, the public involvement process included six major steps (*The Carmelite Plan*, 2001:11–14).

1. *Preliminary briefing*: A step in which announcements were issued to inform the public on the preparation of the Carmelite project and on the intended public involvement process. The announcements were advertised in several languages (principally Hebrew, Arabic, and Russian) in local and national newspapers, and on local television and radio. The announcements were also distributed to neighborhood committees in areas located around the geographical borders of the Carmelite project. High school pupils assisted in this activity and did the rounds of placing the materials in residents' mailboxes. In addition, a detailed exhibition of the project was mounted in City Hall, with information on the public involvement process presented there and in some of the municipality's main departments. All the information was also available on a special Internet site created for this purpose.

2. *Presenting the project to the public*: Two public meetings were held to present the project to the public. An open invitation was distributed to all city and noncity residents, and some 450 people attended both meetings.

At these gatherings the project was presented by the entrepreneurs and by city officials, and feedback from the public was obtained and recorded. In addition, the public gained information on the involvement process, its rationale, and its goals.

3. *Feedback from the public*: Two principal methods were applied to obtain feedback from the public. First, the comments, concerns, questions, and answers voiced during the meetings were recorded and summarized in a separate document. Second, a detailed questionnaire was distributed to all those present at the meetings. This questionnaire included two major sections, one referring to the Carmelite project itself and the other to the public involvement process, its strengths and weaknesses. It is important to mention that despite previous suggestions by the professionals, who were specially hired to conduct the public opinion survey, the committee chose to use a convenient sample of residents rather than a more extensive and representative sample. As a result, many residents who were unable to attend the meetings for various reasons had no reasonable chance to make themselves heard. Finally, a total of 145 completed questionnaires were returned and analyzed. The participants were also asked to indicate if they were interested in further discussion of the project in smaller "discussion groups."

4. *Focus/discussion groups*: An additional phase of hearing the public voice was accomplished through five discussion groups. These forums were composed of independent interested citizens, about twenty-five in each group, around a hundred in all, who had the chance to review the details of the project, to ask questions, to raise concerns, and to suggest alternatives and emendations to various parts in the project. Steps 3 and 4 were managed by objective professionals, and expenses were covered entirely by the entrepreneurs and monitored by the steering committee.

5. *A summary document of public opinions*: The entire public involvement process, as well as the public attitudes, questions, and concerns, were summarized in a comprehensive paper. This summary was given to the entrepreneurs, who were asked to revise their proposal in accordance with the recommendations. The summarizing document was also made public through the media and presented to the local Planning and Building Committee, together with the revised Carmelite plan.

6. *Response by the entrepreneurs—feedback to the public*: The entrepreneurs examined the possibilities of making changes and revisions in the project. They were also asked by the steering committee to present a document in which they would include comments and responses to the public concerns. This document was distributed to the public in ways similar to those described above.

Lessons

Most important, this final step closes a circle in the process of public involvement and collaboration among public administration agencies, private entrepreneurs, citizens, and third sector organizations. It depends on the idea that the revised Carmelite plan will better meet the expectations of the city residents as individuals, interest groups of private or nonprofiting citizens, and the entrepreneurs. The process and its results are also expected to reduce the natural resistance to change in urban planning and development. Being a first experience in the Israeli environment, this collaborative process is also expected to suggest a practical model and guidelines for future similar ventures and decisions on both the local and the national government levels.

The case study of the Carmelite project is thus an example of higher levels of citizens' involvement in the community, and of a potential step toward a stronger urban democratic culture in our modern society. All in all, the collaborative process yielded the following five advantages:

1. An increased sense of participation by city residents and by third sector organizations (green environment movements and other voluntary groups in the community). This is a symbolic contribution of the project, but it is of prime importance due to the potential to increase citizens' trust and partnership with public authorities in similar future projects.
2. Early understanding by city authorities and entrepreneurs of the difficulties that the program carries and of potential ways to adjust it so as to become more coherent with the public interest.
3. Better understanding by public officials that citizens are interested and willing to share knowledge, time, effort, and other resources for the purpose of building quality community life. This advantage contradicts common criticism on the passivissm and lack of interest of citizens in local-level and national-level affairs.
4. As a result of this, public officials identified considerably lower levels of resistance to change in city planning. The experience stimulated a more effective and efficient managerial process of advancing a city construction program through the halls of bureaucracy and public administration.
5. Encouraging a more efficient strategy of policy-making and policy implementation that is based on relevant public inputs into the process from its very early stages.

In the wake of the Carmelite project and other examples of collaboration in modern communities, a question arises. Is there a preferred method and platform for running a successful collaboration or partnership venture? According to Khoury (1993), such processes represent a fragile relationship that depends upon common interest and genuine commitment. Although a desire to do common good must be the basic motivation, goodwill alone cannot ensure a successful partnership. Each partner must bring to the table a real desire to compromise, to cooperate, and to add value to the relationship. In this case, shared values, which touch on every aspect of the collaborative relationship, are critical.

The composition of the team is also important. A balanced and qualified team will contribute significantly to the legitimacy of the project. Many players not directly involved in the collaboration experience will ultimately feel that they have a legitimate voice in the initiative, and it is essential that each partner organization communicate with the players outside the framework of the partnership itself.

A solid collaboration or partnership has the capacity to evolve as the relationship matures or as goals are refocused. This process can result in changes in context and character, and can improve the partnership's ability to bring about significant change. The process of cooperation is itself important, both in building confidence among the partners and in formulating common goals.

The gradual building of trust is a delicate and time-consuming process. Many partnerships are particularly motivated to reach short-term goals or respond to crises. For instance, a partnership between Pratt & Whitney, Inc., and the community of St. Lambert, Quebec, grew out of the company's desire to repair relations with the community following a long and bitter strike. The cooperative efforts of the partners resulted in the renovation of a historic house as a museum. Here, the collaboration process was dictated by the urgency of the cause and the energy level of the relationship. More frequently, partnerships and collaborations develop over time, with trust evolving as part of the maturation process. These partnerships view the achievement of objectives as a longer-term investment, which in our terms may be considered a long-lasting collaboration.

Khoury (1993) further states that although alliances have great potential for success, they have equal potential for failure. Collaborative and partnership ventures fail for many reasons. When they do, the parties are unlikely to try again in the near future.

1. Fear of entrusting control to someone else is one barrier to partnering. Players accustomed to being power brokers are sometimes unable to function in a true partnership because they are used to being in complete control. Others may feel that their knowledge of a particular issue should allow them unlimited control over the partnership. To avoid power struggles, responsibility and accountability should be clarified at the beginning of the relationship.

2. Equity in a collaboration/partnership can be maintained only if all value-adding factors are recognized and appreciated. For example, funding is a key element, but so are the knowledge, expertise, and networks brought to the relationship by all parties involved. All elements of value in the partnership should be identified and periodically reviewed over the duration of the relationship.

3. All stakeholders need a thorough knowledge of the issues that concern the partnership. Each partner must also understand the cultures of the other partners and their stake in the undertaking. A valuable part of the collaborative process should be a frank discussion of the issues, the mutual benefits of the partnership, and the expected outcomes.

4. As mentioned earlier, successful collaborations and partnerships require strong leadership. In fact, poor management within one of the partner organizations can lead to partnership failure. Each management group must seek a balance that reflects both organizational and common interests.

5. Interpersonal conflicts and a high level of organizational politics can arise in collaborations and partnerships. Managers must handle personnel with care, confronting personality difficulties as they occur. Managers should also handle job turnovers carefully, keeping partners informed and finding suitable replacements as soon as possible.

6. Interorganizational dynamics have a profound effect on collaborative processes. Any organization considering collaboration and partnership should be certain of its ability to commit to such a relationship and aware of the potential for internal shifts of policy or strategy. Partners may perceive such shifts as showing a lack of commitment. New governments and administrations, new budgets, and new legislation or corporate mandates often require partners to reassess their strategies and alter existing programs.

7. Perhaps the greatest potential barrier to collaboration projects and partnerships arises from individual beliefs and values. These shape the internal culture of an organization and extend to the relationships outside that organization. For a partnership to work, players must be willing to let go of attitudes that stifle creativity. Attitudes among the stakeholder groups will also have to change if the massive shift needed to meet growing social demand is to be effected. Specifically, leaders in every area of business must become actively involved in recognizing and promoting the importance of the voluntary sector.

THE "HIDDEN SOCIAL HAND": GOVERNANCE, BUSINESSES, AND CITIZENS IN THE SERVICE OF COMMUNITIES AND MODERN SOCIETIES

Looking toward the future of governments and public administration, Ott (1998) argued that "traditional bureaucracy is not an adequate form of governmental organization" and that "the questions now are not whether government bureaucracies should be reformed but whether it is possible to govern through traditional bureaucratic government structures, whether traditional bureaucratic structures can be reformed enough so that we could govern through them, and which of the many alternative models being proposed would be best suited to governing the United States" (p. 540). Similarly, Fox and Miller (1996) argued that some contemporary policy networks and interagency consortia represent sites where discourses on particular issues can be influenced by a variety of interests. They predict a future situation where "think tank experts, legislative staffs, policy analysts, public administrators, interested citizens, process generalists, even elected officials [are] participating together to work out possibilities for what to do next" (p. 149). This book suggests that traditional structures of governments and public administration face reforms that are based on such a vision and on an evolutionary continuum. Such reforms will create a different and more flexible model of governing that combines responsiveness, collaboration, and the ideal type of citizens' ownership.

So far, treating citizens as clients of the public system has definitely worked for the benefit of bureaucracies by illuminating some neglected dimensions in citizens-government/administrative relationships. Among these improvements are (1) the assumption of great responsibility by governments and public administration toward citizens; (2) accountability in and transparency of the public sector operation; (3) the idea that government's action must be continuously monitored to ensure high efficiency, effectiveness, and better economic performance; and (4) recognition that the government's power must depend principally on citizens' support, voice, and satisfaction with the services they receive.

However, in this book I have argued that some adjustment must be made in the process of running modern states by the new generation of public administration. In fact, my view is much in line with the discourse theory of Fox and Miller (1995). In their stimulating book *Postmodern Public Administration: Toward Discourse,* these authors tried to develop an alternative philosophy for both the institutionalist/constitutionalist and the communitarianism approaches to citizens-government/administrative relationships. Instead, they rendered a synthetic (not analytic) idea that the public sphere is an energy field where mixed interests and explanations of reality coexist despite deep contradictions. According to Fox and Miller (1995:101), the discipline of public administration, in theory and in practice, is facing a paradigm shift from bureaucracy (the orthodox type) to public energy fields (the future "new" type). The discourse theory is built upon the public energy explanation, which paves the way for a new model of public administration and policy.

Moreover, while according to Fox and Miller (1995) representative democracy is neither representative nor democratic, it is definitely here to stay for years to come. In such a system citizens cannot be, and do not want to be, in the position of owners in a citizenry coerciveness type of interaction. Citizens give up ownership of government and public administration because of restraints compelled by the structure and culture of modern states. Thus, citizens as owners, defined on my continuum as a "citizenry coerciveness" interaction, is an "ideal type of democracy," one that must remain ideal and never can be implemented practically. Citizens are unwilling, perhaps unable, to become practical owners of the state even if they are the real owners by all democratic and business criteria. Still, they resist being treated as subjects or even as simple voters, as is usually accepted in the old orthodox type of government and public administration. They generally seek practical flexibility between the role of clients/customers and the position of equal partners. Government and public administration, at the other extreme, move between their roles as managers and their proposed mission as citizens' partners. Since the 1990s many governments and public administration systems in America and elsewhere have gladly adopted the role of managing citizens' lives, and do so from a businesslike standpoint. In the coming decades they are likely to face citizens' demands to be treated as equal partners. This shift forward is anticipated to be less readily adopted by government and public administration.

According to Henry Mintzberg, citizens have a variety of relationships with their government: customers, clients, citizens, and subjects. Thus, the label "customer" is particularly confining. Citizens are not mere customers of government, and expect something more than arm's-length trading and something less than the encouragement to consume. As I demonstrated earlier, the NPM approach that calls for a supplier-customer relationship in public affairs is problematic. In many respects the terrorist events of September 11 reflected serious problems with the ways citizens are viewed in our society. As Denhardt and Denhardt noted in their column in the aftermath of the attack, millions of New Yorkers (and folks elsewhere in the country) had a strong desire to get directly and actively involved in responding to the crisis. They had valuable knowledge and skills to contribute, and by building a sense of self-efficacy and community efficacy, this kind of involvement could have helped people deal with the profound vulnerability we are all experiencing. Unfortunately, New York (like many other communities around the country) does not have a "civil society" infrastructure that makes such involvement possible. So people were told to contribute money to charities and spend money in stores, theaters, and restaurants. In other words, they were treated as consumers rather than citizens.

Accordingly, Denhardt and Denhardt argued that those in government can and should play an active role in expanding the idea of democratic citizenship. In their view a start can be made in various governmental agencies simply by treating citizens as citizens, not customers, remembering that in a democracy these people are not just clients or customers; they are "bosses," and as such they deserve no less than full and complete involvement and participation in our work. In addition, government can and should play a more active role in promoting the development of civil society. It should encourage and support efforts to extend a sense of community in neighborhoods, in workplaces, and throughout other social institutions. An expansion of democratic citizenship not only will benefit citizens in their work together, but it will also help build the spirit of public service throughout society—to the benefit of all. In fact, this view perfectly coheres with the position taken in this book. The way toward modern public service cannot, and should not, leave all responsibilities in the hands of servicemen and bureaucracy. It is in the civic society's interest to instill a sense of participatory citizenship and collaboration with public officials in the hearts and minds of the people.

Our suggestion, then, is that a better definition of the citizen-government/administrative relationship must rely upon the conception of collaboration and partnership, if not citizenry ownership and control. Put another way, "government will continue to govern . . . but the more authentic the encounters with citizens will be, the less will government be 'they' and the more will it be 'we'" (Fox and Miller, 1995:128). Hence, this book has attempted in some measure to fill a conceptual and practical gap between perceptions of responsiveness and the quest for productive partnership by citizens, state administrators, politicians, and other social players such as the media and academe. I have portrayed a normative possible interaction among these players in an evolving marketplace arena that will become even more turbulent in the future. The administrative-democratic turmoil will lead to growing and serious risks of citizens' alienation, disaffection, skepticism, and increased cynicism toward government. Such trends are already intensifying, and only a high level of cooperation among all parties in society can potentially guard against these centrifugal forces. Thus, the new generation of public administration will need a different spirit, perhaps a combination of communitarianism, institutionalism, and energism, but in any case one that successfully fosters mutual effort. This movement from a "they" spirit to a "we" spirit is perhaps the most important mission of public administration in our era.

THE NATURE OF COLLABORATION IN MODERN PUBLIC ADMINISTRATION: MIDRANGE SUMMARY, PARTIAL IMPLICATIONS, AND A LOOK TO THE FUTURE

A look toward the future of collaboration in public administration draws its substance from the disciplinary roots of the field. Beyond the legal approach noted by Rosenbloom (1998), which still has many advantages for the study of present-day public administration, the earlier disciplines furnished the essence of the field as a new science in its beginnings. They greatly influenced its formation in subsequent years as well, and thus serve as core elements in the present model of the management of collaboration. Moreover, these disciplines once again bring force to the notion that any practical reform in the public sector needs to rely heavily on organized theoretical thinking.

Political science and policy analysis provided public administration with a core scientific terminology, a macroconceptual framework, a research focus, and a politics-oriented agenda to be developed in later years. In most modern nations public administration is considered mainly a blend of political and organizational knowledge that characterizes large bureaucracies. Sociology contributed the cultural aspect, which is relevant for cross-organizational and cross-national studies (Hofstede, 1980). It also made possible the development of comparative studies and a better understanding of group dynamics and informal structures such as norms or values inside bureaucracies (Schein, 1985). The business approach guided public administration through managerial considerations and individual behaviors in organizations. Traditional management science of the late 1800s and the concentration on the human side of organizations during the early 1900s exerted increasing influence on administrative thinking. A significant increase and extension of managerial influences on public administration thinking as a science and profession occurred during the mid-1980s with the evolution of New Public Management (NPM) trends, which revitalized managerial theory in the public sector. Together, these three disciplines and their appropriate internal integration are essential for better understanding of contemporary modern public services.

At first glance, collaboration of government and public administration with other social stakeholders seems to contradict the essence of bureaucracy. The ideal type of bureaucracy, as set forth by Max Weber, has clearly defined organizational characteristics that have remained relevant down the years. Nonetheless, while public organizations have undergone many changes in the last century, they are still based on the Weberian legacy of a clear hierarchical order, concentration of power among senior officials, formal structures with strict rules and regulations, limited channels of communication, confined openness to innovation and change, and noncompliance with the option of being replaceable (Golembiewski and Vigoda, 2000). These ideas seem to be substantially different from the nature of collaboration, which means negotiation, participation, cooperation, free and unlimited flow of information, innovation, agreements based on compromises and mutual understanding, and a more equal distribution and redistribution of power and resources. According to this analysis, which some may find quite utopian, collaboration is an indispensable part of democracy. It means partnership in which authorities and state administrators accept the role of leaders who need to run citizens' lives better, not because they are more powerful or superior but because this is a mission to which they are obligated. They must see themselves as committed to citizens who have agreed to be led or "governed" on condition that their lives continuously improve.

Still, the theory of collaboration and partnership sometimes fails to cohere with the complex realties that are constantly being built around us. For example, Cloke et al. (2000) suggest that collaboration becomes an influential social tool only with the presence of massive citizenship involvement. However, only citizens and voluntary groups with proper resources and skills are likely to be able to discharge the responsibilities that collaboration and partnership entail (Murdoch and Abram, 1998). In addition, the continuous rise of experimental and often competitive partnership initiatives undermines the potential for policy and action from within the state, and at the same time achieves precious little in terms of establishing an effective alternative service delivery system (Cloke et al., 2000:113; Bassett, 1996).

Hence, it sometimes seems odd to ask for genuine collaboration between those in power and those who delegated power. In many respects, growing citizenry involvement by interest groups, political parties, courts, and other democratic institutions, as well as greater involvement by business firms and the private sector, may only cause bother for politicians in office and state administrators. Too broad an involvement, in the eyes of elected politicians and appointed public officers, may be perceived as interfering with their administrative work. The freedom of public voice is thus limited and obscured by the need of administrators and politicians to govern. Consequently, the public lacks sufficient freedom of voice and influence. While mechanisms of direct democracy are designed to show such impediments the door, modern representative democracy lets them back in through the window. Representative democracy frequently diminishes the motives for partnership with governance. Constitutions, legislatures, federal and local structures, and electoral institutions are in slow but significant decline in many Western societies. They suffer from increasing alienation, distrust, and cynicism among citizens; they encourage passivism and raise barriers to original individual involvement in state affairs (Eisinger, 2000; Berman, 1997). Thus, as a counterrevolutionary course of action, a swelling element in contemporary public administration seeks to revitalize collaboration between citizens and administrative authorities through various strategies (Vigoda, 2002b).

The future of collaboration in public administration is thus quite promising. I have stated elsewhere (Vigoda, 2002a) that during the last century, modern societies accomplished remarkable achievements in different fields, many of them thanks to an advanced public sector. Yet at the dawn of the new millennium, new social problems await the consideration and attention of the state and its administrative system. To overcome these problems and create effective remedies for the new type of state ills, there is a need to increase cooperation and collaboration, and to share information and knowledge among all social parties. As shown in the present book, various models and opportunities for collaboration exist. Public administration bears chief responsibility for making them work effectively and directing them well. The Carmelite project is only one example, and others definitely exist across the globe. Together, they embody a new, vitalizing, and challenging field of action for a modern public sector. Nonetheless, despite citizens' being formal "owners" of the state, they usually remain passive as far as policy-making and policy implementation are concerned. Thus, citizens' ownership will remain a symbolic banner for the relationship between governments and public administration and other social players in a representative democracy. Modern governance and modern public administration will continuously have to battle powerful and centrifugal forces of citizens' passivism as well as the economic- and self-interest-based considerations of the private and third sectors. Hence, a more realistic approach suggests that collaboration can be better used by public administration but it may never be fully applied, for various reasons related to contradicting interests in modern representative democracies. The pragmatic scenario for the years ahead is that governments and public administration, citizens, and the private sector will continuously tango between two types of interaction: the demand for growing responsiveness and the utopia of optimal collaboration.

CONCLUSION

Modern societies of the twenty-first century will undoubtedly face a greater need for collaboration between public administration and other social players. This book has attempted to develop a broader understanding of this process and to put forward some ideas that can advance it. I have suggested that strategic thinking on collaboration, combined with empirical evidence on its chances to endure, is a momentous tool for policy makers, public administrators, managers, and citizens of the developed democracies. I have further argued that an independent activity by public administration, governments, and other social players is no longer sufficient for our complex societies. Instead, an interdisciplinary, integrative, and collaborative strategy should be adopted, and may prove to be the real promise for the years to come.

In line with these ideas, I developed a multidimensional perspective of citizenship behavior that does not necessarily contradict, but indeed blends well with, the trends of new managerialism and NPM. My perspective elaborated on (1) settings of citizenship (national/communal and organizational); (2) levels of analysis (individual and collective); and (3) integration of these dimensions with NPM ideas to create a "spirit of new managerialism." This spirit may be defined as a mutual power of MC1, MC2, MC3, and MC4. It asks that governments take strategic steps to promote citizenship values at all levels and that citizens actively participate in spontaneous initiatives and in the process of social building. Public administration structure and culture must become more flexible and responsive to citizens' needs (Vigoda, 2000b). To achieve this goal, it should become active and entrepreneurial in the initiation of partnerships between public servants and citizens. The focus of NPM should adjust to include the transformation of "goodwill" into "effective operations." In contrast to the "old" managerialism, the new spirit of public management must call for multivariate citizenry action. Public administration, through its professional cadre, should initiate this process and learn its lessons. Investment in spontaneous behavior is low-cost and economical compared with other reform efforts, so it should receive higher priority on the NPM agenda that calls for improved performance of public agencies.

Furthermore, an encouragement of the micro-citizenship pattern may lead to improvement in all other patterns (midi-, macro-, and meta-citizenship). Organizational behavior theory and general management literature can provide additional guidelines as to the nature of this phenomenon and its recommended application in the public sector (Podsakoff and MacKenzie, 1997). Citizenship behavior should be an integral part of NPM as well as of any other reform in the public sector. Similarly, much can be learned from research on communitarianism, organizational citizenship behavior, volunteer groups and programs, the third sector, and various other aspects of individuals' altruistic behavior. As suggested by Kramer (1999) and King and Stivers (1998), building relationships among citizens, administrators, and politicians is a long-term and continuous project. For truly democratic government, administrators and citizens must engage each other directly on a regular basis in full-throated public dialogue, neither side holding back anything important. Democratic public administration involves active citizenship and active administration that uses discretionary authority to foster collaborative work with citizens. In sum, this book has proposed that there is something unique about NPM compared with other managerial practices that makes citizenship behavior especially important to incorporate. Thus, the challenge for governance and new managerialism is a more comprehensive application of this valuable knowledge in public administration strategies. Accordingly, this book has suggested an insight into a wider effective use of the concepts of citizenship and collaboration by citizens in the study of new public managerialism.

The importance and relevance of collaboration for public administration and for citizens of our era are not disputed. While there are equivocal attitudes on the best way to implement collaboration, there is consensus on its necessity. As it progresses, public administration will have to collaborate with a variety of participants and integrate various attitudes and interests to accomplish its challenging tasks. Traditional, albeit effective, techniques of participation in decision-making or negotiation management are expected to grow and mature into a more extensive strategy of collaboration. Ambitious projects and programs for larger groups of citizens will have to rely on collaboration and support the communal "we" rather than an alienated "they" spirit in society. This is a main track that can lead public administration on its way forward.

Appendix
Collaboration with
Public Administration Survey

The University of Haifa
Department of Political Science
Mount Carmel
Haifa, 31905 ISRAEL

Tel: 972-4-8240599
Fax: 972-4-8257785
http://poli.haifa.ac.il/~poliweb

Dear Manager,

This study focuses on collaboration among public sector organizations, private organizations, voluntary and nonprofit bodies, and citizens as individuals. The goal of the study is to learn about the meaning of collaboration and its contribution to the quality of life in modern societies and communities. The following questions ask you to provide some useful information and to express your attitudes and perceptions about collaborative dynamics in the public sector. All information will be kept confidential and anonymity is assured.

Thank you for your cooperation,

1. In your opinion and according to your professional experience, please indicate how much collaboration exists between public administration and private organizations in the following fields:

	Never or almost never	Seldom	Sometimes	Usually	Always or almost always
Education	1	2	3	4	5
Health	1	2	3	4	5
Welfare	1	2	3	4	5
Culture and Sports	1	2	3	4	5
Employment	1	2	3	4	5
Other: _____	1	2	3	4	5

2. In your opinion and according to your professional experience, please indicate how much collaboration exists between public administration and nonprofit organizations, voluntary groups, and citizens in the following fields:

	Never or almost never	Seldom	Sometimes	Usually	Always or almost always
Education	1	2	3	4	5
Health	1	2	3	4	5
Welfare	1	2	3	4	5
Culture and Sports	1	2	3	4	5
Employment	1	2	3	4	5
Other: _____	1	2	3	4	5

3. In your organization, who usually initiates the collaboration process?

1. The public sector organization
2. The other organization (private, voluntary, or citizens themselves)

4. In your opinion, who gains the main benefit as a result of this collaboration?

1. The public sector organization
2. The other organization
3. Both organizations
4. The public

5. In your opinion, how successful is this collaboration?

1. Completely unsuccessful
2. Quite unsuccessful
3. Quite successful
4. Extremely successful

6. The statements below refer to your attitudes toward collaboration between public administration and other parties. Please circle the number from 1 to 5 that most closely reflects your response to each of the sentences.

	Strongly disagree	Disagree	Neither agree nor disagree	Agree	Strongly agree
1. Today, more than ever before, government offices collaborate with each other to improve services for citizens.	1	2	3	4	5

	Strongly disagree	Disagree	Neither agree nor disagree	Agree	Strongly agree
2. The level of collaboration among public administration, private organizations, and voluntary and nonprofit bodies can much improve.	1	2	3	4	5
3. Senior managers in the public sector well understand the advantages of collaboration with other bodies and work to improve these relations.	1	2	3	4	5
4. Many problems at the state level could be solved if public organizations learned to collaborate with the private sector and with voluntary and nonprofit organizations.	1	2	3	4	5
5. The private sector is interested in collaborating with the public sector.	1	2	3	4	5
6. Voluntary and nonprofit organizations are interested in collaborating with the public sector.	1	2	3	4	5
7. Today, more than ever before, the public sector is searching for ways to increase collaboration with private firms and with voluntary organizations.	1	2	3	4	5
8. Personally I am willing to become actively involved in public sector initiatives aimed at improving the quality of life in our nation.	1	2	3	4	5
9. I am willing to spend time in such activities (i.e., take part in citizens committees).	1	2	3	4	5

	Strongly disagree	Disagree	Neither agree nor disagree	Agree	Strongly agree
10. I am willing to bring in knowledge and ideas (e.g., suggest new ways to improve quality of life).	1	2	3	4	5
11. I am willing to bring other people into the collaborative processes.	1	2	3	4	5
12. An advanced state must seek better collaboration between the public sector and other private and voluntary bodies.	1	2	3	4	5
13. In the future, the public sector will be forced to increase collaboration with others in order to reach its goals.	1	2	3	4	5
14. Collaboration between the public sector and the private sector is more important than collaboration between the public sector and voluntary/ nonprofit organizations.	1	2	3	4	5

7. General information

Age: _____

Gender: 1. Man   2. Woman

Tenure in the organization: _____

Years of formal education: _____

Ethnicity: 1. Jewish   2. Muslim   3. Christian   4. Druze   5. Other

Name of organization where you work: _____

Thank you for your cooperation,
The Research Team

References

Almond, G. A., and Verba, S. (1963). *The Civic Culture: Political Attitudes and Democracy in Five Nations: An Analytic Study.* Boston: Little, Brown.

Arsenault, J. (1998). *Forging Nonprofit Alliances.* San Francisco: Jossey-Bass.

Aucoin, P. (1995). *The New Public Management: Canada in Comparative Perspective.* Montreal: IRPP, Ashgate.

Barber, B. (1984). *Strong Democracy: Participatory Politics for a New Age.* Berkeley: University of California Press.

Bardach, E. (1999). *Getting Agencies to Work Together: The Practice and Theory of Managerial Craftsmanship.* Washington, DC: The Brookings Institution.

Bassett, K. (1996). Partnership, business elites in urban politics: New forms of governance in an English city? *Urban Studies, 33,* 539–555.

Batsleer, J. (1995). Management and organizations. In J. D. Smith, C. Rochester, and R. Hedley, eds., *An Introduction to the Voluntary Sector,* pp. 224–248. London: Routledge.

Berman, E. M. (1995). Empowering employees in state agencies: A survey of recent progress. *International Journal of Public Administration, 18,* 833–850.

Berman, E. M. (1996). Local government and community-based strategies: Evidence from a national survey of a social problem. *American Review of Public Administration, 26,* 71–91.

Berman, E. M. (1997). Dealing with cynical citizens. *Public Administration Review, 57,* 105–112.

Bianchi, G. (1997). Training in skills for coping with democracy. *Annals of the American Academy of Political and Social Science, 552,* 114–124.

Blau, P. M. (1964). *Power and Exchange in Social Life.* New York: Wiley.

Boschken, L. H. (1998). Institutionalism: Intergovernmental exchange, administration-centered behavior, and policy outcomes in urban agencies. *Journal of Public Administration Research and Theory, 8,* 585–614.

Boston, J. Martin, J. Pallot, and P. Walsh. (1996). *Public Management: The New Zealand Model.* Oxford: Oxford University Press.

Box, R. C. (1998). *Citizen Governance: Leading American Communities into the 21st Century*. Thousand Oaks, CA: Sage.

Box, R. C. (1999). Running governments like a business: Implications for public administration theory and practice. *American Review of Public Administration*, 29, 19–43.

Bozeman, B. (1993). *Public Management*. San Francisco: Jossey-Bass.

Brief, A. P., and S. J. Motowidlo. (1986). Prosocial organizational behaviors. *Academy of Management Review*, 11, 710–725.

Brinton, M. H. (1994). Nonprofit contracting and the hollow state. *Public Administration Review*, 54, 73–77.

Brown, C. (1999). United Kingdom: Public private partnership. *International Financial Law Review*, July, 25–29.

Brudney, J. L. (1990). *Fostering Volunteer Programs in the Public Sector: Planning, Initiating, and Managing Voluntary Activities*. San Francisco: Jossey-Bass.

Brudney, J. L., and W. D. Duncombe. (1992). An economic evaluation of paid, volunteer, and mixed staffing options for public services. *Public Administration Review*, 52, 474–481.

Bryson, J. M., and B. Crosby. (1992). *Leadership for the Common Good: Tackling Public Problems in a Shared Power World*. San Francisco: Jossey-Bass.

Burnes, B., and R. Coram. (1999). Barriers to partnership in the public sector: The case of the UK construction industry. *Supply Chain Management*, 4, 43–50.

Camp, R. C. (1998). *Global Cases in Benchmarking: Best Practices from Organizations Around the World*. Milwaukee, WI: ASQ Quality Press.

The Carmelite Plan. (2001). Haifa: Haifa Municipality Press.

Carter, N. (1989). Performance indicators: "Backseat driving" or "hands off" control? *Policy and Politics*, 17, 131–138.

Cigler, A. B. (1999). Pre-conditions for the emergence of multicommunity collaborative organizations. *Policy Studies Review*, 16, 87–101.

Cloke, P., P. Milbourne, and R. Widdowfield. (2000). Partnership and policy networks in rural local governance: Homelessness in Taunton. *Public Administration*, 78, 111–133.

Coble, R. (1999). The nonprofit sector and state governments: Public policy issues facing nonprofits in North Carolina and other states. *Nonprofit Management and Leadership*, 9, 293–313.

Cohen, A., and E. Vigoda. (1999). Politics and the workplace: An empirical examination of the relationship between political behavior and work outcomes. *Public Productivity and Management Review*, 22, 389–406.

Cohen, A., and E. Vigoda. (2000). Do good citizens make good organizational citizens? An empirical examination of the effects of citizenship behavior and orientations on organizational citizenship behavior. *Administration and Society*, 32, 566–595.

Cole, I., and B. Goodchild. (1993). Local Housing Strategies in England. CRESR working paper 26. Hallam University, School of Urban and Regional Studies.

Coleman, J. (1989). The dynamics of community controversy. In R. Warren and L. Lyon, eds., *New Perspectives on the American Community*. Chicago: Dorsey Press.

Collin, S. O. (1998). In the twilight zone: A survey of public-private partnership in Sweden. *Public Productivity and Management Review*, 21, 272–283.

Conover, P.J., I. Crewe, and D. D. Searing. (1993). Citizen Identities in the Liberal State. Paper presented at the annual meeting of the American Political Science Association. Washington, DC.

Cotton, J. L., D. A. Vollrath, K. L. Froggat, M. L. Lengnick-Hall, and K. R. Jennings. (1988). Employee participation: Diverse forms and different outcomes. *Academy of Management Review*, 13, 8–22.

Crook, R. (1996). Democracy, participation and responsiveness: A case study of relations between the Ivorian communes and their citizens. *Public Administration*, 74, 695–720.

DHSS. (1979). *Patients First*. London: Her Majesty's Stationery Office.

Drucker, P. (1966). *The Practice of Management*. New York: Harper & Row.

Eisinger, R. M. (2000). Questioning cynicism. *Society*, 37, 55–60.

Ellwood, J. W. (1996). Political science. In D. F. Kettl and H. B. Milward, eds., *The State of Public Management*, pp. 51–74. Baltimore: Johns Hopkins University Press.

Erez, M., C. P. Earley, and L. C. Hulin. (1985). The impact of participation on goal acceptance and performance: A two-step model. *Academy of Management Journal*, 28, 50–66.

Etzioni, A. (1994). *The Spirit of Community*. New York: Touchstone.

Etzioni, A. (1995). *New Communitarian Thinking: Persons, Virtues, Institutions, and Communities*. Charlottesville: University of Virginia Press.

Farnham, D., and S. Horton. (1995). The political economy of public sector change. In David Farnham and Sylvia Horton, eds., *Managing the New Public Services*, pp. 3–26. Basingstoke, UK: Macmillan.

Fisher, R., and W. Ury. (1983). How to fight dirty tricks in negotiations. *Marketing Times*, September–October, 36–40.

Forbes, D. P. (1998). Measuring the unmeasurable: Empirical studies of nonprofit organization effectiveness from 1977 to 1997. *Nonprofit and Voluntary Sector Quarterly*, 27, 122–183.

Fox, C. J., and H. T. Miller. (1996). *Postmodern Public Administration: Toward Discourse*. Thousand Oaks, CA: Sage.

Fox, C. J., and H. T. Miller. (1997). The depreciating public policy discourse. *American Behavioral Scientist*, 41, 64–89.

Fox, C. J., and H. T. Miller. (2001). The epistemic community. *Administration and Society*, 32, 668–685.

Fredericksen, J. P. (1996). Community collaboration and public policy making. *American Behavioral Scientist*, 39, 552–569.

Fredrickson, H. G. (1982). The recovery of civism in public administration. *Public Administration Review*, 42, 501–509.

Fredrickson, H. G. (1997). *The Spirit of Public Administration*. San Francisco: Jossey-Bass.

Gardner, J. (1991). *Building Community*. Washington, DC: Independent Sector.

Garson, G. D., and E. S. Overman. (1983). *Public Management Research in the United States*. New York: Praeger.

Gidron, B., R. M. Kramer, and L. M. Salamon. (1992). *Governments and the Third Sector: Emerging Relationships in Welfare States*. San Francisco: Jossey-Bass.

Glaister, S. (1999). Past abuses and future uses of private finance and public-private partnership in transport. *Public Money and Management*, 19, 29–36.

Golembiewski, R. T. (1995). *Practical Public Management*. New York: Marcel Dekker.

Golembiewski, R. T., and E. Vigoda. (2000). Organizational innovation and the science/craft of management. In M. A. Rahim, R. T. Golembiewski, and K. D. Mackenzie, eds., *Current Topics in Management*, vol. 5, pp. 263–280. Greenwich, CT: JAI Press.

Goodnow, F. J. (1900). *Politics and Administration: A Study in Government*. New York: Russell & Russell.

Goodwin, M. (1998). The governance of rural areas: Some emerging research issues and agendas. *Journal of Rural Studies*, 14, 5–12.

Graham, J. W. (1991). An essay on organizational citizenship behavior. *Employee Responsibilities and Rights Journal*, 4, 249–270.

Grant, T. (1996). Keys to successful public-private partnership. *Canadian Business Review*, Autumn, 27–28.

Grubbs, W. J. (2000). Can agencies work together? Collaboration in public and nonprofit organizations. *Public Administration Review*, 60, 275–280.

Hammer, M., and J. Champy. (1994). *Reengineering the Corporation: A Manifesto for Business Revolution*. New York: Harper Business.

Harrison, L., P. Hoggett, and S. Jeffers. (1995). Race, ethnicity and community development. *Community Development Journal*, 30, 144–157.

Hays, S. W., and R. C. Kearney. (1997). Riding the crest of a wave: The National Performance Review and public management reform. *International Journal of Public Administration*, 20, 11–40.

Hirschman, A. O. (1970). *Exit, Voice and Loyalty*. Cambridge, MA: Harvard University Press.

Hofstede, G. (1980). *Culture's Consequences: International Differences in Work Related Values*. London: Sage.

Hofstede, G. (1991). *Cultures and Organizations*. London: McGraw-Hill.

Hughes, O. E. (1994). *Public Management and Administration*. London: Macmillan.

Hurd, D. (1989). Freedom will flourish where citizens accept responsibility. *The Independent*, September 13.

Huxham, C. (1993a). Pursuing collaborative advantage. *Journal of the Operational Research Society*, 44, 599–611.

Huxham, C. (1993b). Collaborative capability: An intra-organizational perspective on collaborative advantage. *Public Money and Management*, 12, 21–28.

Huxham, C. (1994). Collaborative capability and collaborative maturity. *Management Research News*, 17, 28–29.

Janoski, T., and J. Wilson. (1995). Pathways to voluntarism: Family socialization and status transmission model. *Social Forces*, 74, 271–292.

John, D., D. E. Kettl, B. Dyer, and W. R. Lovan. (1994). What will new governance mean for the federal government? *Public Administration Review*, 54, 170–175.

Joyce, M. S. (1994). Citizenship in the 21st century: Individual self-government. In D. E. Eberly, ed., *Building a Community of Citizens*, pp. 3–10. Lanham, MD: University Press of America.

Kanter, R. M. (1989). *When Giants Learn to Dance: Mastering the Challenge of Strategy, Management, and Careers in the 1990s*. New York: Simon and Schuster.

Kanter, R. M., and D. Summers. (1987). Doing well while doing good: Dilemmas of performance measurement in nonprofit organizations and the need for a multiple-constituency approach. In W. W. Powel, ed., *The Nonprofit Sector: A Research Handbook*, pp. 154–166. New Haven, CT: Yale University Press.

Katz, D., and R. L. Kahn. (1966). *The Social Psychology of Organizations*. New York: Wiley.

Keller, R. T. (1997). Job involvement and organizational commitment as longitudinal predictors of job performance: A study of scientists and engineers. *Journal of Applied Psychology*, 82, 539–545.

Kennedy, S. S., and M. S. Rosentraub. (1999). Public-private partnership, professional sports teams, and the protection of the public's interests. *American Review of Public Administration*, 30, 436–459.

Kermit, P. C. (1994). Collaborative genius: The Regional Planning Association of America. *American Planning Association*, 60, 462–482.

Kettl, D. F. (1993). Public administration: The state of the field. In A. W. Finifter, ed., *Political Science: The State of the Discipline II*, pp. 407–428. Washington, DC: American Political Science Association.

Kettl, D. F., and H. B. Milward, eds. (1996). *The State of Public Management*. Baltimore: Johns Hopkins University Press.

Khademian, A. M. (1998). What do we want public managers to be? Comparing reforms. *Public Administration Review*, 58, 269–273.

Khoury, G. (1993). From patrons to partners: Strategies for the 90s. *Canadian Business Review*, 20, 26–28.

Kilmann, R. H., et al., eds. (1985). *Gaining Control of the Corporate Culture*. San Francisco: Jossey-Bass.

King, C. S., K. M. Feltey, and B. O. Susel. (1998). The question of participation: Toward authentic public participation in public administration. *Public Administration Review*, 58, 317–326.

King, C. S., and C. Stivers. (1998). *Government Is Us: Public Administration in an Anti-government Era*. Thousand Oaks, CA: Sage.

Kramer, R. (1999). Weaving the public into public administration. *Public Administration Review*, 59, 89–92.

Lewin, K. (1936). *Principles of Topological Psychology*. New York: McGraw-Hill.

Lum, L., J. Kervin, K. Clark, F. Reid, and W. Sirola. (1998). Explaining nursing turnover intent: Job satisfaction, pay satisfaction, or organizational commitment? *Journal of Organizational Behavior*, 19, 305–320.

Lynn, L. E. (1996). *Public Management as Art, Science, and Profession*. Chatham, NJ: Chatham House Publishers.

Lynn, L. E. (1998). The new public management: How to transform a theme into a legacy. *Public Administration Review*, 58, 231–237.

Mandell, P. M. (1999). Community collaborations: Working through network structures. *Policy Studies Review*, 16, 43–63.

Marshall, T. H. (1950). *Citizenship and Social Class and Other Essays*. Cambridge: Cambridge University Press.

McKevitt, D. (1998). *Managing Core Public Services*. Oxford: Blackwell.

McPherson, J. M., and T. Rotolo. (1996). Testing a dynamic model of social composition: Diversity and change in voluntary groups. *American Sociological Review*, 61, 179–202.

Michael, H. (1981). Youth, voluntary associations and political socialization. *Social Forces*, 60, 211–223.

Milbrath, L. W. (1965). *Political Participation*. Chicago: Rand McNally.

Milward, H. B., and K. G. Provan. (1998). Principles for controlling agents: The political economy of network structure. *Journal of Public Administration Research and Theory*, 8, 203–221.

Milward, H. B., ed. (1996). Symposium on the hollow state: Capacity, control, and performance in interorganizational settings. *Journal of Public Administration Research and Theory*, 6, 193–196.

Monroe, K. R. (1994). A fat lady in a corset: Altruism and social theory. *American Journal of Political Science*, 38, 861–893.

Morgan, J. (1997). *Glory for Sale: Fans, Dollars, and the New NFL*. Baltimore: Bancroft.

Morrison, E. W. (1996). Organizational citizenship behavior as a critical link between HRM practices and service quality. *Human Resource Management*, 35, 493–512.

Murdoch, J., and S. Abram. (1998). Defining the limits of community governance. *Journal of Rural Studies*, 14, 41–50.

Nalbandian, J. (1999). Facilitating community, enabling democracy: New roles for local government managers. *Public Administration Review*, 59, 187–197.

National Consumer Council. (1986). *Measuring Up: Consumer Assessment of Local Authority Services*. London: The Council.

Nicholson, B. (1998). Private care eases public burden. *Management Today*, August, 5.

Nicol, C. (1998). Collaboration and co-ordination in local government. *Local Government Studies*, 24, 51–66.

Nye, J. S., P. D. Zelikow, and D. C. King, eds. (1997). *Why People Don't Trust Government*. Cambridge, MA: Harvard University Press.

O'Connell, B. (1989). What voluntary activity can and cannot do for America. *Public Administration Review*, 49, 486–491.

Oliver, D., and D. Heater. (1994). *The Foundation of Citizenship*. London: Harvester Wheatsheaf.

Organ, D. W. (1988). *O.C.B.: The Good Soldier Syndrome*. Lexington, MA: Lexington Books.

Organ, D. W., and M. Konovsky. (1989). Cognitive versus affective determinants of organizational citizenship behavior. *Journal of Applied Psychology*, 74, 157–164.

Osborne, D., and T. Gaebler. (1992). *Reinventing Government: How the Entrepreneurial Spirit Is Transforming the Public Sector*. Reading, MA: Addison-Wesley.

Ostrom, E. (1986). An agenda for the study of institutions. *Public Choice*, 48, 2–25.

Ostrom, E. (1993). A communitarian approach to local governance. *National Civic Review*, Summer, 226–233.

O'Toole, L. (1995). Rational choice and policy implementation: Implications for interorganizational network management. *American Review of Public Administration*, 25, 43–57.

O'Toole, L. J., Jr. (1997). Treating networks seriously: Practical and research based agendas in public administration. *Public Administration Review*, 57, 45–52.

Ott, S. (1998). Government reform or alternatives to bureaucracy? Thickening, tides and the future of governing. *Public Administration Review*, 58, 540–545.

Ott, S., A. C. Hyde, and J. M. Shafritz, eds. (1991). *Public Management: The Essential Readings*. Chicago: Nelson-Hall.

Otterbourg, S. (1999). Prepping the next generation. *Across the Board*, 36, 55–56.

Ouchi, W. G. (1981). *Theory Z: How American Business Can Meet the Japanese Challenge*. Reading, MA: Addison-Wesley.

Palfrey, C., C. Phillips, P. Thomas, and D. Edward. (1992). *Policy Evaluation in the Public Sector: Approaches and Methods*. Aldershot, UK: Avenbury.

Palvolgyi, R., and I. Herbai. (1997). Public participation in cooperative planning: A local tax issue in Nagykanizsa, Hungary. *Annals of the American Academy of Political and Social Science*, 552, 75–85.

Pateman, C. (1970). *Participation and Democratic Theory*. London: Cambridge University Press.

Perry, J. L., and K. Kraemer. (1983). *Public Management: Public and Private Perspectives*. Palo Alto, CA: Mayfield.

Peters, G. B. (1996a). Models of governance for the 1990s. In D. F. Kettl and H. B. Milward, eds., *The State of Public Management*, pp. 15–44. Baltimore: Johns Hopkins University Press.

Peters, G. B. (1996b). *The Future of Governing: Four Emerging Models*. Kansas City: University Press of Kansas.

Peters, G. B. (1999). *American Public Policy: Promise and Performance*. New York: Seven Bridges.

Peterson, S. A. (1990). *Political Behavior*. Thousand Oaks, CA: Sage.

Pfeffer, J. (1992). *Managing with Power*. Boston: Harvard Business School Press.

Piliavin, J. A., and H. W. Charng. (1990). Altruism: A review of recent theory and research. *Annual Review of Sociology*, 16, 27–65.

Podsakoff, P. M., and S. B. MacKenzie. (1997). Impact of Organizational Citizenship Behavior on organizational performance: A review and suggestions for future research. *Human Performance*, 10, 133–151.

Pollitt, C. (1988). Bringing consumers into performance measurement. *Policy and Politics*, 16, 77–87.

Pollitt, C., and G. Bouckaert. (2000). *Public Management Reform*. Oxford: Oxford University Press.

Pollitt, C., X. Girre, J. Lonsdale, R. Mul, H. Summa, and M. Waerness. (1999). *Performance or Compliance?* Oxford: Oxford University Press.

Public Management, August 1998, pp. A5–A12.

Putnam, R. (1993). *Making Democracy Work: Civic Traditions in Modern Italy*. Princeton, NJ: Princeton University Press.

Rainey, H. (1990). Public management: Recent development and current prospects. In N. B. Lynn and A. Wildavsky, eds., *Public Administration: The State of the Discipline*, pp. 157–184. Chatham, NJ: Chatham House.

Rhodes, R. (1997). *Understanding Governance: Policy Networks, Governance, Reflexivity and Accountability*. Buckingham, UK: Open University Press.

Rhodes, R.A.W. (1987). Developing the public service orientation, or let's add a soupçon of political theory. *Local Government Studies*, May–June, 63–73.

Rhodes, R.A.W. (1996). The new governance: Governing without government. *Political Studies*, 44, 652–657.

Rimmerman, C. A. (1997). *The New Citizenship: Unconventional Politics, Activism, and Service*. Boulder, CO: Westview Press.

Roberts, N., and R. Bradley. (1991). Stakeholder collaboration and innovation. *Journal of Applied Behavioral Science*, 27, 209–227.

Rosenbloom, D. H. (1998). *Public Administration: Understanding Management, Politics, and Law*. Boston: McGraw-Hill.

Rosenbloom, D. H., D. D. Goldman, and P. W. Ingraham, eds. (1994). *Contemporary Public Administration*. New York: McGraw-Hill.

Rosentraub, M. (1999). *Major League Losers: The Real Costs of Sports and Who's Paying for It*. New York: Basic Books.

Rourke, F. E. (1992). Responsiveness and neutral competence in American bureaucracy. *Public Administration Review*, 52, 539–546.

Sanderson, I. (1999). Participation and democratic renewal in the U.K.: From "instrumental" to "communicative rationality." *Policy and Politics*, 27, 325–341.

Sarason, S. B., and E. M. Lorentz. (1998). *Crossing Boundaries: Collaboration, Coordination, and the Redefinition of Resources*. San Francisco: Jossey-Bass.

Savas, E. S. (1994). On privatization. In F. Lane, ed., *Current Issues in Public Administration*, pp. 404–413. New York: St. Martin's Press.

Schachter, H. L. (1997). *Reinventing Government or Reinventing Ourselves*. Albany: State University of New York Press.

Schein, E. H. (1985). *Organizational Culture and Leadership*. San Francisco: Jossey-Bass.

Schneider, A. L. (1999). Public-private partnership in the U.S. prison system. *The American Behavioral Scientist*, 43, 192–208.

Schwartz, R. (2001). Managing government-third sector collaboration: Accountability, ambiguity, and politics. *International Journal of Public Administration*, 24, 1161–1189.

Shafritz, J. M., and E. W. Russell. (1997). *Introducing Public Administration*. New York: Addison-Wesley Longman.

Smith, C. A., D. W. Organ, and J. P. Near. (1983). Organizational citizenship behavior: Its nature and antecedents. *Journal of Applied Psychology*, 68, 653–663.

Smith, P. (1993). Outcome-related performance indicators and organizational control in the public sector. *British Journal of Management*, 4, 135–151.

Smith, S. R., and M. Lipsky. (1993). *Non-Profits for Hire: The Welfare State in the Age of Contracting*. Cambridge, MA: Harvard University Press.

Snavely, K., and U. Desai. (2000). Municipal government nonprofit sector collaboration in Bulgaria. *American Review of Public Administration*, 31, 49–65.

Sobel, R. (1993). From occupational involvement to political participation: An exploratory analysis. *Political Behavior*, 15, 339–353.

Stewart, J., and S. Ranson. (1994). Management in the public domain. In D. McKevitt and A. Lawton, eds., *Public Sector Management*, pp. 54–70. London: Sage.

Stivers, C. (1994). *Gender Images in Public Administration: Legitimacy and the Administrative State*. Thousand Oaks, CA: Sage.

Stoker, G. (1996). Governance as theory: Five propositions. Department of Government, University of Strathclyde. Mimeo.

Stoker, G. (1997). Public-private partnership and urban governance. In G. Stoker, ed., *Partners in Urban Governance: European and American Experience.* London: Macmillan.

Swindell, D., and M. S. Rosentraub. (1998). Who benefits from the presence of professional sports teams? The implications for public funding of stadiums and arenas. *Public Administration Review*, 58, 11–20.

Terry, L. D. (1998). Administrative leadership, neo-managerialism, and the public management movement. *Public Administration Review*, 58, 194–200.

Thomas, J. C. (1999). Bringing the public into public administration: The struggle continues. *Public Administration Review*, 59, 83–88.

Thomas, P., and C. Palfrey. (1996). Evaluation: Stakeholder-focused criteria. *Social Policy and Administration*, 30, 125–142.

Thompson, A. A., F. B. Tancredi, and M. Kisil. (2000). New partnership for social development: Business and the third sector. *International Journal of Public Administration*, 23, 1359–1385.

Thompson, D. (1983). Bureaucracy and democracy. In Graem Duncan, ed., *Democratic Theory and Practice.* Cambridge: Cambridge University Press.

Toregas, C. (2000). Lessons from the "Y2K and You" campaign for the local government community. *Public Administration Review*, 60, 84–88.

Van Dyne, L., J. W. Graham, and R. M. Dienesch. (1994). Organizational Citizenship Behavior: Construct redefinition, measurement, and validation. *Academy of Management Journal*, 37, 765–802.

Vardi, Y., and Y. Wiener. (1996). Misbehavior in organizations: A motivational framework. *Organization Study*, 7, 151–165.

Verba, S., and N. H. Nie. (1972). *Participation in America.* New York: Harper & Row.

Verba, S., K. L. Schlozman, and H. E. Brady. (1995). *Voice and Equality: Civic Voluntarism in American Politics.* London: Harvard University Press.

Vigoda, E. (2000a). Internal politics in public administration systems: An empirical examination of its relationship with job congruence, organizational citizenship behavior and in-role performances. *Public Personnel Management*, 29, 185–210.

Vigoda, E. (2000b). Are you being served? The responsiveness of public administration to citizens' demands: An empirical examination in Israel. *Public Administration*, 78, 165–191.

Vigoda, E., ed. (2002a). *Public Administration: An Interdisciplinary Critical Analysis.* New York: Marcel Dekker.

Vigoda, E. (2002b). From responsiveness to collaboration: Governance, citizens, and the next generation of public administration. *Public Administration Review*, 62, 527–540.

Vigoda, E., and E. Gilboa. (2002). The quest for collaboration: Towards a comprehensive strategy for public administration. In E. Vigoda, ed., *Public Administration: An Interdisciplinary Critical Analysis*, pp. 99–118. New York: Marcel Dekker.

Vigoda, E., and R. T. Golembiewski. (2001). Citizenship behavior and the spirit of new managerialism: A theoretical framework and challenge for governance. *American Review of Public Administration*, 31, 273–295.

Vroom, V. H. (1964). *Work and Motivation.* New York: Wiley.

Waldo, D. (1968). Scope of the theory of public administration. *Annals of the American Academy of Political and Social Science*, 8, 1–26.

Wallace, S. (1978). Premises of public administration: Past and emerging. In J. Shafritz and A. Hyde, eds., *Classics of Public Administration*, pp. 201–220. Oak Park, IL: Moore Publishing.

Weber, E., and A. M. Khademian. (1997). From agitation to collaboration: Clearing the air through negotiation. *Public Administration Review*, 57, 396–410.

Weikart, L. A. (2001). The Giuliani administration and the New Public Management in New York City. *Urban Affairs Review*, 36, 359–381.

Wheeland, C. M. (1993). Citywide strategic planning: An evaluation of Rock Hill's E. *Public Administration Review*, 53, 65–72.

Wilson, W. (1887). The study of administration. *Political Science Quarterly*, 2, 197–222.

Winkler, F. (1987). Consumerism in health care: Beyond the supermarket model. *Policy and Politics*, 15, 1–8.

Young, B. S., S. Worchel, and D. J. Woehr. (1998). Organizational commitment among public service employees. *Public Personnel Management*, 27, 339–348.

Author Index

Subject Index

About the Author

ERAN VIGODA-GADOT is Senior Lecturer of Public Administration and Organizational Behavior at the Department of Political Science, University of Haifa, Israel.